Pitt Poetry Series

THE PITTSBURGH BOOK OF
CONTEMPORARY AMERICAN

Ed Ochester & Peter Oresick, Editors

5 1 4 2 1

University of Pittsburgh Press
Pittsburgh and London

Published by the University of Pittsburgh Press, Pittsburgh, Pa. 15260
Manufactured in the United States of America
Printed on acid-free paper

Library of Congress Cataloging-in-Publication Data
The Pittsburgh book of contemporary American poetry / Ed Ochester
  and Peter Oresick, editors
      p.   cm.—(Pitt poetry series)
   ISBN 0-8229-3752-2 — ISBN 0-8229-5506-7 (pbk.)
   1. American poetry—20th century. I. Ochester, Ed. II. Oresick, Peter.
III. Series.
PS615.P47   1993
811'.5408—dc20   92-50846
                                                                     CIP

A CIP catalogue record for this book is available from the British Library.
Eurospan, London

A detailed list of acknowledgments begins on page 395.

Contents

To the Reader

This anthology commemorates the twenty-fifth anniversary (1968–1993) of the Pitt Poetry Series, which from modest beginnings has become one of the most prominent poetry publishers in the United States. During this period, first under the editorship of Paul Zimmer and now Ed Ochester, 156 titles by 102 poets were published. When Catherine Marshall, assistant director of the Press and editor-in-chief, first suggested a "best of the Pitt Poetry Series" anthology, we hesitated: How to do justice to so much good work without the book growing unwieldy? We decided, finally, to limit our selections to the forty-five Pitt poets currently in print. (A complete list of titles and poets published appears at the back of this book.) Our goal is to create a Pitt Poetry Series reader that offers generous samplings of each poet's work—about 300 lines—in hopes that the reader will be motivated to buy and read the full-length collections by these outstanding writers.

After studying our selections, however, we realize that this book is more than just a commemorative volume. It seems to us to be as valid a cross-section of contemporary American poetry as we know, with a range of styles and content illustrative of its richness.

Poetry, except for rare moments, has always been a literary orphan in America, with notoriously few readers, and poets in this century have rarely sold well initially. Every few years a critical Jeremiah will explain that poets have betrayed their audiences, and will without a trace of irony spin a new myth of the golden age. To which we say, "What about Whitman? How well did he sell during his lifetime?" Most of the books in the Pitt Poetry Series outsell the early editions of Wallace Stevens and T. S. Eliot—and Whitman—so perhaps *this* is the golden age?

Jeremiah will also tell you that contemporary poets have lost touch with the conventions of traditional verse (though some of our poets, Ronald Wallace and Peter Meinke, for example, have been writing enormously skillful sonnets and sestinas long before the current rise of the New Formalists); and will tell you that American poets have lost touch with life as she is lived (though all of the poets in this anthology write about little else—very few roses of Picardy here); and will tell you that the language of contemporary poetry is so rarefied or so complex as to baffle ordinary readers (though most of the poets here ground their art in a mastery of contemporary American dictions).

Jeremiah will tell you just about anything. He's about as helpful a guide to poetry as Ed Ochester's high school English teacher who, when asked *why* her class had to memorize Masefield's "I must Go Down to the Sea Again," thought for a few moments and said, "Well, when you go to the beach this summer, you'll have something to think about."

Pleasure. One reads poetry for that. And knowledge, too. These poems that follow, whether in well-made free verse (which if good, is never free) or traditional forms, offer the pleasure that well-made artifacts always offer.

And these poems have something to say about the worlds their speakers and authors inhabit. Yes, *worlds:* the poets in the Pitt Series are of all colors, classes, genders, and ethnic backgrounds. No doubt Jeremiah will sputter "politically correct," and imply thereby—as did a white male middle-class poet we heard recently—that only white male middle-class professors write "Poetry." We do like white male middle-class professors (the current editor of the Series is one), but we also believe that the impulse for poetry exists in all people.

Over the years we have been faithful in our task of reading manuscripts from writers outside the usual and established networks. We do publish established writers, but what has always driven the Series is a desire to publish the best new poets, to read manuscripts with an eye for a kind of excellence we haven't seen before. Years ago a friend of ours said to a magazine editor, parodying a cliche of editors, "Why don't you publish some writing you *don't* like for a change, and give us a rest from all this excellence?" We've wanted to do that, to find work that may not initially meet current norms and fashions, but that has power, and that defines its own excellence.

Editing is an art, and we don't intend to theorize our position. We do believe that any reader even nominally interested in poetry will find much that is exciting, moving, and yes, beautiful in this book. It is true about poetry that the reader must be attentive, and it is true the reader must exercise some tolerance until he or she sees where the poem is going. Give the poem the same courtesy as you'd give an interesting stranger; don't judge the person before she has a chance to speak her piece. And don't feel that you have to like everything. Poetry is a subjective art, and you're entitled to skip around. The poems you don't like this year may make emotional sense to you in the future. Or may not. It doesn't matter, really, since the poems don't exist to improve you. They do exist to take your breath away, to make you laugh, to show you yourself in a mirror, to allow you to feel as some other person may feel. Poetry has no more utility than tennis or most sex, though some of the pleasures of both; we wish our high school teachers had told us that years ago.

Ed Ochester
Peter Oresick
December 1992

THE PITTSBURGH BOOK OF
CONTEMPORARY AMERICAN

CLARIBEL ALEGRÍA

Photo by Lars Hansen

Documentary

Come, be my camera.
Let's photograph the ant heap
the queen ant
extruding sacks of coffee,
my country.
It's the harvest.
Focus on the sleeping family
cluttering the ditch.
Now, among trees:
rapid,
dark-skinned fingers
stained with honey.
Shift to a long shot:
the file of ant men
trudging down the ravine
with sacks of coffee.
A contrast:
girls in colored skirts
laugh and chatter,
filling their baskets
with berries.
Focus down.
A close-up of the pregnant mother
dozing in the hammock.
Hard focus on the flies
spattering her face.
Cut.
The terrace of polished mosaics
protected from the sun.
Maids in white aprons
nourish the ladies
who play canasta,
celebrate invasions
and feel sorry for Cuba.
Izalco sleeps
beneath the volcano's eye.

A subterranean growl
makes the village tremble.
Trucks and oxcarts
laden with sacks
screech down the slopes.
Besides coffee
they plant angels
in my country.
A chorus of children
and women
with the small white coffin
move politely aside
as the harvest passes by.
The riverside women,
naked to the waist,
wash clothing.
The truck drivers
exchange jocular obscenities
for insults.
In Panchimalco,
waiting for the oxcart to pass by,
a peasant
with hands bound behind him
by the thumbs
and his escort of soldiers
blinks at the airplane:
a huge bee
bulging with coffee growers
and tourists.
The truck stops in the market place.
A panorama of iguanas,
chickens,
strips of meat,
wicker baskets,
piles of *nances*,
nísperos,
oranges,
zunzas,
zapotes,
cheeses,
bananas,

dogs, *pupusas, jocotes,*
acrid odors,
taffy candies,
urine puddles, tamarinds.
The virginal coffee
dances in the mill house.
They strip her,
rape her,
lay her out on the patio
to doze in the sun.
The dark storage sheds
glimmer.
The golden coffee
sparkles with malaria,
blood,
illiteracy,
tuberculosis,
misery.
A truck roars
out of the warehouse.
It bellows uphill
drowning out the lesson:
A for alcoholism,
B for batallions,
C for corruption,
D for dictatorship,
E for exploitation,
F for the feudal power
of fourteen families
and etcetera, etcetera, etcetera.
My etcetera country,
my wounded country,
my child,
my tears,
my obsession.

The American Way of Life

Bewildered I accepted
the invitation
that other I nearly forgot
offering me fragments of the past
of the present
California swallowed me
its hypnotic tangle
of freeways
crisscrossing
interlocking
vanishing in the stench
of smog.
Had you forgotten
she asks me
the American way of life?
From the plane crossing the bay
floating spiderwebs
arch between Berkeley
and San Francisco
she took me to the Sanctuary
presented me to
the "eternally undocumented,
my compatriots."
Transparent they slide
through Mission Heights
and sometimes in the afternoons
they meet in unsafe houses
and contemplate
the aquatic butterflies
of the yuppies
skimming in circles
around Alcatraz.
Three hundred a week
three hundred undocumented
returned to their deaths
by the Migra.
I climbed the steps at Berkeley
leading to the Campanile
suddenly

amid the groves of academe
between the corrugated trees
that frown down
on the campus
a festive touch of anarchy
banners and slogans
mocking the cloisters
boys in scraggly beards
dressed in rags
lounging on their sleeping bags
the strident squawk
of a cheap PA system
defying the dinosaurs
of the Establishment
the Jewish girl
in solidarity with the blacks
of South Africa
while the other
her Palestinian rival
demanded a homeland
for her people
and they both knew
and I also knew
amid the sacred walls
of Jericho
Joshuas dressed in blue jeans
sounded their trumpets
and the walls shuddered
and the deans trembled
and a blonde girl
spun in tight circles
with her eyes closed
in the sixties
we did it with flowers
with acid and with flowers.
Heading for Los Angeles again
toward the Edenic beaches
of Santa Barbara
by way of Santa Cruz
and Big Sur
be careful

she warns me
they're full of tar
a long line
of drilling platforms
stretching to the horizon
sticky furrows of tar
trapping birds
staining bare feet
and they have to get rid
of the dead birds.
Who's going to vacuum the beach?
Who's going to bury them?
They're cockroaching humanity
the new thinking robots
want to cockroach us.
In east Los Angeles
before the chained gates of Bethlehem Steel
the jobless steelworkers
walk back and forth
their lives suddenly as empty
as the eyeless windows
as insurmountable
as the gates of Bethlehem.
City Hall offers them
a bowl of soup
Washington
a social worker
who urges them
to write poems
to put on
group therapy plays
so they can vomit up
their helplessness.
In a lightning trip
we fly to Gettysburg
we talk of the drunken sprees
of General Grant
of the gentlemanly Lee
neon signs
mark the way
to General Eisenhower's farm

and I remember Guatemala
and I also remember
the Bay of Pigs.
Finally New York
the landscape grows portentous
skyscrapers of steel
and dark glass
skyscrapers with voluptuous curves
they used to be phallic symbols
now they have curvaceous skyscrapers
coquettish skyscrapers
but they're still built of steel
and dark glass.
Down the sidewalk an African
drags his cart
filled with tribal idols
with simulated tribal idols
his friend trails behind
beating on a bongo
two boys
also dark-skinned
defy New York
with their Walkmans
risking their lives
on their skateboards
deaf to the din
of New York
dodging and zigzagging
amid the sharks
with chrome teeth
they're cockroaching humanity
in Rockefeller Center
I remember Sonja Henie
she also flew on her skates
while the old lady in Harlem
kneeling in the rubble
dismantles her plastic tent
and stuffs it
in her shopping bag
and downtown
in the Village

a redhead
in a white tutu
and toe shoes
sobs on the asphalt
her head resting
on the bumper
of a brand new car
and people pass by
with scarcely a glance
and I pass by as well
and don't stop
then more skyscrapers
a Porsche
its yuppie plates proclaiming
I-LUV-ME
the American way of life
shop windows with books
with dresses
art galleries
jewelry stores
the bitch is drunk with blood
with her diadem of rubies
and her drugstore stink
she chews Salvadorans
as if they were Chiclets
chews up Nicaraguans
on her scarlet throne
Lebanese
Chicanos
Chiclets
Chiclets
Chicanos
her golden calves
cost-analyzing wars
her profits are ciphers
and the dead are ciphers
and the war drags on
that endless war
that already reaches
for the stars

and there'll be a rain of fire
and ashes
and the stars shall fall
upon the earth.

DEBRA ALLBERY

Photo by Julie Coash

Produce

No mountains or ocean, but we had orchards
in northwestern Ohio, roadside stands
telling what time of summer: strawberries,
corn, apples—and festivals to parade
the crops, a Cherry Queen, a Sauerkraut Dance.
Somebody would block off a street in town,
put up beer tents and a tilt-a-whirl.

Our first jobs were picking berries.
We'd ride out early in the back of a pickup—
kids my age, and migrants, and old men
we called bums in sour flannel shirts
smash-stained with blueberries, blackberries,
raspberries. Every fall we'd see them
stumbling along the tracks, leaving town.

VACATIONLAND, the signs said, from here to Lake Erie.
When relatives drove up we took them to see
The Blue Hole, a fenced-in bottomless pit
of water we paid to toss pennies into—
or Prehistoric Forest, where, issued machine guns,
we rode a toy train among life-sized replicas
of brontosaurus and triceratops.

In winter the beanfield behind our house
would freeze over, and I would skate across it
alone late evenings, sometimes tripping
over stubble frozen above the ice.
In spring the fields turned up arrowheads, bones.
Those slow-plowing glaciers left it clean and flat here,
scraping away or pushing underground what was before them.

Carnies

That's what we went for, Holly and I,
not for the rides or the games we couldn't win.
What were we then, fourteen, fifteen,
wearing cutoffs and our brothers' workshirts.
Holly tossing her hair as we walked down the midway,
her talking big and me saying nothing, a half step
behind her. But don't you know how deep summer
crawls inside you in a town like that.
You can't keep still, you need fast
fresh air from another place. And if boys
your own age try showing off for you there,
you nod and shrug but keep glancing away.
You look over at the quick swipes of grease
on the jeans of some muscled roustabout unlocking
the safety bars on the Octopus, you watch
the flutter of his T-shirt, the travel of his eyes.
And when he looks at you you're caught
not knowing what to do, and afraid to smile.
You just move on through that broken-down music.
Holly and I, we took our time getting on
and off those rides, we craved that coolness
just an extra second airborne, scrambling
summer and Main Street and a stranger's level gaze.
And you bet we'd take them home with us,
their soft goddamns that followed us out,
and wouldn't we toss all night with them, too.

Assembler

My twentieth summer I got a job in Door Locks
at the Ford plant where my father has worked
for twenty years. Five in the morning
we'd stand tired in the glare and old heat
of the kitchen, my father fiddling with
the radio dial, looking for a clear station.

There weren't any women in my department.
At first the men would ask me to lift
what I couldn't, would speed up the turntable,
juggling the greasy washers and bolts,
winking at each other, grinning at me.
In the break room they would buy me coffee,
study my check to see if I got shorted.
They were glad I was in school and told me
to finish, they said I'd never regret it.
Once I got loaned to Air Conditioners,
worked three days in a special enclosure,
quiet and cool and my hands stayed clean.
Out the window I could see Door Locks,
the men taking salt pills, 110 degrees.

In rest rooms there were women sleeping
on orange vinyl couches, oven timers ticking
next to their heads.

At lunch I'd take the long walk to my father.
I'd see him from a distance, wearing safety glasses
like mine, and earphones, bright slivers of brass
in his hair—him standing alone in strange sulfur light
amidst machines the size of small buildings.
Every twenty minutes he worked a tumbler,
in between he read from his grocery bag of paperbacks.
He would pour us coffee from a hidden pot,
toast sandwiches on a furnace. We sat
on crates, shouting a few things and laughing
over the roar and banging of presses.

Mostly I remember the back-to-back heat waves,
coffee in paper cups that said Safety First,
my father and I hurrying away from the time clocks,
proud of each other. And my last day, moving shy past
their *Good Lucks,* out into 5:00, shading my eyes.

Offering

At night in Vinton County a Satanic cult
is sacrificing farmers' calves and lambs.
My grandmother rubs her hands as she speaks of it
in a voice that absently fingers its words
like the tissue her bony hands grip and twist,
the newspaper she smoothes and folds.

My grandfather, hard of hearing, arthritic,
watches a television that doesn't work.
These days he believes raccoons are living
in their house, that they eat right out of his hand.
He grins at us, alert, remote, as she talks,
and points to a dusty plastic fern,
his few words wrestling with silence.

The light of my grandparents' living room
belongs to no hour or season. It is the light
of the parlor—shades drawn, its kept darkness
a preservative, a hush. But as a child, being quiet
is one of the things I am best at, so that adults
might forget I am there and discuss
what I'm not supposed to hear.

On my lap I'm holding the Sunday comics,
a flat blur of simple colors and letters,
and as I feign reading I can see the robed
and hooded figures circling their altar.
I see the lamb, its legs bound, in moonlight
as bright as this room's daylight is dim.

But it's pure television. I can't believe
the Devil is on this farm any more than I
think God resides in our particular church.
What I do understand is the dead live here—
their pictures are everywhere, their pallid breath.
My grandmother rises to cover the bird cage,
reads to herself from the open Bible beside it.

On the end tables are photographs of two sons lost
to war, to accidents. And on the table before me
is the picture I have colored in Sunday school
that morning, and have given to my grandmother.
Blessed are the meek, it says above my black
and blue planet Earth, suspended between God's
white, idle hands, all of it ours to inherit.

MAGGIE ANDERSON

Photo by Hilary Sio

Country Wisdoms

Rescue the drowning and tie your shoe-strings.
—Thoreau, *Walden*

Out here where the crows turn around
where the ground muds over and the snow fences bend
we've been bearing up. Although

a green winter means a green graveyard
and we've buried someone every month since autumn
warm weather pulls us into summer by the thumbnails.

They say these things.

When the April rains hurl ice chunks onto the banks
the river later rises to retrieve them.
They tell how the fierce wind from the South

blows branches down, power lines and houses
but always brings the trees to bud.
Fog in January, frost in May

threads of cloud, they say, rain needles.
My mother would urge, be careful what you want,
you will surely get it.

More ways than one to skin that cat.
Then they say, Bootstraps.
Pull yourself up.

The Invention of Pittsburgh

That was the year I drove around all the time
talking about poems. I'd eat my lunch in the car
between one public high school and another.
I was so exhausted, preoccupied with gearshifts
and poetry workshops. I forgot to pay
my income taxes and wandered around acting like

I was really earning what they were paying me.
That was the year Ed kept telling me
to eat more squid and, being accommodating,
I tried. I had to eat squid, gelatinous chalk dust,
in every Chinese restaurant in Philadelphia;
in New Hampshire, broiled squid, a double order,
no garnish, no rice. And once in Vermont,
I was so overwhelmed by all the multifoliate
adeciduous trees that I ordered a squid sandwich
in a health food restaurant on Lake Bamboseen
that came to me on whole wheat bread with sprouts.
Then I was in Eugene, on a Saturday in February,
about four o'clock. I asked for a bowl of squid
in a little restaurant on Polk Street
but what I got looked exactly like Pittsburgh,
or the Pittsburgh I suddenly knew that I,
a forty-year-old poet sitting in Oregon
was about to invent from whimsy and weariness.
There were thirty bridges, and thirty highways
followed the rivers. Neighborhoods laced
the hillsides, through detours and freeway
construction around the inclines and concrete tubes,
circuiting the long walls of old mines buried under
the gray Carnegie libraries and the universities,
the closed mills and the steaming slag piles,
the orthodox churches on the North Side
where they bless the cabbages at Easter.
This is what the lonely imagination finds in
squid: the aftertaste of scallops, the texture
of cheap perfume, bright yellow leaves
on the sycamores in the parking lot
off Forbes, kids recumbent with radios
on the lawns of the robber baron's mansions,
intricate lingerie wadded up in a hotel sink
on the Boulevard of the Allies in Pittsburgh,
the tough, sweet city of the workers.

Spitting in the Leaves

In Spanishburg there are boys in tight jeans,
mud on their cowboy boots and they wear huge hats
with feathers, skunk feathers they tell me.
They do not want to be in school, but are.
Some teacher cared enough to hold them. Unlike
their thin disheveled cousins, the boys on Matoaka's
Main Street in October who loll against parking meters
and spit into the leaves. Because of them, someone
will think we need a war, will think the best solution
would be for them to take their hats and feathers,
their good country manners and drag them off somewhere,
to Vietnam, to El Salvador. And they'll go.
They'll go from West Virginia, from hills and back roads
that twist like politics through trees, and they'll fight,
not because they know what for but because what they know
is how to fight. What they know is feathers,
their strong skinny arms, their spitting
in the leaves.

Closed Mill

I'm not going to tell you everything,
like where I live and who I live with.
There are those for whom this would be
important, and once perhaps it was to me,
but I've walked through too many lives
this year, different from my own,
for a thing like that to matter much.
All you need to know
is that one rainy April afternoon,
exhausted from teaching six classes
of junior high school students,
I sat in my car at the top of a steep hill
in McKeesport, Pennsylvania and stared
for a long time at the closed mill.

"Death to Privilege," said Andrew Carnegie,
and then he opened up some libraries,

so that he might "repay his deep debt,"
so that light might shine on Pittsburgh's poor
and on the workers in the McKeesport Mill.
The huge scrap metal piles below me
pull light through the fog on the river
and take it in to rust in the rain.
Many of the children I taught today
were hungry. The strong men who are
their fathers hang out in the bar
across the street from the locked gates
of the mill, just as if they were still
laborers with lunch pails, released
weary and dirty at the shift change.

Suppose you were one of them?
Suppose, after twenty or thirty years,
you had no place to go all day
and no earned sleep to sink down into?
Most likely you would be there too,
drinking one beer after another,
talking politics with the bartender,
and at the end of the day
you'd go home, just as if you had
a paycheck, your body singing
with the pull and heave of imagined
machinery and heat. You'd talk mean
to your wife who would talk mean back,
your kids growing impatient and arbitrary,
way out of line. Who's to say you would not
become your father's image, the way any of us
assumes accidental gestures,
a tilt of the head, hard labor,
or the back of his hand?

From here the twisted lines of wire
make intricate cross-hatchings against
the sky, gray above the dark razed mill's red
pipe and yellow coals, silver coils of metal
heaped up and abandoned. Wall by wall,
they are tearing this structure down.
Probably we are not going to say

too much about it, having as we do
this beautiful reserve, like roses.

I'll say that those kids were hungry.
I would not dare to say the mill won't
open up again, as the men believe.
You will believe whatever you want to.
Once, philanthropy swept across our dying cities
like industrial smoke, and we took everything
it left and we were grateful, for art
and books, for work when we could get it.

Any minute now, the big doors buried under
scrap piles and the slag along this river
might just bang open and let us back inside
the steamy furnace that swallows us
and spits us out like food, or heat
that keeps us warm and quiet
inside our little cars in the rain.

ROBIN BECKER

Photo by Helen Lang

My Father's Heart

My father's heart is on television
at the hospital. Lonely and a little embarrassed, it beats blindly on
the videotape, hoping for the best. Like family
members of a game-show contestant, my mother and I
stand off to the side, proud of the healthy culvert doing its chores.
The doctor explains that this is the artery of
a much younger man, and I think of the parts of my father's
body assembled in a shop from the odds and ends
of others. Now the doctor is speaking
very quickly, as if she could hide
the sad blocked door of the right ventricle,
unable to pass its burden of blood
from one room to another. When the lights go on,
I expect to see it, sore and swollen, counting
off the seconds with its bad arm. My mother
takes a few steps, respectfully, holding
her pocketbook, waiting to be addressed. We have seen
the unshaven face of the heart, the cataract
eyes of the heart, the liver-spotted hands
of the heart. Seated in the cafeteria, my mother whispers
that my father's heart is a miracle, that it has already
been dead and recalled twice.

In Pompano Beach, Florida

Like the inflatable palm tree I gave to my lover,
the palm trees on this golf course whisper
eternal life. A man circles the green and kneels,
divining meaning. He knows the sand
trap and the skein of water with its drowned elements.
I consider his handicap, the fast condition
of the course, the way his partners pause to watch,
like couples gathering on the floor
for a slow dance. Sun on his pastel sweater. Sun
on the roofs of rented cars heading to the beach.

My father passes behind me, assembling his orange, knife,
plate, coffee cup. We do not speak, we respect the old lesions,
thick scar tissue; he takes the kitchen,
leaves me the deck. He is frightened he will die
at the Humana Hospital, out of sight, behind the row
of condominiums and the swimming pool.

Last night, after dancing at J.J.'s Otherside,
we listened to the water
clean itself, traveling along its plastic arteries.
And I awoke to the sound of emergency
in paradise, sirens at six A.M., parting the traffic,
the early runners, the golfers and sleepers
still dreaming of a perfect shot at heaven.

Incarnate

I spot him at the water's edge with his daughter, a revised child from his new, corrected family. Waves roll in and cover my father's feet; waves tumble the heavy brown shoes of brokerage, precarious place settings, camp trunks stuffed with our old clothes. In his mind, my father places each one of us on a separate beach, a shaman scattering the poisons.

He grasps the child's hand. He has become the family man my mother always wanted, dreaming up improvements he will make around the house. When he sees me, he asks forgiveness in a voice he has discovered since he was my father. "Sure," I say. "Sure, Dad." I can see that he is happy and I weep; when he was ours, he hated beaches, he hated being seen. Now he walks like an Old Testament king, splendid David or great King Saul, wise with pain.

The Accident

Because you were in Navaho Nation, which is a nation within a state within a nation, there is nothing you can do. He stood silent, eyes averted, waiting, and when the authorities came, he did not give his name, address, or reason for slamming you clear across the highway from behind. You've gathered clay from every county in the state and trusted the magic of feathers, bone, deer hoof, animal hair. At the pueblos, in the terrible heat, you listened to the drums, penitent, sweat pouring down your face.

But he has no insurance, and the tribal elders and the lawyer from the BIA explain that everyone needs a car or truck in New Mexico, insurance isn't mandatory, you were on Indian land. When you tell me the story, you've changed the point of view. No longer victim, you've become a witness to the accident, to the slaughter of the Indians, to the years of food stamps and lousy jobs. In Shiprock, New Mexico, you stand in his shadow, the only shaded spot for miles.

The Story I Like to Tell

In a drugstore north of Ft. Lauderdale
you stand in line to buy a roll of film, and I'm suddenly
aware of desire, how it fills the body
at inconvenient moments. We stare innocently at the magazines.
We are hours away from making love, months away from summer
in our real home, up north. But here, eighty degrees
in mid-December, reports of bad weather arrive
like messages from a distant star. You know I want you
and you smile, for the inopportune
appeals to you. Come closer. If we can't make love,
I'll tell you a story.
My bedroom opened onto olive trees and grapevines.
It was too hot for sheets. Mornings, she walked naked
around the mill, we drank strong coffee, I watered red
geraniums in the garden. At the sight of my thighs, she gasped.
While Italian cyclists rimmed our hill town,
I swept her with my tongue for hours.

How does it feel? Tales of old lovers, silk beneath denim,
pain and pleasure cresting like a Mediterranean
wave, like the moon slung in a Tuscan window.
Come closer. I know you
like meetings after separations, ambiguous
relations, someone kissing your ear. Let's go
to the beach now; palm fronds quiver on postcards;
pelicans are flying close to shore.
If we can't make love, I'll distract you
with another story
I like to tell, the one set on a distant coast,
in another Romance language.

The Bath

I like to watch
your breasts float like two birds
drifting downstream; you like a book,
a glass of wine on the lip
of the porcelain tub,
your music. It is your way of dissolving
the day, merging the elements of your body
with this body. The room fills with steam
like mist off a river—
as intimate to imagine you
pleasuring yourself: watery fingers, slow
movement into fantasy.
You call me in and take my hand
in your wet hand. I have to shield my eyes
from the great light
coming off your body.
When you ask me to touch you
I kneel by the water like a blind woman
guided into the river by a friend.

SIV CEDERING

Grandmother

baked and cleaned
all day
then washed
herself
in the evening.
Friday

was the best night
of the week.
Grandfather opened the gown
and her breasts
filled his hands
like warm

loaves.
Because the windows
shone, and the sheets
were fresh, her braids
were undone.
When his fingers

opened the folds
of her cunt,
it was like undoing the buttons
and layers of lace
of her high-necked
Sunday
blouse.

Miss Pimberton Of

the Metropolitan
Museum of
Art
has the key
to
Genitalia.
The broken off

parts
of
Greek statues and
Roman gods
are her
curatorship.
From foreign countries

and graves,
papal quarters and
geological digs,
they find their way
to
Miss Pimberton,
who dates

the testicles, measures
penises,
labels all—
and files them
neatly,
deliberately,
working late.

Peaches

There was a contest
once
for the best picture
of a peach

in China

Madame Ling
or was it Ching
sat in some yellow
pollen

then

carefully, again
she sat
upon
a piece of white

paper

Almagest, Last Letter to Zakarias

*What is inconceivable about the universe
is that it should be at all conceivable.*
—Albert Einstein

1

When the synchrotron was being built
at Brookhaven,
I walked through the perfectly circular
underground structure
where particles would be accelerated
and split,
and I thought

of the mounds that were made
for some larger than human
eye,
and of their builders
who were named
after their constructions,
and of Pythagoras
who saw nature exposing
its precise mathematics
while things, according to
the second law, were moving
toward randomness,
and of Ptolemy of Alexandria
who made the most accurate
measurements of the earth
by using instruments devised
for the stars,
and of Gerard of Cremona,
who translated the *Almagest,*
where science had slept
for a thousand years,
and of the knowledge
that still sleeps
in the root of a word
or some old story's
metaphor,
and I knew it doesn't matter
whether the universe exists
without human perception
or not,
for we can conceive of it as fractional
or whole,
the concept of heaven
can enter the human soul
and flow out like water
finding its own
level.

2

Like all who try to harness chaos
with formulas and phrases,
I stand on the edge of the known world.
The smallest particle, the right side
of the brain, the region beyond
our galaxy is waiting.
The names I have used
as spells against the night
lead me to the word *matter.*
And like an alchemist, I juggle
the known elements,
not for gold, but for a unified
theory.

3

I sail out on the black waters
of the sound, the night speckled
with lights. Three miles from shore
I wonder if I can swim
the wave, the ray, the killer shark
home. I lie on my back on the deck
looking up.
And as the homing pigeon knows
by the slant of sunlight, the rotation
of stars, the magnetism of the earth,
how to find its way home,
the word sings through my bones,
as if they too were hollow.

4

The elements
      fuse:
        fire

      with air
   with the earth
floating in the water

of space
Space is
time

measured in distance
Dimension is
a matter

of perception
Change is
the only

constant
Conception
conceives

all
All is
relative

Mother
is the same word as
matter

5

And a stranger in a restaurant
takes me
into the blue waters of
his eyes
to someplace inside
his brain, turning me upside down
like a face in a spoon,
turning me right side up, finding
my colors, the shape of my cheek,
to remember, or not remember,
not knowing I question where
I exist
in my body? in my brain?
in someone else's eyes
where I am tumbling?
Where am I tumbling?

6

Sssshhhh. Any one answer is no
answer. As the wheel
spun out animals and herbs,
genitals, skill and time,
and still spins,
the names of the ancient ones who found
answers
spin
with the remaining questions in
this pinwheel, whirlpool, circle
around the pole.
And like Vainamoinen, who went north
in search of the three runes
that hold the secret of absolute
origin,
I will travel north, in the sign of Gemini.
If the stars would be visible,
I would search for the twins
and name them Possible and Impossible.
But the night will be light.

And there,
where the invisible bear roams,
where the wolf I once created
with the shadow of my hands
walks, I too will walk
naming the impossibilities
that fetter the wolf:

> *the footfall of a cat*
> *the root of a rock*
> *the beard of a woman*
> *the breath of a fish*
> *the spittle of a bird*

to the present but invisible
stars.

LORNA DEE CERVANTES

Photo by Georgia McInnis

Emplumada

em · plu · ma · do   *v.m.,* feathered; in
plumage, as in after molting

plu · ma · da   *n.f.,* pen flourish

When summer ended
the leaves of snapdragons withered
taking their shrill-colored mouths with them.
They were still, so quiet. They were
violet where umber now is. She hated
and she hated to see
them go. Flowers

born when the weather was good—this
she thinks of, watching the branch of peaches
daring their ways above the fence, and further,
two hummingbirds, hovering, stuck to each other,
arcing their bodies in grim determination
to find what is good, what is
given them to find. These are warriors

distancing themselves from history.
They find peace
in the way they contain the wind
and are gone.

Meeting Mescalito at Oak Hill Cemetery

Sixteen years old and crooked
with drug, time warped blissfully
as I sat alone on Oak Hill.

The cemetery stones were neither erect
nor stonelike, but looked soft and harmless;
thousands of them rippling the meadows
like overgrown daisies.

I picked apricots from the trees below
where the great peacocks roosted and nagged

loose the feathers from their tails.
I knelt to a lizard with my hands
on the earth, lifted him and held him
in my palm—Mescalito
was a true god.

Coming home that evening
nothing had changed. I covered Mama on the sofa

with a quilt I sewed myself, locked my bedroom
door against the stepfather, and gathered
the feathers I'd found that morning, each
green eye in a heaven of blue, a fistful
of understanding;

and late that night I tasted
the last of the sweet fruit, sucked the rich pit
and thought nothing of death.

Beneath the Shadow of the Freeway

1

Across the street—the freeway,
blind worm, wrapping the valley up
from Los Altos to Sal Si Puedes.
I watched it from my porch
unwinding. Every day at dusk
as Grandma watered geraniums
the shadow of the freeway lengthened.

2

We were a woman family:
Grandma, our innocent Queen;
Mama, the Swift Knight, Fearless Warrior.
Mama wanted to be Princess instead.
I know that. Even now she dreams of taffeta
and foot-high tiaras.

Myself: I could never decide.
So I turned to books, those staunch, upright men.
I became Scribe: Translator of Foreign Mail,
interpreting letters from the government, notices
of dissolved marriages and welfare stipulations.
I paid the bills, did light man-work, fixed faucets,
insured everything
against all leaks.

3

Before rain I notice sea gulls.
They walk in flocks,
cautious across lawns: splayed toes,
indecisive beaks. Grandma says
sea gulls mean storm.

In California in the summer,
mockingbirds sing all night.
Grandma says they are singing for their nesting wives.
"They don't leave their families
borrachando."

She likes the ways of birds,
respects how they show themselves
for toast and a whistle.

She believes in myths and birds.
She trusts only what she builds
with her own hands.

4

She built her house,
cocky, disheveled carpentry,
after living twenty-five years
with a man who tried to kill her.

Grandma, from the hills of Santa Barbara,
I would open my eyes to see her stir mush
in the morning, her hair in loose braids,

tucked close around her head
with a yellow scarf.

Mama said, "It's her own fault,
getting screwed by a man for that long.
Sure as shit wasn't hard."
soft she was soft

5

in the night I would hear it
glass bottles shattering the street
words cracked into shrill screams
inside my throat   a cold fear
as it entered the house in hard
unsteady steps   stopping at my door
my name   bathrobe   slippers
outside a 3 A.M. mist heavy
as a breath full of whiskey
stop it   go home   come inside
mama if he comes here again
I'll call the police

inside
a gray kitten   a touchstone
purring beneath the quilts
grandma stitched
from his suits
the patchwork singing
of mockingbirds

6

"You're too soft . . . always were.
You'll get nothing but shit.
Baby, don't count on nobody."

—a mother's wisdom.
Soft. I haven't changed,
maybe grown more silent, cynical
on the outside.

"O Mama, with what's inside of me
I could wash that all away. I could."

"But Mama, if you're good to them
they'll be good to you back."

Back. The freeway is across the street.
It's summer now. Every night I sleep with a gentle man
to the hymn of mockingbirds,

and in time, I plant geraniums.
I tie up my hair into loose braids,
and trust only what I have built
with my own hands.

Poem for the Young White Man Who Asked Me How I, an Intelligent, Well-Read Person Could Believe in the War Between Races

In my land there are no distinctions.
The barbed-wire politics of oppression
have been torn down long ago. The only reminder
of past battles, lost or won, is a slight
rutting in the fertile fields.

In my land
people write poems about love,
full of nothing but contented childlike syllables.
Everyone reads Russian short stories and weeps.
There are no boundaries.
There is no hunger, no
complicated famine or greed.

I am not a revolutionary.
I don't even like political poems.
Do you think I can believe in a war between races?
I can deny it. I can forget about it
when I'm safe,

living on my own continent of harmony
and home, but I am not
there.

I believe in revolution
because everywhere the crosses are burning,
sharp-shooting goose-steppers round every corner,
there are snipers in the schools . . .
(I know you don't believe this.
You think this is nothing
but faddish exaggeration. But they
are not shooting at you.)

I'm marked by the color of my skin.
The bullets are discrete and designed to kill slowly.
They are aiming at my children.
These are facts.
Let me show you my wounds: my stumbling mind, my
"excuse me" tongue, and this
nagging preoccupation
with the feeling of not being good enough.

These bullets bury deeper than logic.
Racism is not intellectual.
I can not reason these scars away.

Outside my door
there is a real enemy
who hates me.

I am a poet
who yearns to dance on rooftops,
to whisper delicate lines about joy
and the blessings of human understanding.
I try. I go to my land, my tower of words and
bolt the door, but the typewriter doesn't fade out
the sounds of blasting and muffled outrage.
My own days bring me slaps on the face.
Every day I am deluged with reminders
that this is not
my land

and this is my land.

I do not believe in the war between races

but in this country
there is war.

NANCY VIEIRA COUTO

Living in the La Brea Tar Pits

Each morning she is wheeled into the picture
window of her son-in-law's house,
jammed into her selected viewing space
by the table with the lamp and bowling trophy.
The drapes sweep apart like fronds.

She stretches her neck like a brontosaurus
and watches the neighbors, whose names she doesn't
remember. Across the street
two Volkswagens line up like M&M's,
one yellow, one orange.

               At lunchtime
her daughter broils a small steak, very tender,
saying "Ma, you *must* have meat." But her taste runs
these days to Kellogg's Corn Flakes and baby cereals.
She leans over her plate,
stretching her neck like a brontosaurus,
and mangles a small piece between her tough
gums. The dog waits his turn.

Each evening she is wheeled up close
to the TV in her son-in-law's house.
She watches "Superman" reruns.
In the kitchen, her son-in-law
eats meat and potatoes and talks in a loud voice.
His bowling night—she will have
her daughter to herself. But the TV
picture has gone bad, and the room is dark.
Just last week she could hardly tell if there
were four lovely Lennon sisters, or three.

He returns late—almost eleven—
low scorer on his team. He wants his wife
but there's a dinosaur in his living room, stretching
her neck. It's past her bedtime. He waits his turn.

~

Each morning he looks out of the picture
window of his house. Across the street

---

the neighbors have parked their shiny new Toyotas.
He blinks, as if at something unexpected
and obscene. He moves away,
walking upright, heavy on his bare
heels. He wears pajamas.

                          In the kitchen
he pours orange juice into a paper cup
and takes his medication—two shiny capsules.
His mother-in-law is extinct, and his wife, too.

There is the dog to feed, and he will think of
people to visit. He moves slow, deliberate,
but keeps on moving. The sky is full of birds,
and the Rocky Mountains all have names.

In the evening he turns on the TV
and wedges his fifty-foot frame into his favorite
chair, curling his tail over the armrest.
He watches the third rerun of the Italian
version of *Zorro*. When the horizontal
hold goes haywire, he watches diagonal stripes.

It's not easy to be a tyrannosaurus.
He stands eighteen feet tall, he thuds through life,
what's left. And when he roars, he shows his sharp
stalactites and stalagmites. His grown children
get nervous. He resents them. They wait their turn.

Lizzie

A spinster with a mouth like a dam and a heart
like a gyroscope is seen stirring
the shreds of a drab blue dress of Bedford cord
into the kitchen stove. It is Sunday,

three days after the murders. At the trial
witnesses layer their stories like transparencies.
The dress was new, yes, but of a cheap fabric,
badly soiled with paint around the edges,

best got rid of. And so,
because there is no real evidence against her,
nothing (nothing except a spot of blood
on a white petticoat, in back, beneath the placket,

a—how to put it delicately?—souvenir
of her monthly illness), and because
she has been active in church organizations,
and because she is a woman, and a lady,

they acquit her. She stays in that city
where under every jump rope children mock her
to the music of "Ta-ra-ra-boom-de-ay."
She doesn't say, even once, what she is thinking,

but her heart keeps spinning, spinning. If she calls
herself Lizbeth now, it is only
that she always did like Lizbeth better.
She moves to a gabled mansion on a hill

and drives all over the city in a pony
cart. Her investments multiply like fishes.
She entertains some people from the theatre,
an event that shocks her neighbors.

One autumn when the maples turn oppressively
red, she unlocks her smile for the paperboy
who comes in for milk and cookies on his collection
day and is not afraid, or does not know.

She draws a will, leaving money for the care
of animals. And still later,
when her heart, like a child's toy, is winding down
and slowing on its axis,

she is suddenly very surprised to discover
she cannot remember whether it really was paint
or menstrual blood, or blood,
or whether it matters.

You Bet Your Life

In the beginning, the word
is shown to the audience.
And although it's a common
word, something I see
every day, I don't say it.

We talk about my life,
but he won't take it seriously.

And after I've wagered
all my money, and lost it,
and after I didn't know
who was buried in Grant's tomb
and I've said my good-byes
to Groucho and George
and I'm walking toward the wings
feeling like a failure,

I guess I must say something right
under my breath,
because the ceiling divides
and the duck
comes down and gives me a hundred dollars.

Tea Party

Vassar girls attend teas;
Bridgewater girls give them.
—The Dean of Women

So there you are, in wispy veil and hat,
out to out-Vassar Vassar, macaroons
crumbling from the saucer that you balance
with kid gloves. Dizzy from the bargains
you thought you'd struck, you've swapped your last ounce
of naiveté for that
die-cast innocence the Quaker whalemen

fingered as they steered their weighty payload
toward Boston, their wake a bright divide
unyielding as the double line drawn down
a ledger. *We mind our business, we pray for peace.*
You wobble across the room on high heels,
a ropewalker. The waves are sloped as china
teacups and the ocean churns with whales,
schools of them. With studied legerdemain the
expression on your face
says sugar-and-milk-please when the faux
Indians moccasin up the gangplank
looking *so* familiar. And only when they've sunk
your whole consignment of exotic thus
taxable teas do you lean back, close your eyes,
and let the bloodyolked sun draw delicate ratlines
on your veiled face. They stood for peace, those captains,
and you the initiate stand for your school and your class.

You Have Shown Me a Strange Image, and We Are Strange Prisoners

You grow impatient while I focus, fiddle
with the aperture, forget to cock the shutter.

reflex   Your mouth droops, sets in what I call your pissed-
off look, the look you wear in all your formal
photographs. And if I try to snare you
with wide-angle lens, autofocus, Tri-X,
and flash, all I get is blank surprise
before the mirror flips. The mirror plays
the same old game, I play the same old tricks
badly. Frame after frame you slip through
my viewfinder, leaving not-quite-normal
thumbprints and toothmarks, a pressed
smile under glass, montage built of silver
reckless light. The mirror's in the middle.

~

I shouldn't need to put my faith in magic.
After all, it's only Dektol. I control

chemistry what it does, and why. The paper curls
perceptibly, as if startled in the act
of becoming an egg, a fertile egg with a thin
opalescent shell still unhardened
by the real world. I must not love you enough

or I wouldn't need to put my faith in magic.
Checking the clock, I slide the paper in
with one hand, with the other start a careful
rocking so you'd think I held an ocean
in a tray. In seconds you are born
again against my doubt under the safe
light in a dark room. The fetal curves
of cheek and brow, your embryonic smile
define themselves, darken, assert the shapes
I've captured. Then the hypo eases out
the undertow, teeming with grains of silver
possibilities. Out of the wash you look
remarkably like a photo of yourself,
but not yourself. I must not love you enough.

~

The image doesn't hold without belief.
For all the gentle miracles of silver
safelight we see each other dimly under safe

light in a dark room. Although it's half
hide-and-seek, a trick with lens and mirror,
the image doesn't hold without belief.

And even if I did love you enough
to print full frame for each stroke of the shutter,
we'd see each other dimly under safe

light, for what is love if not a rough
projection from the negative? On paper
the image doesn't hold without belief

in burning, dodging love, and the proof
fades fast. How can we hope for better
than to see each other dimly under safe

NANCY VIEIRA COUTO / 52

light in the dark, cropped in the dark, deaf
to hints of coded detail even pure
image couldn't hold without belief?
We see each other dimly under safe light.

KATE DANIELS

Photo by Elizabeth Knight

Ethiopia

Niobe lives in the desert, too.
She spends her days bent over
like an umbrella, bent over
the little dying things
that make no noise.
Niobe's mouth is so dry
she makes no noise, either.
She cannot talk, cannot moan.
She has given up spitting
in the mouths of those she shelters
from the desert sun. No spit
is left. No water, no rice.
There is only Niobe, always
here and everywhere else,
who cannot help herself, bending over
the dying. She does not feel
like an animal, but perhaps
she is. Others who are as strong
as she do not bend
over dying children. They save
their strength. They talk
to the government men
in the trucks. They walk
away if they can. But Niobe
is different. Niobe
bends over, Niobe
bends.

Bus Ride

Niobe is very old now.
She has hardly anything left
to lose: her teeth, her eyesight
are already gone, her hair's
falling out in gray-black clumps.
All her children are dead.
So when the white man wants

to sit down, and gives her the Look,
she can't tell if it's tiredness
or strength that keeps her fixed
on the plastic seat.   Suddenly
everyone is very quiet.
Heat whirs in through the open windows.
Flies flick on hat brims.
Niobe's eyes are on the floor.
The driver opens the door and tells her
to get out if she won't move back.
But Niobe won't
move back. She's lived
her life. She knows
she's right. Only god can hurt
someone as much
as she's been hurt.
And they aren't god
because they're scared
of her—an old woman
who's almost crushed
with only this much left:
to lift her chin
and look them in their eyes
and shake her head
and sit there, riding
all the way to History.

Not Singing

for Thomas and Andrew

God stopped and the car
kept rolling backward
over the baby's leg.

And then god started again
because it didn't hurt. He lay there
conscious and uncrying. Cinders

mixed in his yellow hair. Tread marks
red on his broken thigh.

When we got to the hospital
I saw that god had stopped
permanently and was never coming back
to visit these children: the two year old
burned everywhere but her face
by her teenage mother. The boy hung
by the neck for wetting the bed.
The little girl with her hands cut off.
An entire hall of bald ones succumbing
to uncured cancers.

When we got to the hospital
I saw the calm, methodical walking
of mothers who knew the truth
and how many days and what the odds
had been from the very beginning.
They were walking constantly through the halls,
sick children slumped in their arms
pushing portable I.V.'s, their hairdos flat,
clothes crumpled and spit up on.
I heard the low telling of favorite stories,
the thousand soothing sounds
that only mothers can make. And then,
in the rare moments when sick children sleep,
the terse trading of hospital stories—
the tracing back of stupid incident
and cruel accident that led them here.
The fathers in their suits or uniforms
coming in after work, standing nervously
beside the tall, white beds and twisting
their caps in their hands or wanting a smoke,
terrified of the supine children
with the far-off look of drugs in their eyes.

Do you know the sound of children
crying in a hospital at night?
You know the smell of a hospital,
and the mechanical, repetitive sounds

of elevators and cardiographs and intravenous pumps.
You remember the hushed voices of visitors,
the uncomfortable feeling of your own good health,
the soundless swoosh of the nurses' shoes,
the drop of air forced from the syringe
before the injection is begun.
But the sound of children crying
in a hospital ward at night? The lights
are turned off early, blinds twirled shut,
toys and crumbs cleared from the sheets.
The children are given their sleeping pills
in sweetened water like soda pop, and the parents
who can stay—those who can leave their other children
home, or those whose child will probably die tonight—
settle on the narrow cots and cannot sleep.

First, there is the steady thump and buzz
of the hospital like a private city that never stops.
Then the whole story of sick children that must be
remembered in spite of oneself.
Every time a little one screamed
and could not be made to feel any better.
All the questions that have no answers.
There is the falsely calm breathing
of tranquilized children,
the terrifying rhythm of all of this.
But medications wear off and pain rises again.
The moon rises, the night gets deeper, the city
quieter and even more indifferent, and the sobbing
of children starts filling the air, inarticulate and immediate.
The nurses listen at the door for this to start
and come in with their tiny flashlights
and ask, *are you in pain* and *where does it hurt?*
The children ask for the soda pop
that makes them go to sleep, something to stop
the ruined thigh from jumping out of its tractioned sling
and unsettling the muscles all over again.
For the parents on the cots, there is nothing to do
but lie there and listen and wait for the next drug
and curse god and feel themselves ripping apart inside
and not coming back together in all the same places.

There is so much misery in the world
it cannot be imagined. This is only
one ward of one hospital in one small city.
Beyond this, there's all the other hospitals
and the untamed places where there are no hospitals
but the same diseases, identical pain. There's war and famine,
all the cruelties and violence we inflict on one another,
all the abstractions we keep unspecific.
Now I want to think of happiness
and love and the cured children who live
and go home. The teddy bear in the wheelchair
and the smiles and tight wrinkles
around the eyes of the tired relatives whose child
is wheeled out of brain surgery alive,
their awkward fingers fluttering helplessly
above the green skullcap.
Instead, I think only how odd it is
that people suffer so much, and always have.
Even in my mostly untouched life, I know the breaking
walls of pain inside, and can never imagine
how those with real tragedies go on.
How strong they must be. How strong
and marvelous everyone must be
to bear so much. I'll never understand
how we endure it all or why this is the only gift
we give back to god: how much it hurt,
how much we stood up straight and took.

TOI DERRICOTTE

Photo by Kathy Keeney

Blackbottom

When relatives came from out of town,
we would drive down to Blackbottom,
drive slowly down the congested main streets—Beubian and
    Hastings—
trapped in the mesh of Saturday night.
Freshly escaped, black middle class,
we snickered, and were proud;
the louder the streets, the prouder.
We laughed at the bright clothes of a prostitute,
a man sitting on a curb with a bottle in his hand.
We smelled barbecue cooking in dented washtubs, and our
    mouths watered.
As much as we wanted it we couldn't take the chance.

Rhythm and blues came from the windows, the throaty voice of
    a woman lost in the bass, in the drums, in the dirty down
    and out, the grind.
"I love to see a funeral, then I know it ain't mine."
We rolled our windows down so that the waves rolled over us
    like blood.
We hoped to pass invisibly, knowing on Monday we would
    return safely to our jobs, the post office and classroom.
We wanted our sufferings to be offered up as tender meat,
and our triumphs to be belted out in raucous song.
We had lost our voice in the suburbs, in Conant Gardens,
    where each brick house delineated a fence of silence;
we had lost the right to sing in the street and damn creation.

We returned to wash our hands of them,
to smell them
whose very existence
tore us down to the human.

Boy at the Paterson Falls

I am thinking of that boy who bragged about the day he threw
    a dog over and watched it struggle to stay upright all the
    way down.
I am thinking of that rotting carcass on the rocks,
and the child with such power he could call to a helpless thing
    as if he were its friend, capture it, and think of the cruelest
    punishment.
It must have answered some need, some silent screaming in a
    closet, a motherless call when night came crashing;
it must have satisfied, for he seemed joyful, proud, as if he had
    once made a great creation out of murder.
That body on the rocks, its sharp angles, slowly took the shape
    of what was underneath, bones pounded, until it lay on the
    bottom like a scraggly rug.
Nothing remains but memory—and the suffering of those who
    would walk into the soft hands of a killer for a crumb of
    bread.

In an Urban School

The guard picks dead leaves from plants.
The sign over the table reads:
Do not take or *touch* anything on this table!
In the lunchroom the cook picks up in her dishcloth
what she refers to as "a little friend,"
shakes it out,
and puts the dishcloth back on the drain.
The teacher says she needs stronger tranquilizers.
Sweat rises on the bone of her nose,
on the plates of her skull under unpressed hair.
"First graders, put your heads down. I'm taking names
so I can tell your parents
which children do not obey their teacher."
Raheim's father was stabbed last week.
Germaine's mother, a junkie,
was found dead in an empty lot.

St. Peter Claver

Every town with black Catholics has a St. Peter Claver's.
My first was nursery school.
Miss Maturin made us fold our towels in a regulation square
    and nap on army cots.
No mother questioned; no child sassed.
In blue pleated skirts, pants, and white shirts,
we stood in line to use the open toilets
and conserved light by walking in darkness.
Unsmiling, mostly light-skinned, we were the children of the
    middle class, preparing to take our parents' places in a
    world that would demand we fold our hands and wait.
They said it was good for us, the bowl of soup, its pasty
    whiteness;
I learned to swallow and distrust my senses.

On holy cards St. Peter's face is olive-toned, his hair near kinky;
I thought he was one of us who pass between the rich and poor, the
    light and dark.
Now I read he was "a Spanish Jesuit priest who labored for the
    salvation of the African Negroes and the abolition of the slave
    trade."
I was tricked again, robbed of my patron,
and left with a debt to another white man.

The Struggle

We didn't want to be white—or did we?
What did we want?
In two bedrooms, side by side,
four adults, two children.
My aunt and uncle left before light.
My father went to the factory, then the cleaners.
My mother vacuumed, ironed, cooked,
pasted war coupons. In the afternoon
she typed stencils at the metal kitchen table.
I crawled under pulling on her skirt.

What did we want?
As the furniture became modern, the carpet deep, the white
ballerina on the mantel lifted her arms like some girl near
terror;
the Degas ballerinas folded softly in a group, a gray sensual
beauty.
What did we push ourselves out of ourselves
to do? Our hands
on the doors, cooking utensils, keys; our hands
folding the paper money, tearing the bills.

The Friendship

I tell you I am angry.
You say you are afraid.
You take your glasses off and lay
them on the table like a sparkling weapon.
I hold my purse in front of me.
Do I love you? Do you love me?
"If we just had time . . ."

You could show me how you wore your hair
pushed forward over one eye, hiding
half of what you knew of beauty.

Poor friendship, why must it sit
at a table where the waitress
is ready to go home? In a city
between tunnels—cracks
of darkness in the sea.

Allen Ginsberg

Once Allen Ginsberg stopped to pee at a bookstore in New
    Jersey,
but he looked like a bum—
not like the miracle-laden Christ with electric atom juice, not
    like the one whose brain is a river in which was plunked the

stone of the world (the one bathing fluid to wash away
    25,000 year half-lives), he was dressed as a bum.
He had wobbled on a pee-heavy bladder
in search of a gas station,
a dime store with a quarter booth,
a Chinese restaurant,
when he came to that grocery store of dreams:
Chunks of Baudelaire's skin
glittered in plastic;
his eyes in sets, innocent
as the unhoused eyes of a butchered cow.
In a dark corner, Rimbaud's
genitals hung like jerky,
and the milk of Whitman's breasts
drifted in a carton, dry as talcum.
He wanted to pee and lay his head
on the cool stacks;
but the clerk took one look
and thought of the buttocks of clean businessmen squatting
    during lunch hour,
the thin flanks of pretty girls buying poetry for school.
Behind her, faintly,
the deodorized bathroom.
She was the one at the gate
protecting civilization.
He turned, walked to the gutter,
unzipped his pants, and peed.
Do you know who that was?
A man in the back came forth.
Soon she was known as
the woman in the store on Main
who said no to Allen Ginsberg;
and she is proud—
so proud she told this story
pointing to the spot outside, as if
still flowed that holy stream.

SHARON DOUBIAGO

Photo by Amy Frenzel

1. Descent: La Violencia

Out the window, Colombia, out the window
the road beneath the window, the mountain village.
Out the window men on white donkeys, women in a crooked door.
Inside the window, back of the bus
I carry our daughter down the Cordilleras, the Andes.
Out the window armed farmers
carry marijuana to market.

Out the window Bogotá, city of thieves.
Out the window, the guns, the revolutionaries,
the lust of the police. Inside the window
the civil war, *you must take turns,* it is whispered,
to sleep. Everyone has had someone
killed.

Out the window the bus descends the continent.
Inside the bus the driver pilots an airplane.
We fly faster than last night's news warning of travel, we fly
over deep green valleys, mist-filled.
He sees around blind curves, he takes us over
flowering rock walls, landslides, a five-year-old boy
building an adobe brick house.
We fly past women washing clothes on a rock, we fly
above the clouds, above the road, how many days and nights
washed-out to Quito, around and around
the Cordillera Centro, how many nights
over the fog, over the coffee plants, over the jungle, the swollen rivers,
the cows and clouds streaming down the mountainside, the dark sky
of the East, over the grass huts perched on the abyss, over
these people who never traverse
to the outside. *If we go slow,*
it is explained,
the bandits will stop us.

Inside I dream I carry your daughter down the world.
Outside the girl Cartagena holds the Spanish explorers

at the continent's northern door
five days after they kill her people.
When they overcome her
every man rapes her
first. Inside our bodies
four hundred years of America.

Out the window a young man is boarding for Popayán.
Inside he falls in love with mi hija Shawn.
He begs us to stop in Ibagué where he lives.
When we say no he falls in love
with the black girl in front of him,
does not get off at Ibagué or Popayán, rides all night
with her to Tulcán.

Out the window Jesus bleeds
real blood and cries
diamond tears
down his naked body.
Out the window is a path
to the highest mountain
made by the crutches and canes of the crippled
who when they reached him
skipped away.

Out the window with each mile the state appears
beneath our tires, the police on the white road.
Inside the bus her uniformed hands
search briskly, professionally
not to admit the flesh, her hands on my breasts,
inside my vagina, I stare into her eyes,
her gunned hip
as she touches my daughter, the quick search
up the thighs. Beyond her
in the aisle, her brothers
search the men.
Outside as inside another woman weeps
for theft, I watch the long white road to Quito.

Out the window, Ibagué, city of music.
Out the window, poinsettia, avocado, banana, bougainvillea.
Out the window terraced mountains, eucalyptus, Easter lily, photo of Ché.

Out the window giant mimosa, smell of wood smoke,
a king dipped in gold, TURBAY Y SOMOZA, LA MISMA CASA!
Out the window clouds, the Spanish violin pouring
through the Western Cordillera.
Out the window the stimulants,
coffee, chocolate, sugar, marijuana.

Inside the red-fringed curtains
she sleeps on my shoulder
having gotten me from you.
Inside the shoulder the heart beats
to your rock n roll fiddle
that cries and wails
down the long continents
in a song I can almost hear
over the curve of earth.

In the front window the driver glows,
a mushroom in his white ruana,
spits to his violin, *gringas!* Inside
you drive me madly around curves, sawing
your instrument, my heart. Inside our daughter dreams
her future, her school, her men, her car.

Inside all night the boy from Popayán
touches through the seat crack
the breasts of the black girl from Tulcán
who travels with her ancient grandma
who gives us queso y pan that we eat
though the driver has warned
take food from no one. *Nada!*
You will be drugged. Then
you will be robbed. Inside
this body I yearn for your hands
on my breasts

as we descend west, south, down
the Western Cordillera, the road washed-out to Equador.
Inside the window of my heart
is a letter I write to you. Out the window
the Aquarius moon rises,

the constellation of your face,
my sprinting twin, mi amor norteamericano,
my Orpheus, you follow us down
the Andean night.

2. Someone waiting for me among the violins

I am with you in the small house of our life.
Musicians, your band of junkies,
one who has already died,
come to play.
But the music is gone from you.
The one who will die next
injects your violin
into his body.

Pregnant, I sweep the floor.
Holy music.
I sweep above you, the three of you,
then under you. Trinity.
Your lady of the broom.
Then through the community
that has come to hear you.

Slowly your violin materializes,
returns to you.
Joyful, with faith, we wait
to see what you will play.
Behind and above I look down
onto your bow
as it searches for the song.
The Earth spins,
sweeping the frail dancers off.
In your beautiful male body of patience,
truth's filament, you wait.
When the music comes, it comes
the great journey from Jupiter and the spheres,
it is more wonderful
than we dreamed.

But I forget myself. In the middle
of your ecstatic song, my sweeping dance,
my broomstick tangles with your bow
and the tragedy of our love,
that I am a mother
that you flee children and love
crescendos, and I find myself
outside our home
with your instrument.

I look down the ancient violin,
the two halves of the hemisphere.
The top begins to melt.
The bottom darkens, erupts
into flames.

3. Demeter and Persephone

In the morning waterfalls and her giggles
falling thousands of feet,
gorges so deep, mud slides,
sunrise, my maiden's shouts
down the greenest, the highest
Andes, silver

fall of the holy river
Guaitara
into and out of
clouds
churning the sun beneath us
music
ringing like a Spanish Piaf
and the brightest, most spectacular
rainbow. She squeals, the boy laughs,
"el arco iris!" the ends of

"the rainbow eye
of God," pour
violet, blue, green, yellow, orange, red

into the pots, godspots, holy *huacas* of two hills, arc
seven huts and people inside
who do not know
the colors that illuminate them.

                                "What
is the Third World?" she asked me
waking to daylight, Impiales, city
of three volcanoes, the headlines
STREET FIGHTING IN CARACAS! Revolutions
all around us, inching
toward Equador, down
the Inca Pipeline
dozens of busses, people
jammed on the tops, hanging off
the bumpers, amazing, waking
to this mass of humanity
beneath the United States

                           I didn't know
you were here

"Our blacks," Mary said in Bogotá
"live mostly on the coasts,
but we do not have prejudice
as you have it

against colors."

4. *Love, love, do not come near the border*

We are the only ones to cross to Equador.

"You must walk across the border"

a natural bridge over the Carchi River
Rumichaca
Royal Bridge of the Incas

Out the window we descend
a long morning to the frontera,

a desolate, colorless canyon,
"the driest, dustiest part
of the Andes," our things heavy,
the light, though early, a glare,
hard and hot.

Armed uniformed men
watch us come.
They lean against their border guard hut,
stroke their guns.
Comment.

Inside the hut naked girls, color of the canyon,
Playboy, Penthouse, Hustler,
are tacked with money
from the nations of the world
to every inch of wall.
The men take our pictures.
Then one tries to take me
to the other hut.
Suddenly, the girls stare down, twist torsos, open
vulvas, open mouths, cry

Mother! Sister!

"*Mi hija!*" I snap, grabbing her.
"*Mi hija!*"

They study our pasaportes.

"*Su madre?*"
They shrug their shoulders. "*Si,
su madre,*" sign our pasaportes,
chagrined

let us leave

STUART DYBEK

Maroon

for Anthony Dadaro, 1946–58

A boy is bouncing a ball off a brick wall after school. The bricks have been painted maroon a long time ago. Steady as a heartbeat the ball rebounds oblong, hums, sponges back round. A maroon Chevy goes by.

Nothing else. This street's deserted: a block-long abandoned factory, glass from the busted windows on the sidewalk mixed with brown glass from beer bottles, whiskey pints. Sometimes the alkies drink here. Not today.

Only the ball flying between sunlit hands and shadowed bricks and sparrows brawling in the dusty gutters. The entire street turning maroon in the shadow of the wall, even the birds, even the hands.

He stands waiting under a streetlight that's trying to flicker on. Three guys he's never seen in the neighborhood before, coming down the street, carrying crowbars.

My Father's Fights

His best
were the two
between Chuck Davey
& Chico Vejar:

Davey, balding,
insurance man
in trunks
with a jab
precise as a surgeon;

Vejar, Latin legs,
legs from where
they grow up playing soccer,
that don't fold,
his own blood
shiny on his gloves;

My father,
in the stuffed chair
facing the Zenith,
throwing so many punches
no one could
get near.

Cherry

Another wedding & Aunt Cherry
            the only thing sexy about it.
        Cousins slide across the dance floor
            stealing bases
                & a look up her dress—
    chiffon fanning dark seamed hose.

This time she's flirting
            with the accordion player who's
        still woozy from World War II,
    while at the bar, the Groom,
                my cousin Tony,
            arm wrestles motorcycle buddies
    who dropped by on the way to Korea.

The Bride, a knocked-up high school girl,
            broods behind the temple
        of a wedding cake;
    her Mamacita, veiled in black mantilla, weeps:
    she's heard the VFW bartender say,
            "Who's the spic?"
            Another scandal . . .

It's getting late,
            Uncle Yosh stamps
        his soused, solo polka.
    Cherry & Accordion Man,
            wearing cellophane hats
                & party noses,
        sway to Harbor Lights.

Father Zwia blesses them
                as they sail by,
         a sound like salt beneath their soles.
(The story goes the priest
has carried a torch for Cherry
since grammar school
             when he was just Wally Zwia,
nobody's father, not this saint
      drunk enough to have removed his collar,
         neck raw as a watchdog's.)

& the Photographer,
         that missing person in all our family pictures,
kneels
         behind the lightning of his bulbs,
      ignoring Bride & Groom,
as he's ignored
      First Communicants and christened infants
      to concentrate his tiny kleig lights
         on Aunt Cherry's legs.

Brass Knuckles

Kruger sets his feet
before Ventura Furniture's plate glass window.
                We're
        outlined in streetlights,
      reflected across the jumbled living rooms,
bedrooms, dining rooms,
            smelling fresh bread
      from the flapping ventilator down the alley
      behind Cross's Bakery.

His fist keeps clenching
(Our jaws grinding on bennies)
             through the four thick rings
         of the knuckles he made me in shop
      the day after I got stomped
            outside St. Sabina's.

*"The idea is to strike like a cobra. Don't follow through. Focus
total power at the moment of impact."*
His fist uncoils
                              the brass
whipped back a centimeter from
                              smashing out my teeth,
            the force waves
                              snapping my head back.
                              "See?" he says,

sucking breath like a diver, toe to toe
with the leopard-skin sofa;
                              I step back
            thinking how a diamond ring cuts glass;
his fist explodes.
                    The window cracks for half a block,
                    knees drop out of our reflections.

An alarm
is bouncing out of doorways,
                              we cut
                  down a gangway of warm bread,
            boots echoing
            through the dim-lit viaduct on Rockwell
where I see his hand
flinging orange swashes off the concrete walls,

blood behind us
like footprints,
                    spoor for cops;
            in a red haze of switches
            boxcars couple,
we jump the electric rail
knowing we're already caught.

Bastille Day on 25th St.

I heard them kick through the door in the next room, the TV explode, sounds and shouts of a struggle and knew I had to exit fast. The goddam window was painted stuck. I grabbed a roll of toilet paper and bashed it out with a muffled tinkle. Someone was already rattling the doorknob with diarrheic abandon, yelling, "Com'on outa der," as I squeezed onto the fire escape.

I went to live with the Old Bum and his gimpy dog under the sidewalk, with Cookie John in his ramshackle boxcar behind the train yards, with the deaf mute who slept on cardboards nestled in the girders beneath the black industrial bridge. We cooked pigeon eggs in a coffee can beside the drainage canal.

Like an underground railroad the mysterious stragglers we feared and envied as kids: the men who always walked through alleys, who lived in lots behind factories, squatting on some small oversight of wilderness in the midst of monstrous cities—hobos, hermits, tramps on the lam, winos and crazies, junkmen and rag peddlers who lived in smoldering dumps on the outskirts of business helped me like brothers.

O Brothers! The secret bombs, fake beards, and dark glasses! Razor blades in the edges of placards, black flags nailed to baseball bats, songs and slogans flinting from teeth used to flinging out curses! Clanking cowbells, bleating tin horns, and penny whistles! Syncopated off-rhythm hooting! Picking up rocks, swept as one through clouds of bursting gas bombs and buckshot into History, snot rags held to our faces, rushing up Rockwell shouting, bust past the barricades, sending cops sprawling, we charge down 25th Street to open the barred asylums, set free the cheering maniacs!

My Neighborhood

Shadows become familiar,
recognizable dangers: Fredju
on the Housing Project roof
tossing off a cat. Swantek
perfecting a pipe gun,
the gang on 22nd playing

endless blackjack in a doorway,
dropping bennies in wine.
Drunks stroll under dying elms
discussing the love of police,
surgeons make house calls,
transactions completed
blood changes hands.
The Mute's FM plays Schubert.
In a Chevy, behind the factory,
a girl reaches both arms
behind her back,
the gesture thrusting her breasts
out like offerings
as the bra unsnaps.
In a basement, on a cot
beside a furnace, a girl
hikes her dress over her head.
Later, she'll spit sperm
into her own bunched underpants
then throw them into the furnace.
She'll walk home alone
on the coldest night of the year,
bare under a flaring skirt,
hair flying, jacket whipping open.
Summer, in a hallway
beneath a 40-watt bulb, a girl
neatly folds her clothes
over the guardrail on the 4th-floor landing.
The elastic impression from her jeans
circles her waist like a scar.
Five guys slouch on the stairs.
They were playing softball,
she was sitting on the swings
when she asked them if they wanted
to see something. *Maybe,* they said.
And in a bathroom, a girl
writes a love letter full of words
her father would kill her for;
rises at 5 A.M. to deliver it herself.
That morning, on the bus to school,
the world blurs as it's read,
then passed to a friend

who reads in disbelief, starts to tremble,
can't be stopped from telling
one guy, then another, until they're all
shouting and laughing, pounding
each other's arms, tearing down
advertisements, rocking the bus.
The driver jumps off.
I have forgotten their names,
the names of the streets we passed,
weather, daydreams, legends,
the precision of fear;
almost forgotten how the winos
looked in the cold,
the language of the Old Country,
stray dogs, grandparents, my brothers.
But the girls are clear
in a world they made a mystery.
What did she think
climbing four flights of stairs,
five boys clumping behind her?
Come with me, she said, I'll show you,
and the hall door closed on noon.
Inside, green walls lit by light bulbs
dim as under water,
light chains laced with frayed wires,
roaches running banisters;
even four stories up
the vibration of traffic, dragsters
gunning the stop sign on 25th;
across the street Mr. Patek
unscrewing the awning with a rusty crank,
dropping the green shadow
across the storefront window
where morning donuts harden in the sun;
a brewery truck curbs up to Andy's Tap,
aluminum kegs thud down a wooden ramp
into a cellar, releasing a must
of cobwebs, ice, and yeast
that Mrs. Kosh pauses to inhale
as she feels her way
along the buildings to church,
refusing to admit she's blind.

JANE FLANDERS

Photo by Chuck Kidd

The House That Fear Built: Warsaw, 1943

The purpose of poetry is to remind us
how difficult it is to remain just one person,
for our house is open, there are no keys in the doors.
—Czeslaw Milosz

I am the boy with his hands raised over his head
in Warsaw.

I am the soldier whose rifle is trained
on the boy with his hands raised over his head
in Warsaw.

I am the woman with lowered gaze
who fears the soldier whose rifle is trained
on the boy with his hands raised over his head
in Warsaw.

I am the man in the overcoat
who loves the woman with lowered gaze
who fears the soldier whose rifle is trained
on the boy with his hands raised over his head
in Warsaw.

I am the stranger who photographs
the man in the overcoat
who loves the woman with lowered gaze
who fears the soldier whose rifle is trained
on the boy with his hands raised over his head
in Warsaw.

The crowd, of which I am each part, moves on
beneath my window, for I am the crone too
who shakes her sheets
over every street in the world
muttering
What's this? What's this?

The Handbell Choir

Twelve children, twelve gray geese in starched
collars, file onstage. Like their bells,
which are set out buffet-style on a long table,
they are graduated. The gym, with its folding chairs
and stale air, seems wrong;
they belong in a cloister or small pond.

The director, also in gray, appears.
They will play "Geese . . ." no, "Sheep May Safely Graze,"
in honor of Bach's three hundredth birthday.
Her raised hand, their rapt stance quiet us,
who suddenly seem to be listening
for a rush of wings. But the advent
is simply that of a sweet chord.

With a flick of the wrist, each bell is rung
then silenced on the breast. No hurry.
They take all the repeats,
arms rising and falling stiffly, like clockwork
hammers sounding over the roofs of Eisenach
on a March day for the baptism of the infant
Johann Sebastian. We think of sheep and lambs
in spitting snow. The church is clammy, water cold
on a baby's head, he cries a bit—
another miraculous, ordinary birth.

Having happened, the past is safe.
This is the dangerous moment, the melody passed
from hand to hand. Tirelessly, ancient-eyed,
they raise their bells as if in blessing, yes,
someone here, now, is blessing us.

Other Lives of the Romantics

1808 Wordsworth dies from fall while hiking in Scotland.

1811 Blake takes concubine.

1818 Byron teaches Shelley to swim.

1819 Shelley has affair (probably platonic) with Miss X. Mary returns to England.

1820 Blake takes second concubine.

1822 Shelley, exhausted after boating mishap, contracts pneumonia. Mary returns to Italy.

1823 Keats marries Fanny Brawne, establishes apothecary practice in Hampstead.

1824 Blake teaches concubines to read, write, color engravings.

1825 Shelly has affair (possibly platonic) with Mme. Y. Mary returns to England.

1826 Byron reunited with Lady Byron; disposes of 8 horses, a mule, 11 dogs, a macaw, 3 peacocks, a monkey, a lamb, and a tyger.

1827 Blake ascends to Heaven.

1830 Coleridge completes "Kubla Khan."

1831 Shelley shows signs of consumption. Mary returns to Italy.

1833 Coleridge completes "Cristabel." Leigh Hunt moves to Chicago and founds *Poetry* magazine.

1834 Coleridge dies after critics pan "Cristabel."

1839 Keats discovers anesthesia.

1840 Shelley dies while leading uprising of croupiers in Monaco.

1845 Keats operates on Byron's Achilles tendon, corrects lifelong limp.

1857 Byron completes "Don Juan" (199 cantos), embraces Calvinism.

1862 Keats dies from drug overdose.

1883 Byron dies in sleep at age 95; posthumous publication of his "Ecclesiastical Sonnets."

Twirling

Spring and the girls are twirling batons,
learning *beginnings* and *endings,*
aerials, swings, salutes, capers, wraps.
Everywhere batons spin and bounce.
The girls' wrists ache. They have chapped
hands, sore claves and thighs.
Twirling drives them to bed early.

Beth Skudder and Mary Lou Ravese,
captains of the varsity twirling team,
send messages: "Use imagination!
It's always nice to see something new."

They will progress with time from *butterflies*
to *tea cup slides* and *rainbow reverses,*
set their wands on fire,
become the hubs of chancy wheels.

In Beth Skudder's dream, she does the
heliocopter on the gym roof,
creating a field of force no one can enter.
Soon she begins to rise, still twirling,
over the track, the trees, the parking lot.

She's a space probe, asking what's out there,
waving good-bye to the twirlers below,
whose bodies shimmer, then dim, like lights
from a little town quickly passed over.

Big Cars

Jonah had his whale but we had sedans.
Finned and simonized they carried us
through the fifties in their plush bellies,
safer than houses and almost as big.

In school we watched movies about them.
Someday they would float or fly,
or sail themselves on swanroads to the sun.

Boys drew nothing else.
They entered "Cars of Tomorrow" contests,
hoping to win trips to Detroit.

I "learned" on a green Buick
with Hydromatic Drive, which I steered
through a neighbor's hedge.
Behind the wheel even girls were men.

We loved our glossy follies.
They had the power of many horses.
Spellbound we whispered their deathless names—
Cadillac, Oldsmobile, Hudson, Chimera, Leviathan.

GARY GILDNER

Photo by Mary Kay Bozanic

First Practice

After the doctor checked to see
we weren't ruptured,
the man with the short cigar took us
under the grade school,
where we went in case of attack
or storm, and said
he was Clifford Hill, he was
a man who believed dogs
ate dogs, he had once killed
for his country, and if
there were any girls present
for them to leave now.
                        No one
left. OK, he said, he said I take
that to mean you are hungry
men who hate to lose as much
as I do. OK. Then
he made two lines of us
facing each other,
and across the way, he said,
is the man you hate most
in the world,
and if we are to win
that title I want to see how.
But I don't want to see
any marks when you're dressed,
he said. He said, *Now.*

Digging for Indians

The first week the soil was clean,
except for a shrew's lobster-
colored jaw, a bull snake caught
in its long final bellow,
and an ocher mouse holding
its head, as if our trowels had given it

a migraine. Then we hit bird-bone
beads, clam shells,

and then we struck a spine.
Digging slowly we followed it
north, toward a stand of cottonwood
overlooking the river and, beyond,
a patch of abandoned pickups and plows
taking the sun.
We stopped
below the shoulder blades for lunch.

Then we resumed, working down
and into the body,
now paring
the dirt like exotic fruit,
now picking between the ribs
as if they were bad teeth
aching with impacted meat.
We were dripping wet,

and slapping at sweat bees
attacking the salt
on our backs—
but he was taking shape,
he was beginning to look,
as his pelvis came through,
like a man. We uncovered
his thighs and brittle, tapering feet,

and then we went for his skull.
Shaving close, slicing off
worms that curlicued
like brains out of place,
we unearthed his hollow expression,
his bony brow,
and finally, in back of his neck,
an arrowhead stuck to the vertebrae.

The ground rumbled under our knees—
quickly we got the Polaroid

and snapped him from several angles—
except for the scattered fingers
we could not have planned a better specimen . . .
Then we wrapped him up in foil.
Tomorrow we would make a plaster cast,
and hang it in the junior college.

Nails

My father, his mouth full of nails,
is building my mother's dream house.

My mother is listing the grief
it cost her, & pointing out how smooth

the woodwork is. To her brothers:
well, the blacks are taking over—

& her cousins passing through from Santa Monica
swear the church is kissing ass. Ah,

a dream house draws the line on many
fronts. (St. Monica, if I remember, wed thou thee

a pagan, no? & brought him in the fold.
& when he died thou set

to work on sonny boy, old dissolute Augustine, right?
Any food in there for thought?)

Meanwhile, time to pour
the basement floor,

& the Ready Mix man plops
his concrete through the future

rec room window, *Lord*
it isn't wet enough to spread!

Just lays there like a load some giant chicken
dropped. My father, mixing figures,

says all hell will hit the fan
if our fannies do not *move*

& sets my little brother on it with the hose
while we grab hoes & shovels, Lord

I liked that part & afterwards
the lump all smooth

we drank our beer & pop
& mopped our sweat,

& talked about What Next.
The future meant:

cut the lumber square,
make the nails go straight

& things will hold.
I loved that logic, saw him prove it—

then he said we're done
& covered up the last nail's head

with wood paste;
everything was smooth.

I moved around a lot
when I left home, making stories up.

In one blockbuster there's a lady says:
"You taste like roofing nails, father."

And: "You're growing shorter!"
Terrific dialogue but not much plot.

Like building dream houses—
no one knows what you mean.

They Have Turned the Church Where I Ate God

They have turned the chuch where I ate God
and tried to love Him into a gym

where as an altar boy I poured water and wine
into the pastor's cup, smelling the snuff
under his lip on an empty stomach

where I kept the wafer away from my teeth
thinking I could die straight to the stars
or wherever it was He floated warm and far

where I swung the censer at Benedictions to the Virgin
praying to better my jump shot from the corner
praying to avoid the dark occasions of sin

where on Fridays in cassock and Windsor knot and flannel pants
I followed Christ to His dogwood cross
breathing a girl's skin as I passed, and another's
trying less and less to dismiss them

where I confessed my petty thefts and unclean dreams
promising never again, already knowing
I would be back flushed with desire and shame

where I stood before couples scrubbed and stiff
speaking their vows, some so hard at prayer
I doubted they could go naked, some so shiny
I knew they already did it and grinned like a fool

where I stood before caskets flanked by thick candles
handing the priest the holy water
feeling the rain trickle down to my face
hearing the worms gnaw in the satin and grinding my teeth

where once a mother ran swooning to a small white box
and refused to let go calling God a liar screaming
to blow breath back in her baby's lungs

They have turned the church where I ate God
into a gym with a stage

where sophomores cross themselves before stepping
on soapboxes for the American Legion
citizenship prize
just as I crossed myself before every crucial free throw
every dream to be good

where on Friday afternoons in the wings
janitors gather to shuffle the deck
or tell what they found in a boy's locker wrapped in foil
or in a girl's love letter composed like maidenhair

where I can imagine pimpled Hamlets
trying to catch chunky Gertrudes at lies
no one believes in except the beaming parents

They have turned the church where I ate God
and tried to love Him into a gym with a stage
where now in my thirty-fourth year I stop
and bend my knee
to that suffering and joy I lost, that play
of pure confusion at His feet.

The High-Class Bananas

The bananas down at the Safeway
were doing OK last week, just as
they'd been doing all along probably,
just lying around on the wood bench
waiting for folks to come by &
look over what they'd like sliced up
on their Grape Nuts in the morning,
or in their raspberry Jello at night,
or maybe what they'd go for after school, plain,
with a big glass of nice cold sweet milk
—to get away from questions like
"How many lights are now on in the 1st place?"
or that other devil, "The fountain pen
was invented 1 century and 1 year
after the balloon. In what year

was the fountain pen invented?"
No, nobody had a lot of grief
over the bananas down at the Safeway,
not the way they just lay there
waiting for you, wanting to make you feel good.
Then somebody, maybe somebody who *knew*
how many lights were now on in the 1st place,
got to thinking, Hey!
why don't we get a merry-go-round
down at the Safeway? A big red carousel
that makes a little pizzazz? a little hubba hubba?
& put the bananas on it! & stick some plastic
leaves on top! & some fuzzy monkeys!
& some palm tress! & everybody pushed up close
said Yeah! They said Yeah! Yeah!
& so now we got high-class bananas
going round & round down at the Safeway.
& you stand there, maybe scratching where it itches,
waiting for your bunch to come around.

ELTON GLASER

Photo by Brian Hurlburt

Cheap Replicas of the Eiffel Tower

"Not altogether a fool," said G—, "but then
he's a poet, which I take to be only one remove
from a fool."
                                        —Edgar Allan Poe

Nuclear ecstasy on the picket line;
Another homily on hominy; the lacquer of tears
Sealing in the wrath of wronged women—

Christ, I'd rather be
Crouched at the slick end of an alley
In the Costa del Sol Bowl-A-Rama and Cocktail Lounge,
Eyeing the 7–10 split,

Than stand up for these anthems
Of amnesia and the undefiled,
Recombinant aesthetics
Backed by the third degree; I'd rather

Hose down the sidewalks of Bourbon Street
After the fatback extravaganza,
Drizzly auditions for the freak parade,

Than plot odes against the birdbath,
Sestinas with the sneer of sequins, as if
I were born fairhaired in Toronto, a town
So dead no one spits on the asphalt.

Elsewhere, they're sweetening theories
For sheep and the French—I can feel
My brain back up with
Dry ironies, romance of the verb,
Those arbitrary accelerations
That flare as though the great bang and spangle
Fused for the 4th of July
Had gone up some muddy midday in March.

Elsewhere, he's putting a new prong
On his pen, buffing an ego
Big as a beerwagon horse; and she,
Profile moist to the moon, has mistaken

The patois on the patios
For the dark spirals of praise. O let them
Spank the words with their tongues,
Until passion pours out
Smoke corrosive on the brain.

Still riddled by the heart's assignments,
The midnight secrets of the lips,
I want only to
Board the last bus to Parnassus,
Hoping there to take on
The torque and surefoot, the rank shag
Of the mountain goat, whose impervious gaze
Angles up the slant, scarp to white ledge:
Beauty once more mounted by the beast.

Blues for the Nightowl

What must a man do in this house
to get a drink? Your birds back up
against the liquor cabinet, their goldtone cages
blocking the door. I don't want candy bottled
by Italian girls with their beads and depilatories,
or rare Shanghai decanters of three-penis wine.
Bring out the sweet mulekick of bourbon,
plummet and catapult of cheap gin. It's not so much
the thirst that bothers me, no dusty tongue,
but the long hole that empties into emptiness.
Take down that barricade of seedball peckerwits,
crack out the ice, the taxing seals, and let me
pour this life until it laps against the end.

Coroner

Cold mornings, he would warm his hands
In the steam clouding from a corpse
Wheeled in after love went bad
Three feet behind its skull. And then

Coffee, black and sweet, to keep down
The bile backed up from the night before.

With the chest hacked free and the organs
Slouched out like mutant amoebas, he would
Cradle the heart as if some pulse
Still pumped, his palms spread under
The valves slapped shut, the blood
Crawling through his knuckles to the steel groove.

And then the brain, that braided ball
Of sin and intuition, slides out on its own
Slick pulp, the stem ragged where the lead
Peeled back the core, the text, and left
A mind draining into darkness. How bright
The slab glares, white tiles and the tools sharp!

And if some chill breaks late through him,
It shudders out like sweat, as the body turns
Stubborn under his prying knife, the hard remains
A strata of earthtones, a rainbow of pain.
What secrets lie bare and split to the eye?
Snicker of scissors as the clock ticks down.

Confluences at San Francisco

—MLA, 1987

From the high line spun over us, we hang on to
The clang of cable cars
As the damp city drops downhill, steeped
In fog and the sharp ascension
Of a pyramid whose stones inter the soul
Of money, whose shadow falls across
The Marxist cash bar and the hiring stalls.

In the glass house of the Hilton, they're raising
The ghost of Derrida, they're plotting
The Empowerment of the Disembodied, in one hand

A cluster of bloody nuts, in the other
The secondhand theories—so many thin breasts
Supporting the beards and tweeds,
So many daring to be glib and equivocal!

In the unwindowed rooms, the voices summon up
A future banked behind the podiums,
As the past grinds its teeth into dust,
Into a dead tongue
That wags against the waste, the forced accounts,
The grievances so old and heavy
Even the bay's salt air can't bear them away.

Far from any session of sweet silent thought, we feel
The pressure crowd inside our heads
Like the giant hissing cockroach of Madagascar;
And suddenly remember that parakeet
Who pecked on marijuana seeds until he sang
A wobbly daylong obbligato to the cage—
One more small mind spent in its own making.

Revelation: The Movie

I'd give it five stars,
if there were any left, so many having
flamed out in the firmament.
This flick's a cross between
Apocalypse Now and the leather resurrections
of some S & M cock-opera called
Bound to Come. You'll know the hero
by his dropdead looks, his sword of hairy righteousness,
his big bazooka for the jezebels:
he puts the *mess* back in *Messiah*.
But it's more than just
another pic of pecs and peckers;
this hardball boxoffice-buster has it all—

toads and hailstones, locusts gunning in
like a motorcycle gang, bad grammar in the overbite;
a woman with eagle wings, her hair the color of
gold tried in the fire of a bottomless pit;
candles and sandals and rods of iron;
an angel with a chain, and four more
cornered up the back alleys of the earth,
and seven angels hellbent on mayhem, and in the crowd scenes
a cram of angels, a mob, a ring, a rout—
O angels up the wazoo! And odors and ointments,
fornications on the wormwood waterbed; a soundtrack
flat-out into hyperdrive, warp of the turbo tubas,
red smears from the trumpet, flimflam on the drum;
and blood strangling out of the winepress; dragons in heat;
machine-edge of the Oscar-copping lines; beasts
with more heads than a college of liberal arts,
each one expelling a brimstone breath;
and dogs and sorcerers and whores; and a choir
goosed up in its robes and haloes, like a dago pope on cocaine,
warbling of Armageddon and the man.

I wish I had ten points locked in on the net;
I wish I had the in-flight option,
earphone rentals on the nonstop routes; I wish I had
half the popcorn handle, gnawed and scorched.
This baby will break out
in every burg on earth, no bargains at the matinee,
no passes, no refunds, full fare in the balcony,
and the promos dragging them in—the spuds
and the mall zombies, cornwise heifers from the heartland,
downtown jailbait on the make, the high and the Holy Rollers—
they'll all freeze in their seats, eyeballs wired
from the teaser to *The End,* each pair scanning for
the flash of a name and a new address, as the credits
crawl up the dark drop of the afterlife.

DAVID HUDDLE

Photo by Marion Ettlinger

Town History, 1917

J. C. Lawson,
my great-grandfather,
came there poor,
built up a livery
stable, a funeral
parlor, a watch repair
shop, and a general
store. In 1917,
when my daddy had sat
in his lap all morning,
my great-grandfather
walked outside,
got shot, and died
that afternoon.
A posse was sent
from Wytheville,
but they didn't catch
Fred Hill until he
gave himself up
the next morning.
My daddy was 7
at the time, and Aunt
Elrica, in her teens,
went into shock
and clasped her hand
over my daddy's mouth
to stop his crying.
She almost smothered
him before he could
get her hand pried
loose.

Holes Commence Falling

The lead & zinc company
owned the mineral rights
to the whole town anyway,
and after drilling holes

for 3 or 4 years,
they finally found the right
place and sunk a mine shaft.
We were proud
of all that digging,
even though nobody from
town got hired. They
were going to dig right
under New River and hook up
with the mine at Austinville.
Then people's wells
started drying up just like
somebody'd shut off a faucet,
and holes commenced falling,
big chunks of people's yards
would drop 5 or 6 feet,
houses would shift and crack.
Now and then the company'd
pay out a little money
in damages; they got a truck
to haul water and sell it
to the people whose wells
had dried up, but most
everybody agreed the
situation wasn't
serious.

My Daddy, Whenever He Went Some Place

Brought gifts
home for me
and my brother
until once the bag
from the 5 & 10
had hammers in it,
which my brother
liked just fine,
took his out
to the back porch
steps, started

driving nails
right away, but
which for some
reason nobody
understands, me
least of all,
offended me,
made me cry
a long time,
and it didn't
take us long
to get used
to the fact
that after that
whenever he
went some place
my daddy was
damn sure
coming back
empty-handed.

Almost Going

Uncle Bill had been there
and said it had
a lovely climate,
so my father applied
for a high-paying job
at a mine in Cyprus.
He and my mother talked
to my brother and me
about it, let us stay
up past our bedtimes.
For several weeks
the house was full
of sunlight, and we
laughed about everything,
but a letter came
turning him down,

and we were relieved,
Mother saying we had
no business in Cyprus
anyway, because she'd
grown up right
in that same house
where we lived,
had married my father
when she was 15,
and he'd grown up
over at Grandmama's
across the field.
We took family trips
to Williamsburg,
Washington, D.C.,
and our favorite one
of all, the Great
Smoky Mountains.

Delivering the Times, 1952–1955

80 papers
was all there was
in the whole town,
a 4-mile walk
before school
and 3 dogs
I had to watch out for.
Crow Jim King
broke me in.
He showed me
how to blow snot
out of one side
of my nose holding
the other side shut
with my finger.
In 2 years
I saved $90,
sent off to a Roanoke

pawnshop
for that gold-plated
trumpet Daddy
had to teach me how
to play. And even
though Sunday
was a heavy load,
I walked that route
every day until
I had to start
catching the bus
to the consolidated
high school.

Gregory's House

It was a testimony
to something that
could make my daddy
mad even talking about
it, how when one side
of the house collapsed
they just stopped using
those rooms, and when
the front porch dropped
off Gregory was upset
because he had to do
his drinking in the
kitchen with the kids
whining all around him
and the TV turned up so
loud he couldn't half
concentrate. And they
say when the outhouse
folded over one January
Gregory cut a hole in
the floor and was happy
not to have to make that
trip in cold weather.

But every Saturday
morning they sent out
one dirty-fisted child
to pay me for the paper.
Until that Sunday I
threw a heavy, rolled-up
one too high and up onto
the roof, and it fell
right on through, and
the next Saturday Gregory
himself came out to the
fence and cussed me and
said I owed him damages
for knocking a hole in
his house.

Miss Florence Jackson

Mother said thirty years ago
Miss Jackson had been a handsome
soft-haired girl getting
her certificate from Radford
and coming back home
to teach high-school math.
But I had trouble seeing back
past that loose flesh
that flapped on her arm
when she wrote staccato
on the blackboard.
They moved the high school
20 miles away to the county seat,
but she stayed there
taught sixth grade
like a kind of basic training,
and got the boys
to make her new paddles
every time she broke an old one.
James Newman,
drawing pictures of her,

called her "old goose bosom,"
and Bernard Burchett said
she had a voice
like a good sharp hatchet.
Grimmer than God one morning
she told us there would be no more
wrestling matches
between the boys and the girls
during recess,
and that put a permanent
stop to it.
In class I told a joke
my grandaddy had told Peaks
and I hadn't understood
about a cow and a bull
and a preacher,
and she sent me to Mr. Whitt's office.
He made me go back
and tell her I was sorry,
to which she replied
she was too.
Angry in Geography she told
us the explanation for birth control:
"People have a choice
about whether or not
to have children."
They say Miss Jackson
mellowed out
just before she died,
but I was always afraid of her,
everybody was.

LAWRENCE JOSEPH

Then

Joseph Joseph breathed slower
as if that would stop
the pain splitting his heart.
He turned the ignition key
to start the motor and leave
Joseph's Food Market to those
who wanted what was left.
Take the canned peaches,
take the greens, the turnips,
drink the damn whiskey
spilled on the floor,
he might have said.
Though fire was eating half
Detroit, Joseph could only think
of how his father,
with his bad legs, used to hunch
over the cutting board
alone in light particled
with sawdust behind
the meat counter, and he began
to cry. Had you been there
you would have been thinking
of the old Market's wooden walls
turned to ash or how Joseph's whole arm
had been shaking as he stooped
to pick up an onion,
and you would have been afraid.
You wouldn't have known
that soon Joseph Joseph would stumble,
his body paralyzed an instant
from neck to groin.
You would simply have shaken your head
at the tenement named "Barbara" in flames
or the Guardsman with an M-16
looking in the window of Dave's Playboy Barbershop,
then closed your eyes
and murmured, This can't be.

You wouldn't have known
it would take nine years
before you'd realize the voice howling in you
was born then.

Do What You Can

In the Church of I AM she hears there is a time to heal,
but her son, Top Dog of the Errol Flynn gang,

doesn't lay down his sawed-off shotgun,
the corn she planted in the field where

the Marvel Motor Car factory once was
doesn't grow with pigweed and cocklebur.

When someone in the Resurrection Lounge laughs,
"Bohunk put the 2-foot dogfish in the whore's hand,"

someone's daughter whispers, "Fuck you,"
places a half-smoked cigarette in her coat pocket,

swings open the thick wooden door and walks
into air that freezes when it hears frost

coming from Sault Sainte Marie. Driving, I see
a shed of homing pigeons, get out of my car to look.

I answer, "What you care?" to a woman who shouts, "What you want?"
Beside the Church of St. John Nepomocene

an old man, hunched and cold, prays, "Mother of God"
to a statue of the Virgin Mary

surrounded by a heart-shaped rosary
of 53 black and 6 white bowling balls.

Where the Ford and Chrysler freeways cross
a sign snaps, 5,142,250,

the number of cars produced so far this year in America.
Not far away, on Beaufait Street,

a crowd gathers to look at the steam
from blood spread on the ice. The light red,

I press the accelerator to keep the motor warm.
I wonder if they know

that after the jury is instructed
on the Burden of Persuasion and the Burden of Truth,

that after the sentence of 20 to 30 years comes down,
when the accused begs, "Lord, I can't do that kind of time,"

the judge, looking down, will smile and say,
"Then do what you can."

Curriculum Vitae

I might have been born in Beirut,
not Detroit, with my right name.
Grandpa taught me to love to eat.
I am not Orthodox, or Sunni,
Shiite, or Druse. Baptized
in the one true Church, I too
was weaned on Saint Augustine.
Eisenhower never dreamed I wore
corrective shoes. Ford Motor Co.
never cared I'd never forgive
Highland Park, River Rouge, Hamtramck.
I memorized the Baltimore Catechism.
I collected holy cards, prayed
to a litany of saints to intercede
on behalf of my father who slept
through the sermon at 7 o'clock Mass.
He worked two jobs, believed
himself a failure. My brother
believed himself, my sister denied.

In the fifth grade Sister Victorine,
astonished, listened to me recite
from the Book of Jeremiah.
My voice changed. I wanted women.
The Jesuit whose yellow fingers
cracked with the stink of Camels
promised me eternal punishment.
How strange I was, with impure thoughts,
brown skin, obsessions.
You could tell by the way I walked
I possessed a lot of soul,
you could tell by the way I talked
I didn't know when to stop.
After I witnessed stabbings
outside the gym, after the game,
I witnessed fire in the streets.
My head set on fire in Cambridge,
England, in the Whim Café.
After I applied Substance and Procedure
and Statements of Facts
my head was heavy, was earth.
Now years have passed since I came
to the city of great fame.
The same sun glows gray on two new rivers.
Tears I want do not come.
I remain many different people
whose families populate half Detroit;
I hate the racket of the machines,
the oven's heat, curse
boss men behind their backs.
I hear the inmates' collective murmur
in the jail on Beaubien Street.
I hear myself say, "What explains
the Bank of Lebanon's liquidity?"
think, "I too will declare
a doctrine upon whom the loss
of language must fall regardless
whether Wallace Stevens
understood senior indebtedness
in Greenwich Village in 1906."
One woman hears me in my sleep

plead the confusions of my dream.
I frequent the Café Dante, earn
my memories, repay my moods.
I am as good as my heart.
I am as good as the unemployed
who wait in long lines for money.

In the Age of Postcapitalism

The disabled garment worker
who explains to his daughter
he's God the Holy Spirit
and lonely and doesn't care
if he lives or dies;
the secret sarcoma shaped like a flower
in the bowels of a pregnant woman;
ashes in the river, a floating chair,
long, white, shrieking cats;
the watch that tells Zurich,
Jerusalem, and Peking time;
and the commodities broker
nervously smiling, mouth slightly twitching
when he says to the police he's forgotten
where he left his Mercedes:
everything attaches itself to me today.
Thirty million—the American
Broadcasting Corporation World News
conservatively estimates—
murders already this century.
Whether the public debt
may have affected case history
Number 51's excuse that she was abandoned
on the pier by a dolphin
and the question "What Has Become of
the Question of 'I' "
are topics for discussion
at the Institute for Political Economy.
I know all about the transmigration of souls.
I know about love and about strife.

To delight in a measured phrase,
to bank the rage in the gut,
to speak more softly,
to waken at three in the morning to think only of her
—in the age of postcapitalism.
Yellow and gray dusk thickens around the Bridge.
Rain begins to slant between
the chimneys and the power plant.
I don't feel like changing,
or waiting anymore either,
and I don't believe we're dreaming
this October sixth, in New York City,
during the nineteen eighties.

That's All

I work and I remember. I conceive
a river of cracked hands above Manhattan.

No spirit leaped with me in the womb.
No prophet explains why Korean women

thread Atomic Machinery's machines
behind massive, empty criminal tombs.

Why do I make my fire my heart's blood,
two or three ideas thought through

to their conclusions, make my air
dirty the rain around towers of iron,

a brown moon, the whole world?
My power becomes my sorrow.

Truth? My lies are sometimes true.
Firsthand, I now see the God

whose witness is revealed in tongues
before the Exchange on Broad Street

and the transfer of 2,675,000,000 dollars
by tender offer are acts of the mind,

and the calculated truths of First
National City Bank. Too often

I think about third cousins in the Shouf.
I also often think about the fact that

in 1926, after Céline visited
the Ford Rouge foundry and wrote

his treatise on the use of physically
inferior production line workers,

an officially categorized "displaced person"
tied a handkerchief around his face

to breathe the smells and the heat
in a manner so as not to destroy

his lungs and brain for four years
until he was laid off. I don't

meditate on hope and despair.
I don't deny the court that rules

my race is Jewish or Abyssinian.
In good times I transform myself

into the sun's great weight, in bad times
I make myself like smoke on flat wastes.

I don't know why I choose who I am:
I work and I remember, that's all.

JULIA KASDORF

Photo by Carol Shadford

Vesta's Father

Mom's in the kitchen telling stories
from before she was born, how Vesta figured
if her father quit smoking, he'd save enough
to buy new winter coats that she and her sisters
would not be ashamed to hang in the anteroom
of Locust Grove Mennonite Church,
where the ladies couldn't help but smell smoke
when the girls pressed around the mirror
to jab pins in their buns and straighten prayer coverings.
He drank, too. Deer season each year
when he went with the Hoot Owls to their camp
on Back Mountain, someone always brought him home, drunk,
to his wife, who had spells when she couldn't stop crying.
The bishop found out he wore a baseball cap
and made him confess that worldliness
to the whole congregation. And when he died,
with whiskey on his nightstand,
he was buried by the Lutherans.

Tears gleam on Mother's cheeks
as she traces the grain in the table boards,
but I am not weeping like his wife or daughters.
The sins of the fathers won't be visited
on my generation. I say there is no shame
in lying among Lutherans where folks are allowed
to put flowers on graves, his plot in plain view
of those mountains that rise dark and silent
as old Mennonites standing in pews—
black-stockinged women on one side,
black-suited men on the other—
those mountains so high they slow the sunrise
and hurry the night.

When Our Women Go Crazy

When our women go crazy, they're scared there won't be
enough meat in the house. They keep asking
but how will we eat? Who will cook? Will there be enough?
Mother to daughter, it's always the same
questions. The sisters and aunts recognize symptoms:
       she thinks there's no food, same as Mommy
       before they sent her away to that place,
       and she thinks if she goes, the men will eat
       whatever they find right out of the saucepans.
When our women are sane, they can tomatoes
and simmer big pots of soup for the freezer.
They are satisfied arranging spice tins
on cupboard shelves lined with clean paper.
They save all the leftovers under tight lids
and only throw them away when they're rotten.
Their refrigerators are always immaculate and full,
which is also the case when our women are crazy.

Dying with Amish Uncles

The ground was frozen so hard
his sons used a jackhammer to pry
open a grave in the rocky field
where Grossdaadi's wife and daughter
lay under the streaked stones
that tell only last names:
Yoder, Zook, Yoder.

Amish uncles, Grossdaadi's sons,
shoveled earth on the box;
stones clattered on wood then quieted
while we sang hymns to the wind.
Bending over the hole,
Uncle Kore wouldn't wipe
his dripping nose and chin.

Ten years later when we gather
for July ham and moon pies,

the uncles stand to sing
Grossdaadi's favorite hymns.
At *"Gott ist die Liebe,"*
they almost laugh
with the tears running
into their beards;
Abe and Mose and Ben
do not wipe them.

Their voices come deep as graves
and unashamed of shirtsleeves
or suspenders. Seeing them cry
that brave, I think the uncles
mustn't die, that they'll stay
with those of us who must,
being so much better than we are
at weathering death.

Leftover Blessings

His dinner on the stove, Grandpa smirked at our jar
of pickled eggs and beets, "Old maids' picnic,
party for hens." They still let Bertha come
since she married so late and someone so mean.
(Who could begrudge all those children a mother,
besides it was she who taught that proud Amishman
to drive in her own new, black Plymouth.)

They had a spot under the hemlocks
by a stream on Back Mountain, the Valley's
leftover blessings: Elsie and Miriam,
the three Stayrook sisters who crocheted and sang,
and Mary and Loamie who lived on the home farm
like girls—calling all the chickens by name,
milking goats and Rosie the cow by hand,
feeding geese and guinea hens just for fun.
Winters they hooked rugs from wool rags,
heating only one room in that great, dark house.

The only child among women, I couldn't imagine
them young or waiting for dates, though I'd seen
the photograph from Rehoboth or one of the ocean cities—
five of them lined up, laughing in the surf,
thin, dark-haired, hiking their skirts.
I never guessed they might have chosen
to stay with women.

I only felt the weight of the way
they heaped my plate and touched my hair,
or the picnic games they made only for me.
How they cheered while I raced against
invisible children, sparing me the indignity
of three-legged relays, bestowing balloons
and butterscotch. So much for just one child,
I thought. This is what it means to be a blessing,
enough love left over to give prizes for nothing,
for just showing up, being young, being born
the granddaughter of a man someone married.

Uncle

At nine I knew what Jesus would do
if he got C.O. just for being born
Mennonite. He'd go anyway, like you.

In the name of peace, he'd race
an ambulance through the screaming streets
of Saigon. He'd grow a moustache to show
he wasn't a soldier—a speck
on the camera lens, Grandpa insisted.

He'd take a generator to a village
in the hills where golden children
would run behind him yelling, "Mother Fucker."

He'd thrust brilliant green blades
of rice into the fields where men's legs

and the torsos of water buffaloes exploded
when plows struck bombs in the mud.

When the planes returned, he'd load
whomever he could into the only car,
drive to a refugee camp, and there give up
at last, as you gave up bearing that war
on your tall, blond body.

Lost across the continents for months,
you returned to us, the uncle of someone else,
gaunt as a corpse, pale and haunted.
And when you could barely finish
a child's portion at Howard Johnson's,
that was the only miracle I could grasp.

Mennonites

We keep our quilts in closets and do not dance.
We hoe thistles along fence rows for fear
we may not be perfect as our Heavenly Father.
We clean up his disasters. No one has to
call; we just show up in the wake of tornadoes
with hammers, after floods with buckets.
Like Jesus, the servant, we wash each other's feet
twice a year and eat the Lord's Supper,
afraid of sins hidden so deep in our organs
they could damn us unawares,
swallowing this bread, his body, this juice.
Growing up, we love the engravings in *Martyrs Mirror*:
men drowned like cats in burlap sacks,
the Catholic inquisitors,
the woman who handed a pear to her son,
her tongue screwed to the roof of her mouth
to keep her from singing hymns while she burned.
We love Catherine the Great and the rich tracts
she gave us in the Ukraine, bright green winter wheat,
the Cossacks who torched it, and Stalin,
who starved our cousins while wheat rotted

---

in granaries. We must love our enemies.
We must forgive as our sins are forgiven,
our great-uncle tells us, showing the chain
and ball in a cage whittled from one block of wood
while he was in prison for refusing to shoulder
a gun. He shows the clipping from 1916:
Mennonites are German milksops, too yellow to fight.
We love those Nazi soldiers who, like Moses,
led the last cattle cars rocking out of the Ukraine,
crammed with our parents—children then—
learning the names of Kansas, Saskatchewan, Paraguay.
This is why we cannot leave the beliefs
or what else would we be? why we eat
'til we're drunk on shoofly and moon pies and borscht.
We do not drink; we sing. Unaccompanied on Sundays,
those hymns in four parts, our voices lift with such force
that we lift, as chaff lifts toward God.

What I Learned from My Mother

I learned from my mother how to love
the living, to have plenty of vases on hand
in case you have to rush to the hospital
with peonies cut from the lawn, black ants
still stuck to the buds. I learned to save jars
large enough to hold fruit salad for a whole
grieving household, to cube home-canned pears
and peaches, to slice through maroon grape skins
and flick out the sexual seeds with a knife point.
I learned to attend viewings even if I didn't know
the deceased, to press the moist hands
of the living, to look in their eyes and offer
sympathy, as though I understood loss even then.
I learned that whatever we say means nothing,
what anyone will remember is that we came.
I learned to believe I had the power to ease
awful pains materially like an angel.
Like a doctor, I learned to create
from another's suffering my own usefulness, and once

you know how to do this, you can never refuse.
To every house you enter, you must offer
healing: a chocolate cake you baked yourself,
the blessing of your voice, your chaste touch.

ETHERIDGE KNIGHT

Photo by McGuire Studios

Hard Rock Returns to Prison from the Hospital for the Criminal Insane

Hard Rock / was / "known not to take no shit
From nobody," and he had the scars to prove it:
Split purple lips, lumbed ears, welts above
His yellow eyes, and one long scar that cut
Across his temple and plowed through a thick
Canopy of kinky hair.

The WORD / was / that Hard Rock wasn't a mean nigger
Anymore, that the doctors had bored a hole in his head,
Cut out part of his brain, and shot electricity
Through the rest. When they brought Hard Rock back,
Handcuffed and chained, he was turned loose,
Like a freshly gelded stallion, to try his new status.
And we all waited and watched, like a herd of sheep,
To see if the WORD was true.

As we waited we wrapped ourselves in the cloak
Of his exploits: "Man, the last time, it took eight
Screws to put him in the Hole." "Yeah, remember when he
Smacked the captain with his dinner tray?" "He set
The record for time in the Hole—67 straight days!"
"Ol Hard Rock! man, that's one crazy nigger."
And then the jewel of a myth that Hard Rock had once bit
A screw on the thumb and poisoned him with syphilitic spit.

The testing came, to see if Hard Rock was really tame.
A hillbilly called him a black son of a bitch
And didn't lose his teeth, a screw who knew Hard Rock
From before shook him down and barked in his face.
And Hard Rock did *nothing*. Just grinned and looked silly,
His eyes empty like knotholes in a fence.

And even after we discovered that it took Hard Rock
Exactly 3 minutes to tell you his first name,
We told ourselves that he had just wised up,
Was being cool; but we could not fool ourselves for long,
And we turned away, our eyes on the ground. Crushed.
He had been our Destroyer, the doer of things

We dreamed of doing but could not bring ourselves to do,
The fears of years, like a biting whip,
Had cut deep bloody grooves
Across our backs.

He Sees Through Stone

He sees through stone
he has the secret eyes
this old black one
who under prison skies
sits pressed by the sun
against the western wall
his pipe between purple gums

the years fall
like overripe plums
bursting red flesh
on the dark earth

his time is not my time
but I have known him
in a time gone

he led me trembling cold
into the dark forest
taught me the secret rites
to make it with a woman
to be true to my brothers
to make my spear drink
the blood of my enemies

now black cats circle him
flash white teeth
snarl at the air
mashing green grass beneath
shining muscles

ears peeling his words
he smiles

he knows
the hunt   the enemy
he has the secret eyes
he sees through stone

The Idea of Ancestry

1

Taped to the wall of my cell are 47 pictures: 47 black
faces: my father, mother, grandmothers (1 dead), grand-
fathers (both dead), brothers, sisters, uncles, aunts,
cousins (1st & 2nd), nieces, and nephews. They stare
across the space at me sprawling on my bunk. I know
their dark eyes, they know mine. I know their style,
they know mine. I am all of them, they are all of me;
they are farmers, I am a thief, I am me, they are thee.

I have at one time or another been in love with my mother,
1 grandmother, 2 sisters, 2 aunts (1 went to the asylum),
and 5 cousins. I am now in love with a 7-yr-old niece
(she sends me letters written in large block print, and
her picture is the only one that smiles at me).

I have the same name as 1 grandfather, 3 cousins, 3 nephews,
and 1 uncle. The uncle disappeared when he was 15, just took
off and caught a freight (they say). He's discussed each year
when the family has a reunion, he causes uneasiness in
the clan, he is an empty space. My father's mother, who is 93
and who keeps the Family Bible with everybody's birth dates
(and death dates) in it, always mentions him. There is no
place in her Bible for "whereabouts unknown."

2

Each fall the graves of my grandfathers call me, the brown
hills and red gullies of mississippi send out their electric
messages, galvanizing my genes. Last yr / like a salmon quitting
the cold ocean-leaping and bucking up his birthstream / I

hitchhiked my way from LA with 16 caps in my pocket and a
monkey on my back. And I almost kicked it with the kinfolks.
I walked barefooted in my grandmother's backyard / I smelled
    the old
land and the woods / I sipped cornwhiskey from fruit jars with
    the men /
I flirted with the women / I had a ball till the caps ran out
and my habit came down. That night I looked at my grandmother
and split / my guts were screaming for junk / but I was almost
contented / I had almost caught up with me.
(The next day in Memphis I cracked a croaker's crib for a fix.)

This yr there is a gray stone wall damming my stream, and when
the falling leaves stir my genes, I pace my cell or flop on my bunk
and stare at 47 black faces across the space. I am all of them,
they are all of me, I am me, they are thee, and I have no children
to float in the space between.

The Warden Said to Me the Other Day

The warden said to me the other day
(innocently, I think), "Say, etheridge,
why come the black boys don't run off
like the white boys do?"
I lowered my jaw and scratched my head
and said (innocently, I think), "Well, suh,
I ain't for sure, but I reckon it's 'cause
we ain't got nowheres to run to."

Feeling Fucked Up

Lord she's gone done left me done packed / up and split
and I with no way to make her
come back and everywhere the world is bare
bright bone white   crystal sand glistens
dope death dead dying and jiving drove

her away made her take her laughter and her smiles
and her softness and her midnight sighs—

Fuck Coltrane and music and clouds drifting in the sky
fuck the sea and trees and the sky and birds
and alligators and all the animals that roam the earth
fuck marx and mao fuck fidel and nkrumah and
democracy and communism fuck smack and pot
and red ripe tomatoes fuck joseph fuck mary fuck
god jesus and all the disciples fuck fanon nixon
and malcolm fuck the revolution fuck freedom fuck
the whole muthafucking thing
all i want now is my woman back
so my soul can sing

Welcome Back, Mr. Knight: Love of My Life

Welcome back, Mr. K: Love of My Life—
How's your drinking problem?—your thinking
Problem? you / are / pickling
Your liver—
Gotta / watch / out for the
"Ol Liver": Love of My Life.
How's your dope
Problem?—your marijuana, methadone, and cocaine
Problem / too?—your lustful problem—
How's your weight problem—your eating problem?
How's your lying and cheating and
Staying out all / night long problem?
Welcome back, Mr. K: Love of My Life
How's your pocket / book problem?—your / being
broke problem? you still owe and borrowing mo'
25 dollar problems from other / po / poets?
Welcome back, Mr. K: Love of My Life.
How's your ex-convict problem?—your John Birch
Problem?—your preacher problem?—your fat
Priests sitting in your / chair, saying
How racist and sexist they / will / forever / be
Problem?—How's your Daniel Moynihan

Problem?—your crime in the streets, runaway
Daddy, Black men with dark shades
And bulging crotches problem?
How's your nixon-agnew—j. edgar hoover
Problem?—you still paranoid? still schizoid?—
Still scared shitless?
How's your bullet-thru-the-brain problem?—or
A needle-in-your-arm problem?
Welcome back, Mr. K:—Love of My Life.
You gotta watch / out for the "Ol Liver."
How's your pussy
Problem?—lady-on-top—
smiling like God, titty-in-your-mouth
Problem? Welcome back, Mr. K:
Love of My Life. How's your peace
Problem?—your no / mo' war
Problem—your heart problem—your belly / problem?—
You gotta watch / out for the "Ol Liver."

Dark Prophecy: I Sing of Shine

And, yeah, brothers
while white / america sings about the unsink-
able molly brown
(who was hustling the titanic
when it went down)
I sing to thee of Shine
the stoker who was hip enough to flee the fucking ship
and let the white folks drown
with screams on their lips
(jumped his black ass into the dark sea, Shine did,
broke free from the straining steel).
Yeah, I sing to thee of Shine
and how the millionaire banker stood on the deck
and pulled from his pockets a million dollar check
saying Shine Shine save poor me
and I'll give you all the money a black boy needs—
how Shine looked at the money and then at the sea
and said jump in mothafucka and swim like me—

And Shine swam on—Shine swam on—
and how the banker's daughter ran naked on the deck
with her pink tits trembling and her pants roun her neck
screaming Shine Shine save poor me
and I'll give you all the pussy a black boy needs—
how Shine said now pussy is good and that's no jive
but you got to swim not fuck to stay alive—
And Shine swam on Shine swam on—

How Shine swam past a preacher afloating on a board
crying save *me* nigger Shine in the name of the Lord—
and how the preacher grabbed Shine's arm and broke his stroke—
how Shine pulled his shank and cut the preacher's throat—
And Shine swam on—Shine swam on—
And when the news hit shore that the titanic had sunk
Shine was up in Harlem damn near drunk

Rehabilitation & Treatment in the Prisons of America

The Convict strolled into the prison administration building to get assistance and counseling for his personal problems. Inside the main door were several other doors proclaiming: Doctor, Lawyer, Teacher, Counselor, Therapist, etc. He chose the proper door, and was confronted with two more doors: Custody and Treatment. He chose Treatment, went in, and was confronted with two more doors: First Offender and Previous Offender. Again he chose the proper door and was confronted with two *more* doors: Adult and Juvenile. He was an adult, so he walked through that door and ran smack into two *more* doors: Democrat and Republican. He was democrat, so he rushed through that door and ran smack into two *more* doors: Black and White. He was Black, so he rushed—*ran*—through that door—and fell nine stories to the street.

BILL KNOTT

Photo by Rochelle Nameroff

Ant Dodger

A suicide applicant
Who braces himself out
On a high ledge at noon
While busy peeking down

Noticed an ant crawling
Dottily on the ledge
Right
There near his left toe

Below crowds all pushed
Oblivious babbling
Omniscient like in the movies
Out whooshy doors

But his gaze halt ant
Ant the true ant
He dimly remembers
Not like them

So now
He hesitates
A million stories up
Shifts weight trying

Make his mind up
Distantly deciding
Whether to step
Before he jumps

On it
Or not

Two Vietnam Poems: 1966

1
(End) of (Summer)

I'm tired of murdering children.
Once, long ago, they wanted to live;
now I feel Vietnam the place
where rigor mortis is beginning to set-in upon me.

I force silence down the throats of mutes,
down the throats of mating-cries of animals who know they are
    extinct.
The chameleon's death-soliloquy is your voice's pulse;
your scorched forehead a constellation's suicide-note.

A phonograph needle plunges through long black hair,
and stone drips slowly into our veins.
The earth has been squandered by the meek.
And upsidedown in the earth someone walks upon my soles
    when I walk.

A baby is crying.
In the swaddling-pages
a baby.

"Don't cry. No Solomon's-sword can
divide you from the sky.
You are one. Fly."

I'm tired, so tired.
I have sleep to do.
I have work to dream.

2
Voi(poem)ces

"mercy . . . mercy" From face to face
a child's voice bounces, lower and lower;
continues its quest
underground.

Bloodspurts lessening . . . hoofbeats of animals
stalked to their birth by the sun, fade. It is a bright
edgeless morning, like a knife that to be cleaned
is held under a vein.

I blink away the stinging gleam
as my country sows desert upon Vietnam.
We, imperious, die of human thirst
—having forgotten tears are an oasis.

"help . . . help" From heart to heart
a heartbeat staggers, looking for a haven.
Bereft. It is easier to enter heaven
than to pass through each others' eyes,

pores,
armor,
like merciful sperm, cool water, the knife-
thrust of tears. . . . It is easier
to go smoothly insane—like a Detroit car—
than to stammer and hiccup help.

And this poem is the easiest thing of all:
it floats upon children's singing, out of the bloodstream;
a sunbeam shoulders it, carries it away.
There is nothing left.
                    "please . . . please"

Shorts/Excerpts

I keep a TV monitor on my chest
so that all who approach me can see themselves
and respond appropriately.

        ~

It was that kind of day
The kind that goes through you
like a skewer but is okay as long
as there's someone beside you

waiting ready to lick the skewer
when it emerges from you

~

I only keep this voice to give to anything afraid of me

~

. . . [the] saint who hung himself
With a noose tied to his halo

~

The only face I will never find between my teeth
continues to quote me . . .

[The eyes, built on a ruins which is
the skull, rise.]

Sonnet

The way the world is not
Astonished at you
It doesn't blink a leaf
When we step from the house
Leads me to think
That beauty is natural, unremarkable
And not to be spoken of
Except in the course of things
The course of singing and worksharing
The course of squeezes and neighbors
The course of you tying back your raving hair to go out
And the course of course of me
Astonished at you
The way the world is not

At the Crossroads

The wind blows a piece of paper to my feet.

I pick it up.

It is not a petition for my death.

Funny Poem

death loves rich people
more than us poor
coffin salesmen look down their sniffs
shoot their cuffs
at us

funeral directors obit-pages priests
all want classy
can't afford
a headstone
a silk lining
daily lawn mowers flowers plus
catering service for the worms
they get mortally insulted

and you know it's funny
while I never
believed that stuff about god
loving
the poor so much
made so many

I never believed that stuff about god
but this
death preferring the rich thing you know
it's kind of funny but you know
I believe it
it makes sense

in fact
I think we
should start a movement
our slogan would be
GIVE DEATH WHAT IT WANTS

yes
let's lend it a helpin' hand
be neighborly
it makes sense
since what death seems to want is
the dead
i.e. the rich

Death

Going to sleep, I cross my hands on my chest.
They will place my hands like this.
It will look as though I am flying into myself.

Feeding the Sun

One day we notice that the sun
needs feeding. Immediately
a crash program begins: we fill rockets
with wheat, smoke-rings, razor blades, then,
after long aiming
—they're off. Hulls specially alloyed
so as not to melt before the stuff
gets delivered we pour cattle rivers windmills,
aborigines etcet into the sun which
however, grows stubbornly
smaller, paler. Finally
of course we run out of things to feed the thing,
start shipping ourselves. By now
all the planets-moons-asteroids and

so on have been shoveled in though they're
not doing much good it's
still looking pretty weak, heck, nothing helps!
Now the last few of us left lift off.
The trip seems forever but then, touchdown.
Just before entering we wonder,
will we be enough. There's
a last-second doubt
in our minds: can we,
can this final sacrifice, our broughten crumb,
satiate
it—will a glutteral belch burst out then at last,—
and will that Big Burp
be seen by far-off telescopes,
interpreted as a nova,
by those other galaxies,
those further stars which have always seemed even more starving
than ours?

TED KOOSER

Photo by William Stafford

Flying at Night

Above us, stars. Beneath us, constellations.
Five billion miles away, a galaxy dies
like a snowflake falling on water. Below us,
some farmer, feeling the chill of that distant death,
snaps on his yard light, drawing his sheds and barn
back into the little system of his care.
All night, the cities, like shimmering novas,
tug with bright streets at lonely lights like his.

At the Office Early

Rain has beaded the panes
of my office windows,
and in each little lens
the bank at the corner
hangs upside down.
What wonderful music
this rain must have made
in the night, a thousand banks
turned over, the change
crashing out of the drawers
and bouncing upstairs
to the roof, the soft
percussion of ferns
dropping out of their pots,
the ballpoint pens
popping out of their sockets
in a fluffy snow
of deposit slips.
Now all day long,
as the sun dries the glass,
I'll hear the soft piano
of banks righting themselves,
the underpaid tellers
counting their nickels and dimes.

Selecting a Reader

First, I would have her be beautiful,
and walking carefully up on my poetry
at the loneliest moment of an afternoon,
her hair still damp at the neck
from washing it. She should be wearing
a raincoat, an old one, dirty
from not having money enough for the cleaners.
She will take out her glasses, and there
in the bookstore, she will thumb
over my poems, then put the book back
up on its shelf. She will say to herself,
"For that kind of money, I can get
my raincoat cleaned." And she will.

Self-Portrait at Thirty-Nine

A barber is cutting the hair;
his fingers, perfumed by a rainbow
of bottled oils, blanket the head
with soft, pink clouds. Through these,
the green eyes, from their craters, peer.

There's a grin lost somewhere
in the folds of the face, with a fence
of old teeth, broken and leaning,
through which asides to the barber
pounce catlike onto the air.

This is a face which shows its age,
has all of the coin it started with,
with the look of having been counted
too often. Oh, but I love
my face! It is that hound of bronze

who faithfully stands by the door
to hold it open wide—on light,
on water, on leafy streets
where women pass it with a smile.
Good dog, old face; good dog, good dog.

The Very Old

The very old are forever
hurting themselves,

burning their fingers
on skillets, falling

loosely as trees
and breaking their hips

with muffled explosions of bone.
Down the block

they are wheeled in
out of our sight

for years at a time.
To make conversation,

the neighbors ask
if they are still alive.

Then, early one morning,
through our kitchen windows

we see them again,
first one and then another,

out in their gardens
on crutches and canes,

perennial,
checking their gauges for rain.

At the End of the Weekend

It is Sunday afternoon,
and I suddenly miss
my distant son, who at ten
has just this instant buzzed
my house in a flying
cardboard box, dipping
one wing to look down over
my shimmering roof, the yard,
the car in the drive. In his room
three hundred miles from me,
he tightens his helmet,
grips the controls, turns
loops and rolls. My windows
rattle. On days like this,
the least quick shadow crossing
the page makes me look up
at the sky like a goose,
squinting to see that flash
that I dream is his thought of me
daring to fall through the distance,
then climbing, full throttle, away.

How to Make Rhubarb Wine

Go to the patch some afternoon
in early summer, fuzzy with beer
and sunlight, and pick a sack
of rhubarb (red or green will do)
and God knows watch for rattlesnakes
or better, listen; they make a sound
like an old lawnmower rolled downhill.
Wear a hat. A straw hat's best
for the heat but lets the gnats in.
Bunch up the stalks and chop the leaves off
with a buck knife and be careful.
You need ten pounds; a grocery bag
packed full will do it. Then go home

and sit barefooted in the shade
behind the house with a can of beer.
Spread out the rhubarb in the grass
and wash it with cold water
from the garden hose, washing
your feet as well. Then take a nap.
That evening, dice the rhubarb up
and put it in a crock. Then pour
eight quarts of boiling water in,
cover it up with a checkered cloth
to keep the fruit flies out of it,
and let it stand five days or so.
Take time each day to think of it.

Ferment ten days, under the cloth,
sniffing of it from time to time,
then siphon it off, swallowing some,
and bottle it. Sit back and watch
the liquid clear to honey yellow,
bottled and ready for the years,
and smile. You've done it awfully well.

A Widow

She's combed his neckties out of her hair
and torn out the tongues of his shoes.
She's poured his ashes out of their urn
and into his humidor. For the very last time,
she's scrubbed the floor around the toilet.
She hates him even more for dying.

Shooting a Farmhouse

The first few wounds are nearly invisible;
a truck rumbles past in the dust
and a .22 hole appears in the mailbox
like a fly landing there.
In a month you can see sky
through the tail of the windmill.
The attic windows grow black and uneasy.
When the last hen is found shot in the yard,
the old man and his wife move away.

In November, a Land Rover
flattens the gate like a tank
and pulls up in the yard. Hunters spill out
and throw down their pheasants like hats.
They blow out the rest of the windows,
set beer cans up on the porch rails
and shoot from the hip.
One of them walks up and yells in,
"Is anyone home?" getting a laugh.

By sunset, they've kicked down the door.
In the soft blush of light,
they blast holes in the plaster
and piss on the floors.

When the beer and the shells are all gone,
they drive sadly away,
the blare of their radio fading.
A breeze sighs in the shelterbelt.
Back in the house,
the newspapers left over from packing
the old woman's dishes
begin to blow back and forth through the rooms.

Year's End

Now the seasons are closing their files
on each of us, the heavy drawers
full of certificates rolling back
into the tree trunks, a few old papers
flocking away. Someone we loved
has fallen from our thoughts,
making a little, glittering splash
like a bicycle pushed by a breeze.
Otherwise, not much has happened;
we fell in love again, finding
that one red feather on the wind.

LARRY LEVIS

Photo by Kent Miles

The Widening Spell of the Leaves

—The Carpathian Frontier, October, 1968
—for my brother

Once, in a foreign country, I was suddenly ill.
I was driving south toward a large city famous
For so little it had a replica, in concrete,
In two-thirds scale, of the Arc de Triomphe stuck
In the midst of traffic, & obstructing it.
But the city was hours away, beyond the hills
Shaped like the bodies of sleeping women.
Often I had to slow down for herds of goats
Or cattle milling on those narrow roads, & for
The narrower, lost, stone streets of villages
I passed through. The pains in my stomach had grown
Gradually sharper & more frequent as the day
Wore on, & now a fever had set up house.
In the villages there wasn't much point in asking
Anyone for help. In those places, where tanks
Were bivouacked in shade on their way back
From some routine exercise along
The Danube, even food was scarce that year.
And the languages shifted for no clear reason
From two hard quarries of Slavic into German,
Then to a shred of Latin spliced with oohs
And hisses. Even when I tried the simplest phrases,
The peasants passing over those uneven stones
Paused just long enough to look up once,
Uncomprehendingly. Then they turned
Quickly away, vanishing quietly into that
Moment, like bark chips whirled downriver.
It was autumn. Beyond each village the wind
Threw gusts of yellowing leaves across the road.
The goats I passed were thin, gray; their hind legs,
Caked with dried shit, seesawed along—
Not even mild contempt in their expressionless,
Pale eyes, & their brays like the scraping of metal.
Except for one village that had a kind
Of museum where I stopped to rest, & saw
A dead Scythian soldier under glass,

Turning to dust while holding a small sword
At attention forever, there wasn't much to look at.
Wind, leaves, goats, the higher passes
Locked in stone, the peasants with their fate
Embroidering a stillness into them,
And a spell over all things in that landscape,
Like. . . .
                    That was the trouble; it couldn't be
Compared to anything else, not even the sleep
Of some asylum at a wood's edge with the sound
Of a pond's spillway beside it. But as each cramp
Grew worse & lasted longer than the one before,
It was hard to keep myself aloof from the threadbare
World walking on that road. After all,
Even as they moved, the peasants, the herds of goats
And cattle, the spiralling leaves, at least were part
Of that spell, that stillness.
                                    After a while,
The villages grew even poorer, then thinned out,
Then vanished entirely. An hour later,
There were no longer even the goats, only wind,
Then more & more leaves blown over the road, sometimes
Covering it completely for a second.
And yet, except for a random oak or some brush
Writhing out of the ravine I drove beside,
The trees had thinned into rock, into large,
Tough blonde rosettes of fading pasture grass.
Then *that* gave out in a bare plateau. . . . And then,
Easing the Dacia down a winding grade
In second gear, rounding a long, funneled curve—
In a complete stillness of yellow leaves filling
A wide field—like something thoughtlessly,
Mistakenly erased, the road simply ended.
I stopped the car. There was no wind now.
I expected that, & though I was sick & lost,
I wasn't afraid. I should have been afraid.
To this day I don't know why I wasn't.
I could hear time cease, the field quietly widen.
I could feel the spreading stillness of the place
Moving like something I'd witnessed as a child,
Like the ancient, armored leisure of some reptile

Gliding, gray-yellow, into the slightly tepid,
Unidentical gray-brown stillness of the water—
Something blank & unresponsive in its tough,
Pimpled skin—seen only a moment, then unseen
As it submerged to rest on mud, or glided just
Beneath the lustreless, calm yellow leaves
That clustered along a log, or floated there
In broken ringlets, held by a gray froth
On the opaque, unbroken surface of the pond,
Which reflected nothing, no one.
                                        And then I remembered.
When I was a child, our neighbors would disappear.
And there wasn't a pond of crocodiles at all.
And they hadn't moved. They couldn't move. They
Lived in the small, fenced-off backwater
Of a canal. I'd never seen them alive. They
Were in still photographs taken on the Ivory Coast.
I saw them only once in a studio when
I was a child in a city I once loved.
I was afraid until our neighbor, a photographer,
Explained it all to me, explained how far
Away they were, how harmless; how they were praised
In rituals as "powers." But they had no "powers,"
He said. The next week he vanished. I thought
Someone had cast a spell & that the crocodiles
Swam out of the pictures on the wall & grew
Silently & multiplied & then turned into
Shadows resting on the banks of lakes & streams
Or took the shapes of fallen logs in campgrounds
In the mountains. They ate our neighbor, Mr. Hirata.
They ate his whole family. That is what I believed,
Then . . . that someone had cast a spell. I did not
Know childhood was a spell, or that then there
Had been another spell, too quiet to hear,
Entering my city, entering the dust we ate. . . .
No one knew it then. No one could see it,
Though it spread through lawless miles of housing tracts,
And the new, bare, treeless streets; it slipped
Into the vacant rows of warehouses & picked
The padlocked doors of working-class bars
And union halls & shuttered, empty diners.

And how it clung! (forever, if one had noticed)
To the brothel with the pastel tassels on the shade
Of an unlit table lamp. Farther in, it feasted
On the decaying light of failing shopping centers;
It spilled into the older, tree-lined neighborhoods,
Into warm houses, sealing itself into books
Of bedtime stories read each night by fathers—
The books lying open to the flat, neglected
Light of dawn; & it settled like dust on windowsills
Downtown, filling the smug cafés, schools,
Banks, offices, taverns, gymnasiums, hotels,
Newsstands, courtrooms, opium parlors, Basque
Restaurants, Armenian steam baths,
French bakeries, & two of the florists' shops—
Their plate glass windows smashed forever.
Finally it tried to infiltrate the exact
Center of my city, a small square bordered
With palm trees, olives, cypresses, a square
Where no one gathered, not even thieves or lovers.
It was a place which no longer had any purpose,
But held itself aloof, I thought, the way
A deaf aunt might, from opinions, styles, gossip.
I liked it there. It was completely lifeless,
Sad & clear in what seemed always a perfect,
Windless noon. I saw it first as a child,
Looking down at it from that as yet
Unvandalized, makeshift studio.
I remember leaning my right cheek against
A striped beach ball so that Mr. Hirata—
Who was Japanese, who would be sent the next week
To a place called Manzanar, a detention camp
Hidden in stunted pines almost above
The Sierra timberline—could take my picture.
I remember the way he lovingly relished
Each camera angle, the unwobbling tripod,
The way he checked each aperture against
The light meter, in love with all things
That were not accidental, & I remember
The care he took when focusing; how
He tried two different lens filters before
He found the one appropriate for that

Sensual, late, slow blush of afternoon
Falling through the one broad bay window.
I remember holding still & looking down
Into the square because he asked me to;
Because my mother & father had asked me please
To obey & be patient & allow the man—
Whose business was failing anyway by then—
To work as long as he wished to without any
Irritations or annoyances before
He would have to spend these years, my father said,
Far away, in snow, & without his cameras.
But Mr. Hirata did not work. He played.
His toys gleamed there. That much was clear to me. . . .
That was the day I decided I would never work.
It felt like a conversion. Play was sacred.
My father waited behind us on a sofa made
From car seats. One spring kept nosing through.
I remember the camera opening into the light. . . .
And I remember the dark after, the studio closed,
The cameras stolen, slivers of glass from the smashed
Bay window littering the unsanded floors,
And the square below it bathed in sunlight. . . . All this
Before Mr. Hirata died, months later,
From complications following pneumonia.
His death, a letter from a camp official said,
Was purely accidental. I didn't believe it.
Diseases were wise. Diseases, like the polio
My sister had endured, floating paralyzed
And strapped into her wheelchair all through
That war, seemed too precise. Like photographs . . .
Except disease left nothing. Disease was like
An equation that drank up light & never ended,
Not even in summer. Before my fever broke,
And the pains lessened, I could actually see
Myself, in the exact center of that square.
How still it had become in my absence, & how
Immaculate, windless, sunlit. I could see
The outline of every leaf on the nearest tree,
See it more clearly than ever, more clearly than
I had seen anything before in my whole life:
Against the modest, dark gray, solemn trunk,

The leaves were becoming only what they had to be—
Calm, yellow, things in themselves & nothing
More—& frankly they were nothing in themselves,
Nothing except their little reassurance
Of persisting for a few more days, or returning
The year after, & the year after that, & every
Year following—estranged from us by now—& clear,
So clear not one in a thousand trembled; hushed
And always coming back—steadfast, orderly,
Taciturn, oblivious—until the end of Time.

The Poem You Asked For

My poem would eat nothing.
I tried giving it water
but it said no,

worrying me.
Day after day,
I held it up to the light,

turning it over,
but it only pressed its lips
more tightly together.

It grew sullen, like a toad
through with being teased.
I offered it all my money,

my clothes, my car with a full tank.
But the poem stared at the floor.
Finally I cupped it in

my hands, and carried it gently
out into the soft air, into the
evening traffic, wondering how

to end things between us.
For now it had begun breathing,
putting on more and

more hard rings of flesh.
And the poem demanded the food,
it drank up all the water,

beat me and took my money,
tore the faded clothes
off my back,

said Shit,
and walked slowly away,
slicking its hair down.

Said it was going
over to your place.

IRENE McKINNEY

Photo by A. B. Paulson

Twilight in West Virginia:
Six O'Clock Mine Report

Bergoo Mine No. 3 will work: Bergoo Mine
No. 3 will work tomorrow. Consol. No. 2
will not work: Consol. No. 2 will not
work tomorrow.

Green soaks into the dark trees.
The hills go clumped and heavy
over the foxfire veins
at Clinchfield, One-Go, Greenbrier.

At Hardtack and Amity the grit
abrades the skin. The air is thick
above the black leaves, the open mouth
of the shaft. A man with a burning

carbide lamp on his forehead
swings a pick in a narrow corridor
beneath the earth. His eyes flare
white like a horse's, his teeth glint.

From his sleeves of coal, fingers
with black half-moons: he leans
into the tipple, over the coke oven
staining the air red, over the glow

from the rows of fiery eyes at Swago.
Above Slipjohn a six-ton lumbers down
the grade, its windows curtained with soot.
No one is driving.

The roads get lost in the clotted hills,
in the Blue Spruce maze, the red cough,
the Allegheny marl, the sulphur ooze.

The hill-cuts drain; the roads get lost
and drop at the edge of the strip job.
The fires in the mines do not stop burning.

Deep Mining

Think of this: that under the earth
there are black rooms your very body

can move through. Just as you always
dreamed, you enter the open mouth

and slide between the glistening walls,
the arteries of coal in the larger body.

I knock it loose with the heavy hammer.
I load it up and send it out

while you walk up there on the crust,
in the daylight, and listen to the coal-cars

bearing down with their burden.
You're going to burn this fuel

and when you come in from your chores,
rub your hands in the soft red glow

and stand in your steaming clothes
with your back to it, while it soaks

into frozen buttocks and thighs.
You're going to do that for me

while I slog in the icy water
behind the straining cars.

Until the swing-shift comes around.
Now, I am the one in front of the fire.

Someone has stoked the cooking stove
and set brown loaves on the warming pan.

Someone has laid out my softer clothes,
and turned back the quilt.

Listen: there is a vein that runs
through the earth from top to bottom

and both of us are in it.
One of us is always burning.

Sunday Morning, 1950

Bleach in the foot-bathtub.
The curling iron, the crimped, singed hair.
The small red marks my mother makes
across her lips.

Dust in the road, and on the sumac.
The tight, white sandals on my feet.

In the clean sun before the doors,
the flounces and flowered prints,
the naked hands. We bring
what we can—some coins,
our faces.

The narrow benches we don't fit.
The wasps at the blue hexagons.

And now the rounding of the unbearable
vowels of the organ, the O
of release. We bring
some strain, and lay it down
among the vowels and the gladioli.

The paper fans. The preacher paces,
our eyes are drawn to the window,
the elms with their easy hands.

Outside, the shaven hilly graves we own.
Durrett, Durrett, Durrett. The babies there
that are not me. Beside me,

Mrs. G. sings like a chicken
flung in a pan on Sunday morning.

. . . This hymnal I hold in my hands.
This high bare room, this strict accounting.
This rising up.

Visiting My Gravesite: Talbott Churchyard, West Virginia

Maybe because I was married and felt secure and dead
at once, I listened to my father's urgings about "the future"

and bought this double plot on the hillside with a view
of the bare white church, the old elms, and the creek below.

I plan now to use both plots, luxuriantly spreading out
in the middle of a big double bed. —But no,

finally, my burial has nothing to do with my marriage, this lying here
in these same bones will be as real as anything I can imagine

for who I'll be then, as real as anything undergone, going back
and forth to "the world" out there, and here to this one spot

on earth I really know. Once I came in fast and low
in a little plane and when I looked down at the church,

the trees I've felt with my hands, the neighbors' houses
and the family farm, and I saw how tiny what I loved or knew was,

it was like my children going on with their plans and griefs
at a distance and nothing I could do about it. But I wanted

to reach down and pat it, while letting it know
I wouldn't interfere for the world, the world being

everything this isn't, this unknown buried in the known.

Chrysanthemums

You may want to cut them down. You may want to use a knife,
and pare the brown leaves away. Your hands will smell
of their deep yellow voices and funeral air.
We sat in the parlor and stared at the shrinking petals.
All of us did; it was the same funeral. You could
inhale that spiced air and be glad, as glad
as you ever were, or anyone could be, seeing

such perfect convolutions. If I handed you
this whole load of chrysanthemums could you take
the dark air, the pointed, spiny wealth
of ragged scent? The magenta ones, burnt crocus,
are whited at the tips. In my room today
I have gathered three water glasses full,
and two white cups of just blossoms.

I wanted them in here with me. I dragged them
into my cave. There are many more outside,
but that is another story. This is what I can have,
these clusteral visions, the very last of the year.
White, with the tiny mustard spot in the center,
magenta starfish out of the sea, and gold,
for all it's worth. And that is enough for now.

This is a room, made in the touching human custom,
with windows and doors. How pitiful this is.
We gather outside for lunch under the elm
surrounded by chrysanthemums. Inside, I change
the water every day and pour away the rank juice
seeping from the stems. Aunt Avah lay in her coffin
like a locust husk while we talked of our houses
and rooms and read the cards on the flowers.

Rapt

This is the part where after a few minutes
the audience asks the time, thinks about dinner
and going off alone to contemplate all this.

The actor watches through a crack
in the shutter as his wife unfolds her creamy
legs and the young doctor smoulders and blazes

above her. The actor turns
from the window in a spasm of grief
and paces the long room in a shaft

of golden light. He takes too long
to reach the green brocaded armchair, where
he slumps with his face in his hands, too long.

What are we to do while we wait for his recovery?
We can listen to the drone of the swelling violins.
We can watch the clear flame of the lamp

flickering. It's excessive, this protraction
of something so readily apparent.
And what are we to do while he stares off

to the right at the white stucco wall, the round
milky globe in the center of the table, while
he considers his large blunt hands, while

nothing is being advanced? And isn't grief specific
to death, and not to such continued throbbing
in the body, such a slow pull on the action

of the heart? All of us wish we could
rise in a body and leave at this point.
After all, haven't we set ourselves up

for this to see what happens? And nothing
is happening, except he has retracted
himself across the long red rug, and is staring

through his fingers at the white bed across
the way, where his wife lies curled like
a sated child and the dark young man is getting

dressed. This grief endures as long as we
can imagine. We know he'll weep sooner
or later, that he'll blow out the lamp at some
point, and relight it later in the night.

The Dance

At first she led them out onto the floor
and they wanted to leave this open place
where they were judged. They remembered
the tiny rooms and windows, the puzzles
and blocks, the humming that could fill
their heads when they sat alone and rocked
with their arms around their knees.
But she held the girl's hand and lifted it
as the music rose. The girl was smooth
and round and cleft like a peach, her
mongoloid eyes were cheerful and slant,
and she stumbled until she felt
the lift of the song.

And then she led the man whose hands
wanted to smash, one against the other,
to the girl, and raised their hands
together as the music came again.
She showed them how to ease into
the bend and sway, and left them.

And now a woman aged by a strange disease
is moving with a veil which has become
the wind she's watching toss her up and
up above her bony knees and bent back
in black tights. She knows the wave
grows, and the paralyzed who can only
move an eyelid are swung about in
their chairs by the mute, who smile
at them in joy that will not be named,
and is not only in the movement
but in the summoning-up and offering
to all who care to see
the self that hovered in the shadowy halls
and has now emerged with all
its marks and scars still on it,
held out for anyone to touch.
They lifted up their arms, they lifted
up their faces, Lord, and danced.

They know they are being watched
by the whole, who they felt they could
not be, who have turned to them now
that their light is pouring out, and
they dance so gently because it is
forever, now. The ones who came
to watch are joining, they enter
the gentle rain, it is rising and
falling on us.

We lifted up our arms, we lifted
up our damaged faces, Lord,
and danced.

PETER MEINKE

Photo by Jeanne Meinke

(Untitled)

this is a poem to my son Peter
whom I have hurt a thousand times
whose large and vulnerable eyes
have glazed in pain at my ragings
thin wrists and fingers hung
boneless in despair, pale freckled back
bent in defeat, pillow soaked
by my failure to understand.
I have scarred through weakness
and impatience your frail confidence forever
because when I needed to strike
you were there to be hurt and because
I thought you knew
you were beautiful and fair
your bright eyes and hair
but now I see that no one knows that
about himself, but must be told
and retold until it takes hold
because I think anything can be killed
after a while, especially beauty
so I write this for life, for love, for
you, my oldest son Peter, age 10,
going on 11.

Supermarket

My supermarket is bigger than your supermarket. That's
what America's all about. Nowhere am I happier,
nowhere am I more myself. In the supermarket, there
you feel free. Listen: the carts roll
on their oiled wheels, the cash register sings
to the Sound of Music, the bag boys are unbearably polite!
Everywhere there are lies, but in the supermarket we speak truth.
The sallow young man by the cornstarch bumps my cart,
I tell him, There are always two brothers. One is
hardworking, serious. The other is good-looking but worthless;
he drinks, he is a natural athlete, he seduces Priscilla
Warren whom the older brother loves, and then abandons her.
Yes, cries the sallow young man, O my god yes!
Everywhere there are lies, I lie to my classes, I say,
Eat this poem. Eat that poem. *Good* for you.
I say, Sonnets have more vitamins than villanelles,
I give green stamps for the most vivid images.
But in the supermarket truth blows you over like a clearance sale.
I meet Mrs. Pepitone by the frozen fish, dark circles
under her dark eyes. I tell her, If we had met 16 years earlier
in the dairy section perhaps, everything would have been different.
Yes! Mrs. Pepitone cracks a Morton pie in her bare hands, lust
floods the aisles, a tidal wave, everyone staring
at everyone else with total abandon; Mr. Karakis is streaking
through the cold cuts! Outside, the lies continue.
We lie in church, we say
Buy Jesus and you get Mary free. If you have faith
you can eat pork, dollar a chop.
We give plaid stamps for the purest souls.
I meet Sue Morgan by the family-sized maxi-pads. Or
is it mini-pads?—Or is it mopeds? In the supermarket
everything sounds like everything else. I tell her,
You can see azaleas even in the dark, the white ones
glow like the eyes of angels. I tell her, Azaleas
are the soul of the South, you kill all azaleas
Jimmy Carter will shrivel like a truffle. Yes,
she exclaims, Hallelujah! And still the lies
pile up on the sidewalk, they're storming
the automatic doors. Mr. Hanratty the manager throws himself

in front of the electronic beam, he knows this means
he will be sterile forever, but the store comes first:
the lies retreat to the First National Bank
where they meet no resistance. Meanwhile,
in the supermarket I am praising truth-in-advertising
laws, I am trying to figure the exact price per ounce,
the precise percentage of calcium propionate. And
for you, my tenderest darling, to whom I always return
laden with groceries, I bring Spaghetti-O's and chocolate
kisses, I tip whole shelves into my cart, the bag boys
turn pale at my approach, they do isometric exercises.
But I know this excess is unnecessary,
I say, My friends, think Small, use the 8-item line, who
needs more than 8 items? All you really need is
civility, honesty, courage, and 5 loaves of wheatberry bread.
Listen friends, Life is no rip-off, the oranges are full of
juice, their coloring the best we can do, why do you think
we live so long?   So long.

My dear friends, the supermarket is open. Let us begin.

The Death of the Pilot Whales

Every few years, down at the Florida Keys,
where bones chew the water like mad dogs
and spit it bubbling out on yellow sand,
the sea darkens, and we crane toward the skies,
toward the airplanes casting their shadows,
but there are no planes and those dark shadows
are not shadows, but mark the silent forms
of pilot whales charging the shore like wild
buffalo charging a train, driving toward
reef and sand till the foam sprays red
below the rainbow stretching from sea to land.

The fierceness of it all, unstoppable,
those broad flukes churning the water, that buried
brain and heart set inflexibly on their last
pulsing, the energy and beauty of all that
flesh turning away from its cold fathomless
world, like the negative of some huge
lemming following god knows whose orders
in a last ordered chaos of frantic obedience
stronger than love. With what joy and
trembling they hunch up the beach,
shred themselves on shoals, what sexual
shudders convulse them at that sweet moment
when they reach—at last!—what
they have burned to meet.

And we, who may be reminded of thoughts
we wish not to think, we tow them back to sea,
cut them open, and they sink.

The Poet, Trying to Surprise God

The poet, trying to surprise his God
composed new forms from secret harmonies,
tore from his fiery vision galaxies
of unrelated shapes, both even & odd.
But God just smiled, and gave His know-all nod
saying, "There's no surprising One who sees
the acorn, root, and branch of centuries;
I swallow all things up, like Aaron's rod.

So hold this thought beneath your poet-bonnet:
no matter how free-seeming flows your sample
God is by definition the Unsurprised."
"Then I'll return," the poet sighed, "to sonnets
of which this is a rather pale example."

"Is that right?" said God. "I hadn't realized. . . ."

Sonnet on the Death of the Man Who Invented Plastic Roses

The man who invented the plastic rose
is dead. Behold his mark:
his undying flawless blossoms never close
but guard his grave unbending through the dark.
He understood neither beauty nor flowers,
which catch our hearts in nets as soft as sky
and bind us with a thread of fragile hours:
flowers are beautiful because they die.

Beauty without the perishable pulse
is dry and sterile, an abandoned stage
with false forests. But the results
support this man's invention; he knew his age:
a vision of our tearless time discloses
artificial men sniffing plastic roses.

Helen

A mad sculptor in our park
has fashioned there, in writhing bronze,
the old story of Leda and the swan.
There, the trees are cool and dark
and men may sit and contemplate
the myriad forms that love can take.

And on the cement pedestal, between
the burning figures and the cool grass,
is scrawled in printing recognizably obscene,
Helen Goldberg is a good peece of ass.

Ah, Helen Goldberg, your mortal lover
has proved false, and, what is worse,
illiterate. Tell me, did he hover
swanlike above your trembling skirts
in a burst of light and shadow,
or were you surprised by a shower
of gold, shining like El Dorado
in your surrendering hour?

But probably you shifted your gum from one side
to the other while he had trouble
with his skin-tight pants (not yours)
and you hoped later he'd give you a ride
on his cycle—and anyway love's a bubble
that bursts like gum in feminine jaws.

There should be a moral here, and yet
I'd be willing to bet
there was no swan back then, either,
just a story that brown-haired Leda
made up for her mother to explain
why she was late again,
and her lovely daughter didn't hatch from an egg,
but was born in the same inelegant way

as Helen Goldberg, whose pointed breasts
and bottom-twitching walk
devastated all of 77th Street West,
Troy 23, New York.

CAROL MUSKE

Photo by Kevin Major Howard

The Wish Foundation

O holy talk show host,
who daily gives us twenty minutes,
no holds barred, on loneliness,

who has provided, for my particular
amusement, this fat hairy man
in a T-shirt that says he likes sex,

pronouncing himself an "impressionistic
person": describe now for us the child
sent by the Wish Foundation. Hold up

her photograph, say haltingly, that
she died and is buried here,
as per her last request: to fly to

Los Angeles. Then to fly forever beneath
its shocked geologic expression.
To land in Los Angeles, like Persephone

descending the sunset stairs, out of a sky
the color of pomegranate, and through the curved glass
of the ambulance hatch—to be photographed through

the lengthening reflections of exit signs. Persephone
crossing eight lanes, in the rapids of pure oxygen,
descending, recasting the tidy shape of elegy.

Under the overpass, where kids throw
things down on cars, through the gates
and over the machined hills to machined

stones: descending to be where she wished to be.
Where on clear days you can see the city.
Where you can see down the coast

to the cones of the reactor, settling
on the slide, down to the famous rides
of the famous amusement park

where they load the kids into bolted seats
and spin them around a center fixed, but
on a moving foundation. O talk show host,

somebody had to imagine it: how
they would slide hard into what happens.
Fear and desire for more fear. No despair,

would you say? but that sense of black acceleration,
like a blacker wish. I'd say Grief put that new
dress on her. Grief combed her adorable hair.

Then: *which hand* said friendly old Death.
And she stepped away from the foundation
into a sky that all my life, dear

host, I've seen fill and refill
with indifferent valediction: overhead
those stupid planes from the base

flying wing to wing and their shadows
on the earth, somebody's stupid
idea of perfect symmetry.

The Eulogy

The man in the black suit delivers a eulogy
each page he turns, turns
a page of light on the ceiling,

because death mimics us, mocking
the eye's cowardly flight
from the flower-covered coffin

to the framed photo of the bereaved, alive.
It is not night.
It is California.

There are hibiscus dropping
their veined shrouds
on the crushed-stone path outside.

A gold cuff link blazes
as the eulogist raises his hands.

Shadows alter the ceiling,
the readable text.
There are two ways to meet death,

he says. One fearful,
the other courageous.
One day purposeful, the next hopeless,

A young man died because he had sex.
The eulogist speaks of soldiers under fire,
the cowards and the heroes.

The woman next to me cannot stop
weeping. I can find no tears inside
me. The cuff links beam

signals at us, above us.
The sun through the skylight
grows brighter and brighter:

Watch now, God.
Watch the eulogist raise his hands.
The rays, like your lasers,

blind the front rows.
The gifts love gives us!
Some of us flinch, some do not.

Intensive Care

—for Kathy and Jim

Then, at 3 A.M. I see her bend
over the stricken infant, her face
that face reproduced for us so many times

in art, as a historical moral:
whose love endureth even death,
whose beauty is forebearance.

Her face that mask of serenity
I see now derives simply
from a shattered will.

There is nothing left of pain or panic—
The TV on the wall tuned to a sitcom.
Her faith in life folded once, twice,

then passed, like a flag
over a lowering coffin,
into her waiting hands.

Far back in its unthinking regions
the brain latches its black shutters
against such improving light

as reason or resignation—the angel
beckoning at the burning gate.
She sees no reason not to draw up

the eyelids, to find herself
reflected in new immensity—
not mother but madonna,

not this child but that other child,
thriving again and returned here
for her to hold and sing to.

Perfectly formed in her arms,
blessed and saved, till the attendants
notice her powerful blind gaze,

till the machines start their desperate,
high-pitched complaints.

Pediatrics

When she came to visit me, I turned my face to the wall—
though only that morning, I'd bent my head at the bell
and with the host on my tongue, mumbled thanks.

Cranked up, then down in my bed—
I told the nurses jokes,
newly precocious, but too old

at twelve, to be anything
but a patient. I slouched in my robe
among the other child-guests of St. Joseph,

the parrot-eyed scald masks,
the waterheads and harelips,
the fat girl with the plastic shunt.

The old crippled nun on her wheeled
platform dispensed her half-witted blessings,
then was gone like the occasional covered gurneys

sliding by my numbered door. Gone
told me I'd go away too—
orderly as dusk in the brick courtyard:

the blank windows curtained one by one.
I could not abide that yearning face
calling me home. Like the Gauls,

in my penciled translations: I saw
Caesar was my home. Through the streets
of the occupied city, his gold mask rose, implacable.

In the fervent improvisational style of the collaborator—

I imagined pain not as pain
but the flickering light embedded
in the headboard, the end

of the snake-wire uncoiling from
the nurses' station. The painkiller winked
in its paper cup, its bleak chirp

meant respect should be paid
for the way I too wielded oblivion,
staring at the wall till six,
my gifts unopened in her lap,

the early dark deepening between us.

Wyndmere, Windemere

> Weep, for the world's wrong
> —Dirge, *Shelley*

The world's wrong, mother,
Shelley said it when, at the end,
he got it right. And you, who knew
every word of his by heart, agreed.

The washed dresses stood on thin air.
You plucked them with distracted grace,
a wind-mother, a plane appearing
between the sun and me, its wings spread

in a stunned arc where the mind still
trails in bright windows of vertigo:
you held me close, you let me go.

We sat on the back step and read
together, not like two, but one
being split apart in some dream
abattoir: I could feel that violence

shudder under my nails, and looked away
from the page, as if the backyard,
the blue stalks of rhubarb, the red
swing, could stop the invisible

passage of one being through another,
the march of infant clothes
on the line, beheaded.

You said, "I'm a tough farm girl
from Wyndmere, nothing fazes me."
Nothing fazed me either, I said.
You drew your town in the dust,

then the thin spires of wind
that grew so tall they split
us up. Now, on a plane, I fly
beside myself. I read

because you said to. The years
pull, dazed as a line of print,
afloat in the life jacket of prose.
Poetry's the air we drown in together,

mother, poetry's the turning room,
the clear field mined with words
you read first. In Wyndmere, you said,
federal men waited by the dry well

with a paper, with justice
that could turn you outlaw.
In the wind, on the back step,
I heard the words of poets

who got it right again and again,
in a world so wrong,
it measures only loss
in those crosses of thin air,

in the blowdown and ascent
of the separator, the mother,
whose face catches once,
then turns from me, again and again.

August, Los Angeles, Lullaby

The pure amnesia of her face,
newborn, I looked so far
into her that, for a while,

the visual held no memory.
Little by little, I returned
to myself, waking to nurse

those first nights in that
familiar room where all
the objects had been altered

imperceptibly: the gardenia
blooming in the dark
in the scarred water glass,

near the phone my handwriting
illegible, the patterned lamp-
shade angled downward and away

from the long mirror where
I stood and looked at
the woman holding her child.

Her face kept dissolving
into expressions resembling
my own, but the child's was pure

figurative, resembling no one.
We floated together in the space
a lullaby makes, head to head,

half-sleeping. *Save it,*
my mother would say, meaning
just the opposite. She didn't

want to hear my evidence
against her terrible optimism
for me. And though, despite her,

I can redeem, in a pawnshop
sense, almost any bad moment
from my childhood, I see now

what she must have intended
for me. I felt it for *her*,
watching her as she slept,

watching her suck as she
dreamed of sucking, lightheaded
with thirst as my blood flowed

suddenly into tissue that
changed it to milk. No matter
how close I press, there is a

texture that moves between me
and whatever might have injured
us then. Like the curtain's sheer

opacity, it remains drawn
over what view we have of dawn
here in this onetime desert,

now green and replenished,
its perfect climate
unthreatened in memory—

though outside, as usual,
the wind blew, the bough bent,
under the eaves, the hummingbird

touched once the bloodcolored hourglass,
the feeder, then was gone.

LEONARD NATHAN

Photo by Andrew Nathan

Body Count

So many women are murdered because some man
failed with his first love, and so many men
failed with their first love because some woman
has not understood, and so many women have not
understood because some man has taught them wrong,
and so many men have taught wrong because no one,
not man or woman, knew the truth, and if
you lose count, go back to the very start,
a cold shadowy place before fire,
where a gene of loneliness tries to unite with a gene
of hope and the slightest miscalculation ends
in a present full of numbers laid side by side,
as lovers who failed, as bodies in a morgue.

At the Well

Does this water
taste of oil to you?

They say drink
what you don't use in the car.

Do these pipes
serving the wrong thirst
reach down to the wrong assumption
so pumping a septic mix
into the pitcher?

They say it's all a waste
anyhow
so accept it.

Do you feel bad
swallowing that?

They say this numbness
is life adapting to new conditions.

The numb parts of me
believe them.

Letter

Dear Antigone,
after going over all the arguments
pro and con, I'm as divided as ever,
but when the last word dies away,
I know you're right.

Everybody does,
that's why Creon has to bury you
every time the state can't make children
obey the letters of the law
that don't spell love.

And that's why I stand here watching it all,
glad no one has asked me to help,
my littlest daughter's hand in mine,
her eyes looking up with a sad trust,
already forgiving.

Breathing Exercises

My mother phoning from far off:
How are you? How are you really? Really?

A long dumbness fills with breathing.
How much does she want to know? Really?

I'm fine, fighting, making passes,
Doing my job. Does that sound right?

No, it sounds as if somebody bugged
The phone and I'm talking for the bugger.

Which reminds me: I'm Leonard Nathan whose grandpa
Changed his last name—too Jewish.

I'm not Leonard Nathan, I'm hiding
Down here and have fooled the psychiatrists.

You know what I do? I breathe slyly.
It's nice to breathe, that's the spirit.

Wonderful. Inside Leonard
Nathan is a little spirit.

Rocks in the desert also breathe—
More spirits, and water breathes deep.

If somebody screws your mouth shut, whistle
Through your nose. For God's sake, keep breathing.

Inhale fifteen seconds, thinking
OM, hold ten, exhale fifteen.

Grandpa scares me holding his breath.
His last address was an oxygen tent.

My belly rises and falls, tidal,
But the phone ringing can freeze me solid.

Hello, this is a rock calling
From the floor of the sea, your great grandma.

Hello, this is an empty bottle
Calling from the desert: I'm going crazy.

Put Father on. He's watching the Jets
Blow somebody right out of the stadium.

He breathes deep in himself, precious
To himself. Daddy's a real rock.

My son is inhaling a whole sky
Of filth. He hates telephones and ideas.

I ask, are you there? Mere breathing
Answers. That also scares me.

Listen, I'll breathe with you, inhale
For Grandpa, exhale for a grandchild unborn.

Sometimes I get the cadence of things
And breathe with them, like music, but not.

They paraphrased Hsieh Ho: "The life
Of the spirit in the rhythm of things." Nope.

You can't paraphrase. You can't say anything.
You live in a tent deep under water.

And someone just stopped breathing again.
Grandpa, names change nothing but words!

This is a prayer to your absence. Hear me.
I lean close. I hiss. I breathe into you.

Out of the stupid air of the desert
I made it and the musculature of the sea.

It is so much wind, but I want it back,
Sucking it out of your life, my spirit.

My mother won't hear. She listens far off
To her self. That's how I am really.

Hole

The mouse crawled through it,
the snake after him
and you're next.

Did you think
because Socrates went through
and Saint Francis
it was going to be bigger?

They also squeezed every hope
into its least possibility,
shedding layer after layer
to slide, tongue flicking,
into the rank darkness.

O yes,
the self is that small.

The Election

How did the stones vote
this time?

They voted for hardness
and few words

as the trees voted
for slow growth
upward and a shedding
of dead dependents.

And the men?

They voted against
themselves again
and for fire
which they thought they
could control,
fire
which voted for blackened stumps
and no more elections.

Coup

That chair
isn't yours anymore.

Noon
when bells shed iron
on the dusty sleep of the poor
we took your chair.

The Republic
is now a wall
for you to die against
and (after a whitewash)
a background
for our smiles.

No hard feelings.

So?

So you aren't Tolstoy or Saint Francis
or even a well-known singer
of popular songs and will never read Greek
or speak French fluently,
will never see something no one else
has seen before through a lens
or with the naked eye.

You've been given just the one life
in this world that matters
and upon which every other life
somehow depends as long as you live,
and also given the costly gifts of hunger,
choice, and pain with which to raise
a modest shrine to meaning.

SHARON OLDS

Photo by Thomas Victor

Satan Says

I am locked in a little cedar box
with a picture of shepherds pasted onto
the central panel between carvings.
The box stands on curved legs.
It has a gold, heart-shaped lock
and no key. I am trying to write my
way out of the closed box
redolent of cedar. Satan
comes to me in the locked box
and says, *I'll get you out. Say*
My father is a shit. I say
my father is a shit and Satan
laughs and says, *It's opening.*
Say your mother is a pimp.
My mother is a pimp. Something
opens and breaks when I say that.
My spine uncurls in the cedar box
like the pink back of the ballerina pin
with a ruby eye, resting beside me on
satin in the cedar box.
Say shit, say death, say fuck the father,
Satan says, down my ear.
The pain of the locked past buzzes
in the child's box on her bureau, under
the terrible round pond eye
etched around with roses, where
self-loathing gazed at sorrow.
Shit. Death. Fuck the father.
Something opens. Satan says
Don't you feel a lot better?
Light seems to break on the delicate
edelweiss pin, carved in two
colors of wood. I love him too,
you know, I say to Satan dark
in the locked box. I love them but
I'm trying to say what happened to us
in the lost past. *Of course,* he says
and smiles, *of course. Now say: torture.*
I see, through blackness soaked in cedar,

the edge of a large hinge open.
Say: the father's cock, the mother's
cunt, says Satan, *I'll get you out.*
The angle of the hinge widens
until I see the outlines of
the time before I was, when they were
locked in the bed. When I say
the magic words, Cock, Cunt,
Satan softly says, *Come out.*
But the air around the opening
is heavy and thick as hot smoke.
Come in, he says, and I feel his voice
breathing from the opening.
The exit is through Satan's mouth.
Come in my mouth, he says, *you're there*
already, and the huge hinge
begins to close. Oh no, I loved
them, too, I brace
my body tight
in the cedar house.
Satan sucks himself out the keyhole.
I'm left locked in the box, he seals
the heart-shaped lock with the wax of his tongue.
It's your coffin now, Satan says.
I hardly hear;
I am warming my cold
hands at the dancer's
ruby eye—
the fire, the suddenly discovered knowledge of love.

Quake Theory

When two plates of earth scrape along each other
like a mother and daughter
it is called a fault.

There are faults that slip smoothly past each other
an inch a year, with just a faint rasp

like a man running his hand over his chin,
that man between us,

and there are faults that get stuck at a bend for twenty years.
The ridge bulges up like a father's sarcastic forehead
and the whole thing freezes in place, the man between us.

When this happens, there will be heavy damage
to industrial areas and leisure residence
when the deep plates
finally jerk past
the terrible pressure of their contact.

                                  The earth cracks
and innocent people slip gently in like swimmers.

Indictment of Senior Officers

In the hallway above the pit of the stairwell
my sister and I would meet at night,
eyes and hair dark, bodies
like twins in the dark. We did not talk of
the two who had brought us there, like generals,
for their own reasons. We sat, buddies
in wartime, her living body the proof of
my living body, our backs to the vast
shell hole of the stairs, down which
we would have to go, knowing nothing
but what we had learned there,

                                so that now
when I think of my sister, the holes of the needles
in her hips and in the creases of her elbows,
and the marks from the latest husband's beatings,
and the scars of the operations, I feel the
rage of a soldier standing over the body of
someone sent to the front lines
without training
or a weapon.

The Sisters of Sexual Treasure

As soon as my sister and I got out of our
mother's house, all we wanted to
do was fuck, obliterate
her tiny sparrow body and narrow
grasshopper legs. The men's bodies
were like our father's body! The massive
hocks, flanks, thighs, elegant
knees, long tapered calves—
we could have him there, the steep forbidden
buttocks, backs of the knees, the cock
in our mouth, ah the cock in our mouth.
                Like explorers who
discover a lost city, we went
nuts with joy, undressed the men
slowly and carefully, as if
uncovering buried artifacts that
proved our theory of the lost culture:
that if Mother said it wasn't there,
it was there.

Station

Coming in off the dock after writing,
I approached the house,
and saw your long grandee face
in the light of a lamp with a parchment shade
the color of flame.

An elegant hand on your beard. Your tapered
eyes found me on the lawn. You looked
as the lord looks down from a narrow window
and you are descended from lords. Calmly, with no
hint of shyness you examined me,
the wife who runs out on the dock to write
as soon as one child is in bed,
leaving the other to you.

Your long
mouth, flexible as an archer's bow,
did not curve. We spent a long moment
in the truth of our situation, the poems
heavy as poached game hanging from my hands.

The Language of the Brag

I have wanted excellence in the knife-throw,
I have wanted to use my exceptionally strong and accurate arms
and my straight posture and quick electric muscles
to achieve something at the center of a crowd,
the blade piercing the bark deep,
the haft slowly and heavily vibrating like the cock.

I have wanted some epic use for my excellent body,
some heroism, some American achievement
beyond the ordinary for my extraordinary self,
magnetic and tensile, I have stood by the sandlot
and watched the boys play.

I have wanted courage, I have thought about fire
and the crossing of waterfalls, I have dragged around

my belly big with cowardice and safety,
my stool black with iron pills,
my huge breasts oozing mucus,
my legs swelling, my hands swelling,
my face swelling and darkening, my hair
falling out, my inner sex
stabbed again and again with terrible pain like a knife.
I have lain down.

I have lain down and sweated and shaken
and passed blood and feces and water and
slowly alone in the center of a circle I have
passed the new person out
and they have lifted the new person free of the act

and wiped the new person free of that
language of blood like praise all over the body.

I have done what you wanted to do, Walt Whitman,
Allen Ginsberg, I have done this thing,
I and the other women this exceptional
act with the exceptional heroic body,
this giving birth, this glistening verb,
and I am putting my proud American boast
right here with the others.

Seventh Birthday of the First Child

The children were around my feet like dogs,
milling, nipping, wetting, slavering,
feed sieving from their chops like plankton.

I slid on their messes, I found their silky bodies
asleep in corners, paws fallen
north, south, east, west,
little sexes gleaming.

Ankle-deep in their smell, their noise,
their crisis, their noses cold and black
or going soft with fever, I waded, I slogged.

Crowding around my toes like tits,
they taught me to walk carefully,
to hold still to be sucked.
I worked my feet in them like mud
for the pleasure.

And suddenly there is a head at my breastbone
as if one of the litter had climbed
onto the branch of a dwarf tree
which overnight grew to here
bearing you up, daughter, with your dark
newborn eyes. You sit in the boughs,
blossoms breaking like porcelain cups around you.

The Unjustly Punished Child

The child screams in his room. Rage
heats his head.
He is going through changes like metal under deep
pressure at high temperatures.

When he cools off and comes out of that door
he will not be the same child who ran in
and slammed it. An alloy has been added. Now he will
crack along different lines when tapped.

He is stronger. The long impurification
has begun this morning.

The Mother

In the dreamy silence after bath,
hot in the milk-white towel, my son
announces that I will not love him when I'm dead
because people can't think when they're dead. I can't
think at first—not love him? The air outside the
window is very black, the old locust
beginning to lose its leaves already . . .
I hold him tight, he is white as a buoy
and my death like dark water is rising
swiftly in the room. I tell him I loved him
before he was born. I do not tell him
I'm damned if I won't love him after I'm
dead, necessity after all being
the mother of invention.

ALICIA SUSKIN
OSTRIKER

Photo by J. P. Ostriker

In the Twenty-Fifth Year of Marriage, It Goes On

1

Damn it, honey, neither one of us
Is the victim of the other one, how
About admitting that for starters?

I am thinking about taking
My Jewish mama tragedy mask and your clever
White man scientist mask and—say what what?

Why is this woman laughing
Her horse teeth sticking out
After you've behaved your worst
Possible bullying self, and she
With reason muttered "Why don't
You kill yourself," and you
Ripped through our old friend's screen
Where you sat on his kitchen sill
Three stories up
Threw yourself out his window?

Pleasant September evening
Seasonally warm
A roof
Under it, but I didn't
Know that, did you? Melodramatic, I always
Wanted to live the artist's
Melodramatic life, next time
I'll do the startling thing
I'll have the knife in my teeth
I'll be the star
You can be the horrified one.

2

Damn it, honey, you say
You wish you'd died rather
Than that I'd been raped
And it makes me grind my teeth.
The fact is, I was raped, and stayed
Alive by my wits, in spite of the guy's
Six-inch knife, nor for
A moment do I think
Rape is a fate
Worse than death, what an absurd
Notion, nor were you
Even home, at the time, to "protect"
Me—can it be that not "protecting"
Me is what's bugged you for
What is it, ten years?
What is this love of death among you men?
Why not wish *I* died? Why
Should anybody at all die? Fact:
You weren't there, it wasn't your fault,
I stayed alive, I saved myself
From death then, from self-loathing later
That wanted to suck me into its toilet
Wanted to clothe me in slime if I'd let it.

3

Honey, I am not your thing, your property.
You are not my gallant knight, you are
Supposed to be my friend.
But you insult me
You insult life
So I argue, so I drunkenly rant, so you composedly
Explain it is your own
Life you don't care about, which is
Still insulting, so
I say "Why don't you kill yourself
Then," and you do
Your angry performance—I've crossed you!
So what else is new?

4

Very quiet for a day, two days.
Yom Kippur, of all days,
During which we repent
Not at all, but want to plant
Repentance in the other.
Both of us angry, and
Under the anger, sorrow,
Fear.

Possibly we touched
The silted bottom.
I find I grow sleepy, a bear, a snake.
I anticipate winter.

5

Recovery. It isn't buried, but
Whom would I wrestle with if not with you.
Don't throw me out any
More windows, you say. Check
Out that Kundalini
Energy I reply, and
We seem to be joking and
Making love, we seem
Peculiarly mirthful together, as if
We had a tiny secret, like children
Or we'd died and been reborn
—Which is the sort of junky talk I do not
Ever believe—as if
It doesn't matter how mad
We are, how mad at each other
As if we are in this marriage for life,
Life that is always surprising us,
As my father used to say,
With some kind of kick in the tail.

I Brood About Some Concepts, for Example

A concept like "I," which I am told by many
Intellectual experts has no

Signification outside of language.
I don't believe that, do you? Of course not.

If I kick myself, do I not
Hurt my foot, and if I fuck

A friend, or even if I masturbate,
Do I not come? Somebody does,

I think it's me, I like to call her "me,"
And I assume you like to call the one

Who comes (it is sweet, isn't it,
While birth and death are bitter, we figure,

But sexuality, in the middle there, is so
Sweet!) when you come, "me" and "I" also,

No harm in that, in fact considerable
Justice I feel, and don't you also feel?

Coito ergo
Sum, you remark. Good, so that settles it

With or without the words. . . .
Meanwhile the errant philosopher

Whatsisname, the eminent Marxist/Lacanian
Linguist, the very lettered one,

Whose very penis leaks
Alphabets, the poor creature, perhaps

Doesn't come at all, doesn't
Like cakes and ale, really

Can't taste them, doesn't
Feel pain and pleasure, is afraid to

Touch himself, or admit it—oh, it is
Turning white all around him,

Look at it turning white all around him
Like a special effect in a film,

A kind of confetti blizzard—he won't admit it—
Frowning, tapping, I assume he is a man,

The keys, the dry air
Filling up with signs around him,

Rather frightening, white and whispering, and faintly
Buzzing, the colors draining

Gradually from him
And the rectangles of windowpane—

Oh, this is
Shocking, an X ray flash a sort of

'Twenties black and white, the scholar
A skeleton! The skull grinning

As skulls do! Merely a flash,
But yes, I am convinced there is no

"I" there, I assume I am seeing language,
So that is what he intended, they intended

To disclose. The thing itself. . . .

A Meditation in Seven Days

1

Hear O Israel
the Lord our God
the Lord is One
—Deuteronomy 6:4

If your mother is a Jew, you are a Jew
—Here is the unpredictable

Residue, but of what archaic power
Why the chain of this nation matrilineal

When the Holy One, the One
Who creates heaven and earth from formless void

Is utterly, violently masculine, with his chosen
Fathers and judges, his kings

And priests in their ritual linen, their gold and blue,
And purple and scarlet, his prophets clothed only

In a ragged vision of righteousness, angry
Voices promising a destructive fire

And even in exile, his rabbis with their flaming eyes
The small boys sent to the house of study

To sit on the benches
To recite, with their soft lips, a sacred language

To become the vessels of memory,
Of learning, of prayer,

Across the vast lands of the earth, kissing
His Book, though martyred, though twisted

Into starving rags, in
The village mud, or in wealth and grandeur

Kissing his Book, and the words of the Lord
Became fire on their lips

—What were they all but men in the image
Of God, where is their mother

~

The lines of another story, inscribed
And reinscribed like an endless chain

A proud old woman, her face desert-bitten
Has named her son: laughter

Laughter for bodily pleasure, laughter for old age triumph
Hagar the rival stumbles away

In the hot sand, along with her son Ishmael
They nearly die of thirst, God pities them

But among us each son and daughter
Is the child of Sarah, whom God made to laugh

~

Sarah, legitimate wife
Woman of power

My mother is a Jew, I am a Jew
Does it teach me enough

In the taste of every truth a sweeter truth
In the bowels of every injustice an older injustice

In memory
A tangle of sandy footprints

2

Whoever teaches his daughter Torah,
teachers her obscenity.
—Rabbi Eleazer

If a woman is a Jew
Of what is she the vessel

If she is unclean in her sex, if she is
Created to be a defilement and a temptation

A snake with breasts like a female
A succubus, a flying vagina

So that the singing of God
The secret of God

The name winged in the hues of the rainbow
Is withheld from her, so that she is the unschooled

Property of her father, then of her husband
And if no man beside her husband

May lawfully touch her hand
Or gaze at her almond eyes, if when the dancers

Ecstatically dance, it is not with her,
Of what is she the vessel

If a curtain divides her prayer
From a man's prayer—

3

We shall burn incense to the queen of heaven,
and shall pour her libations as we used to do,
we, our fathers, our kings and our princes, in
the cities of Judah and in the streets of
Jerusalem. For then we had plenty of food and
we were all well and saw no evil.
                                    —Jeremiah 44:17

Solomon's foreign wives, and the Canaanite daughters
Who with Ishtar mourned the death of Tammuz

Who *on the high places, under every green tree, and alongside*
The altars set fig boughs, images of Ashtoreth

Who *offered incense to the queen of heaven*
And sang in a corner of the temple, passing from hand to hand

In token of joy the fruited branch, body
Of the goddess their mothers loved

Who made cakes bearing her features
And their husbands knew

The Lady of Snakes
The Lady of Lilies

She who makes prosper the house
Who promulgates goodness, without whom is famine

Cursed by the furious prophet, scattered screaming
Burned alive according to law, for witchcraft

Stoned to death by her brothers, perhaps by men
She has nakedly loved, for the free act of love

In her city square
Her eyes finally downcast

Her head shaved
Is she too the vessel of memory

4

For out of Zion shall go forth the law, and the
word of the Lord from Jerusalem. And he shall
judge among the nations, and shall rebuke many
people: and they shall beat their swords into
plowshares, and their spears into pruninghooks:
nation shall not lift up sword against nation,
neither shall they learn war any more.
—Isaiah 2:3–4

Here is another story: the ark burned,
The marble pillars buried, the remnant scattered

A thousand years, two thousand years
In every patch of the globe, the gentle remnant

Of whom our rabbis boast: *Compassionate sons
Of compassionate fathers*

In love not with the Law, but with the kindness
They claim to be the whole of the Torah

Torn from a whole cloth
From the hills of Judea

That ran with sweetness, and from the streams
That were jewels, yearning for wholeness, next

Year in Jerusalem, surely, there would be
Milk and honey, they could see

The thing plainly, an ideal society
Of workers, the wise, the holy hill flowing

Finally with righteousness—
Here they are, in the photographs of the 1880s,

The young women, with their serious eyes
Their lace collars and cameo brooches

Are the partners of these serious young men
Who stand shaven, who have combed their hair smoothly

They are writing pamphlets together, which describe
In many little stitches the word *shalom*

They have climbed out of the gloomy villages
They have kissed the rigid parents good-bye

Soon they will be a light to the nations
They will make the desert bloom, they are going to form

The plough and pruninghook Isaiah promised
After tears of fire, of blood, of mud

Of the sword and shame
Eighty generations

Here in their eyes the light of justice from Sinai
And the light of pure reason from Europe

5

> *I intend to convict God for murder, for he is
> destroying his people and the Law he gave them
> from Mount Sinai. I have irrefutable proof in
> my hands.*
>> —Elie Wiesel, *The Gates of the Forest*

> *And Esau said unto his father, Hast thou but
> one blessing, my father? Bless me, even me also,
> O my father. And Esau lifted up his voice, and
> wept.*
>> —Genesis 27:38

Does the unanswered prayer
Corrode the tissue of heaven

Doesn't it rust the wings
Of the heavenly host, shouldn't it

Untune their music, doesn't it become
Acid splashed in the face of the king

Smoke, and the charred bone bits suspended in it
Sifting inevitably upward

Spoiling paradise
Spoiling even the dream of paradise

6

Come, my friend, come, my friend
Let us go to meet the bride
—Sabbath Song

And in between she would work and clean and
cook. But the food, the food: salmon croquettes,
clam cakes, casseroles, cream puffs, sweet and
sour meatballs, and then, through the years, as
you and your sister left and money was looser,
escalating in gourmet finesse, spinach crepes,
sole amandine, soufflés and vichyssoise and
chiffon pie. O the visits were filled with food.
—Melanie Kaye/Kantrowitz

Not speculation, nothing remote
No words addressed to an atomic father

Not the wisdom of the wise
Nor a promise, and not the trap of hereafter

Here, now, through the misted kitchen windows
Since dawn the dusk is falling

Everywhere in the neighborhood
Women have rushed to the butcher, the grocer

With a violet sky she prepares the bread, she plucks
And cooks the chicken, grates the stinging horseradish

These are her fingers, her sinewy back as she scrubs
The house, her hands slap the children and clean them

Dusk approaches, wind moans
Food ready, it is around her hands

The family faces gather, the homeless
She has gathered like sheep, it is her veiny hands

That light the candles, so that suddenly
Our human grief illuminated, we're a circle

Practical and magical, it's
Strong wine and food time coming, and from outside time

From the jewelled throne
Of a house behind history

She beckons the bride, the radiant
Sabbath, the lady we share with God

Our mother's palms like branches lifted in prayer
Lead our rejoicing voices, our small chorus

Our clapping hands in the here and now
In a world that is never over

And never enough

7

> *For lo, the winter is past; the rain is over and*
> *gone; The flowers appear on the earth; the time*
> *of the singing of birds is come.*
> —Song of Solomon 2:11–12

What can I possess
But the history that possesses me

With whom must I wrestle
But myself

And as to the father, what is his trouble
That leaves him so exhausted and powerless

Why is he asleep, his gigantic
Limbs pulseless, dispersed over the sky

White, unnerved
No more roar

He who yesterday threatened murder, yanking
At his old uniform, waving his dress sword

He's broken every glass in the house, the drunkard
He's snapped the sticks of furniture, howling

And crying, liquor spilled everywhere
He's staggered to the floor, and lies there

In filth, three timid children prod him
While screwing their faces up from the stink

That emanates from his mouth—
He has beaten them black and blue

But they still love him, for
What other father have they, what other king—

He begins to snore, he is dreaming again
How outside the door a barefoot woman is knocking

Snakes slide downhill in the forest
Preparing to peel themselves in rebirth, wriggling

Fiddlehead ferns uncurl, a square of blue sky
Flings its veil, pale mushrooms

Raise their noses after the downpour
A breeze rustles through her yellow dress

Don't come back, he whispers in his sleep
Like a man who endures a nightmare

And in my sleep, in my twentieth-century bed
It's that whisper I hear, *go away,*

Don't touch, so that I ask
Of what am I the vessel

Fearful, I see my hand is on the latch
I am the woman, and about to enter

GREG PAPE

Photo by Marnie Prange

Indian Ruins Along Rio de Flag

I'm learning how to read the rocks,
how to tell the difference between
those that lie where the magma
cooled and hardened, and those
that are the ruined walls of homes.

They lived here because of the river.
They sang the river where the sun shone,
where the night sky glittered.
I can almost hear them sometimes
when I cross the river.

Now it's a pitiful stream
lined with red and white signs
that read contaminated—an open
sewer we call Rio de Flag.
No one knows what they called it.

No one knows what they sang
when they saw the river of fire.
When the fire cooled and the dead
were sung they planted corn and squash
in the cinders and bathed their children

in the river and built their homes
of rocks that once were fire.

I'm learning how to watch the birds
as they fly off into the distance
until they turn into distance,
into nothing I can see, like spirits,
and then go on watching, as they must have,

until something in the distance
turns into birds again.

Storm Pattern

On my living room wall hangs a Navajo rug
handwoven by Virginia Yazzie. A Storm Pattern
with a black and white border, through which
the spirit line passes, a design like silhouettes

of mesas on the Colorado Plateau. Within the border
it's red, Ganado red, with black and white
figures, the sacred water bugs, the mountains
and the clouds, and the intersecting lightning bolts

that shoot out from the center to the four corners.
I love to look at it hanging on my wall.
I love to run my fingers over the wool.
Virginia Yazzie raised and tended the sheep

and sheared the wool and spun it by hand,
mixing in a little hair from her goats.
She dyed the wool and she built the loom
on which to weave it. She made up

this variation on the old pattern, and
she took pleasure in the work of her hands.
But there's coal and uranium and maybe oil
on her land, and the government says she

and her family have to move, relocate
is the word they use, to Flagstaff or Winslow
or Tuba City. Think of Virginia Yazzie
with the relocation blues. Imagine her

telling the government she'll never move.
Then remember the water bugs, the mountains,
the clouds, the lightning, the border through which
the spirit line passes, the storm pattern in her eyes.

Street Music

He's got a radio on his shoulder.
And for him it's playing rivets
and lasers. On its way to the river
there's a scent of lacquer
rising from the sewer.
He walks through it like a man
without a nose, though he is a boy
and his nose is a beauty
stitched across the bridge.

There's a bridge for trains
stitched over the street
where he walks into shadow
wearing his inscrutable face
and his hard sounds
like the body
he's growing into.

In the park men are waiting
to offer him money
for a few minutes of his body,
and women are waiting
to sell him a few minutes of theirs.
And there are other citizens
along Muhammed Ali Boulevard waiting.
And the river waits.

In one cycle of traffic lights
he's walking shoulder deep
in the blue of a siren
dying down Hill Street in Louisville.
In his nimbus of sound
he turns as blue as one of the citizens
of the river. But who knows
what he's thinking
or where he's going?
He's walking his music
through the streets.

The Minotaur Next Door

They are very small, my neighbors.
Sometimes I imagine them as a single creature
arguing and worrying and tearing itself apart.
That first night I heard her moaning
I imagined the sort of scene this city
is famous for. I didn't know she had a husband.
I hadn't seen him yet. I thought she might be
alone, or worse, a rapist or burglar, some
screwed-up half-man having broken in, having
robbed and beaten and violated her, having just
fled, or was about to flee . . . It was up to me.
I had to do something. I ran out into the night
and stopped. There she was in her bright kitchen,
in the faded flowers of her bathrobe walking
back and forth behind the window making that sound
with each deliberate breath. It was clear
she needed more than what I was willing to be.
Tonight again she moans, a sound I will not try
to put on the page, a constriction of blood
and breath, a complaint and a pain as monotonous
and worn as the words she shouts at her husband
in the afternoon: *My life is a living hell.*
I can imagine for her no loveliness, only
the diversion of a meal or the still moments
before the television when, perhaps, without speaking
he brings her a glass of water. I do nothing
but believe her. Just as once there was a man
with the body of a bull, or a bull with the body
of a man, and that creature made of halves turned
on itself or on another, these houses and these
streets and this woman, although they are exhausted,
will not tire, will not sleep.

Dinner on the Miami River

Diesel fumes rise
from boats idling along the dock.
Storm clouds offshore to the south
reflect the pink light of sunset.
We order pink wine to celebrate
the light. We sit without speaking
watching a school of mullet jump
and wheel through rainbow streaks
of oil on the water. We order
oysters, steamed clams, fried
grouper chunks, black beans and rice.
I feel as if we are moving,
but it is an old boat passing
slowly. It doesn't look seaworthy.
It sits low in the water loaded
with stolen bicycles and plastic
buckets roped on the deck
and makeshift cabin, bulging
under tarps—a Haitian trader
setting out for the homeland.
A fire burns in an oil drum
on the foredeck. The engine
coughs a column of black smoke.
It's a ghost ship. No captain.
No crew. Only the wood of the boat
is alive with color, hand painted
layer upon layer, white
streaked with rust along the bow,
trimmed with green, yellow, red
to wake the dead and frighten off
the gray spirits of the sea.
I watch the water imagining
what floats here; hard drugs
in plastic bags, bales of marijuana,
bodies, and this overloaded boat
where now a woman emerges
from under a tarp, a red rag
tied around her hair, a pipe
between her teeth, and sits

down by the oil drum to smoke
in the last light. Thief,
ghost-to-be, I raise my glass
in a toast to safe passage.
She nods her pipe and turns
her fierce eyes toward the sea.

In Line at the Supermarket

Here you've got time to think.
Between the breath mints
and the glamour magazines
you can feel yourself growing old
as you read the headlines
of the non-newspapers: "Country Doctor
Performs Head Transplant on Alien"
or something homier, "Passionate Groom
Kills Bride with First Kiss."
You're growing old alright,
but you'll never be as old
as the woman who runs her shopping cart
up against your hip bone
and keeps on pushing until you
have to say "Stop!" She stares at you
through the faintest blue haze,
her face ancient, perverse,
and you wonder what she sees.
The couple in front of you
have time to debate their selections.
"We don't need a ham this big," he says,
as he holds it under her nose.
"Yes we do" and she places her fingertips
on the ham and pushes it back down,
lightly, to the stalled conveyor.
They are younger than you are,
but it's hard to tell how much younger.
They too, look worn and tired.
You stare at her spiked yellow hair
and her bare shoulders

just a breath away. On her left
shoulder a tattoo, like a brand,
that says *Mike* in shaky cursive.
You wonder if this man is Mike.
You think about slavery.
There was a man you worked with once
whose style was cool, ironic
like dry ice. He referred to his
night shift job as a slave.
"This my second slave" he said,
meaning he had a day job too,
meaning we have to become caricatures
of ourselves in order to do these jobs,
in order to live like this.
You wonder what Mike does
for a living. You stare at the tattoo
on his arm, a skull
with wings where the ears were,
and under that, in case you don't
get it, written in ribbony script,
all capitals, the word *DEATH*.
For some reason you want to laugh
but don't because Mike, if that's
his name, has just turned to you
out of boredom, and in a friendly voice
you wouldn't have expected
says, "Man, this place is slow,
but I'd rather shop here
than that Pantry Pride down the street.
My old lady went there last week
for groceries, and when she came out
the car was stripped, wheels and everything.
That's a bad neighborhood, man,
you never know who you're gonna meet."

Birds of Detroit

I came to visit my friend.
　　　In Detroit, Steve said, a street
kid might stop you with a gun
　　　in hand and say "Check it in"
which means he wants your wallet,
　　　your coat, or your life. I thought,
in Detroit you might see a
　　　few sparrows pecking at things
in the gutter, or a lone
　　　crow drifting over traffic.
You might imagine buzzards
　　　staring from windows above
you as you hold on to your
　　　life and hand over your coat
and wallet. Downtown, alone,
　　　you might notice stacked cages,
parakeets someone forgot
　　　to feed on the back wall at
Woolworth's, or imagine the
　　　people who live like pigeons,
wingless in the alley on
　　　the other side of the wall.
You might find yourself watching
　　　a cockatiel languishing
in the smoky pink light of
　　　a strip joint, or a parrot
chained to his bar-perch swaying
　　　from side to side saying Hey
buddy into a mirror.

Hey buddy, Steve said, let's go
　　　see the city. So we drove
around the neighborhoods, saw
　　　the statue of the Pope in
Hamtramck, lunched at Zukin's
　　　Deli, shopped La Colmena
(beehive) in the barrio.
　　　On Belle Isle we walked in wind
between countries, Canada

to the south, saw buffleheads,
canvasbacks, and goldeneyes
on the river riding waves
steadfastly into the wind.
We talked of the past and the
way time and work had moved us
to different cities. Mallards
dabbled in cold winter ponds,
and Canada Geese grazed in
a field beyond a chain link
fence. One goose wore a Coke can
on its neck like a collar.

In the parking lot a man
fed Wonder Bread to the gulls.
His family watched from an old
Chevy wagon, rusted out
at the fenders. He tore off
a piece and threw it into
the wind where a gull caught it
and wheeled away to swallow
as another circled in
to catch the next piece. Around
and around they went, a gear
made of gulls to turn the kids
tame until all the bread was
gone and the man let the sack
slip from his hand into the wind.

KATHLEEN PEIRCE

Photo by David Ross

Near Burning

1

My sister singing the Kyrie
from Beethoven's Mass in C Major
at Saint Clement's in Chicago, on tape,
through headphones, in Iowa, in bed, dark,
my pillow, the room suddenly perceptibly cooler,
those tears crawling sideways down exactly
to the mark where her voice passes in.

2

Pulling the steaming teacup
easily from the end table,
lightly, so easily through
the space above my baby in my lap,
toward my mouth.

3

Those Yellowstone fires making Iowa hazy.
Dusk. Mercy. That sound the jay made leaving
the empty feeder.

The Alcoholic's Son at Ten

wants to be finished waiting in the car. He ate his pear
as slowly as he could.
The shame that he has learned just recently,
while even its ugliness would not love him,
makes his best desires strange. Holding
the core inside his mouth, he rolls the window down.
The father-air flies out. Though the car weaves, the world still
passes sideways as it should.
He throws that one thought out to many marks, and leans
to spit his pear. Being gone, it can't reveal the joy
of leaving. But it does.

Quilts

1. Maple Leaf

You have to quit talking. You have to
love color with scissors and pins.
You have to poke at the needle's eye as if
everything depends on being entered, you have to pinch
the tool for hours, every day for months, guiding
the in and out, knowing you can never love the repetition enough.

You have to think like a tree thinks
and worry over the shape of leaves,
each one separately and equally like God.
You have to think of the history
of your old skirt, around you and before you,
how all cloth starts in the clattering machine.
You have to think of chlorophyll and the silent coming of leaves.
You have to join these two by entering more and again
by thinking smaller each time until you come across
thread and thread and the winding cell line.

You have to love the bed enough
to sew it the fanciest dress, knowing
all night no one sees it, in darkness
colors never matter, stitches disappear.
You have to believe in presence as the light goes.
The colors won't pool into groups of like kinds,
the leaves will not fall and they point toward you.

2. Flying Geese

Repeating the exhaustible prayer, the woman sews, inserted
into history, keen on marking traceable time.
The sameness of these stitches! Ten per inch marry
the prints to the sweet blue field.

She must have known where she was going, she must have
known she was moving forward through
the blessed familiar, the way
a clock touches each of its numbers lovingly,
new mice find the kitchen every winter, blood
finds its way in the body.
She must have known what things looked like, she
must have had it to here with mystery,
she must have wanted to hold still,
she must have known she was able to do it
when she brought the birds down.

Farmers

Never able to enter
green, they did
what they knew how,
turned everything
to rooms, every
field a low room
with four corners,
four green points
to start
and rest from being
in love with green.
In one green room
in a big square house
a farmhouse whitewashed
white,
because to paint
a farmhouse green
would be too much
a valentine
to the field.
Also, being human,
there was that need
of a returning place
when so much is denied.

Need Increasing Itself by Rounds

The way Lorene and I went back
For blackberries, the same hill
But hotter, the way I said
Doesn't that haze down there look like snow,
The way she said *no*.
The way we left the good canes
To the bottom of the hill, the way she climbed
Inside them like before, the way my kettle felt
Hanging on my waist, the way she'd brought two,
The way she kept turning in the same place,
The way the dollar was wet in my blouse, the way
The berries were swollen underneath, the way she pulled
Her hood up, the way her hands were, under the leaves,
The way I could only keep picking by thinking we were dying,
The way she kept talking when the plane went over, the way
She kept turning in the same place, the way the first few
Sounded in the second gallon bucket,
The way I had to toss her bucket over
The same way I gave the ditch a vase of zinnias
Every day, the way I had cut them, the way
The colors pom-pommed, the way their water smelled by evening,
The way I thought they couldn't hurt me, the way my husband
Sounded, sobbing in his sleep, a boy or a little horse getting bigger,
The way I glued the leg on the wooden horse again,
The left hind, the way it had been lying on its side too long,
The way the same place breaks, the way we seem to stop sleeping,
The way thorns work, the way sleep comes.

DAVID RIVARD

Photo by Michaela Sullivan

How It Will Always Seem

—for David Guenette

Last night in Fall River in Lafayette Park,
Near a dilapidated tin tot-slide, and after
He'd snorted angel dust, my friend wanted to swing
At me with a two-by-four. Both of us sweating

Like crazy. For one brief moment, on that glass-
Wracked playground asphalt, a transitory
Instant, it seemed something—pure, engaging—
Which he despised on sight and wanted to smash,

Had revealed itself. But, look, it was really
Just two girls in cutoffs and halter tops.
They'd drunk and flirted with us all night.
Not visions, holy or demonic, even with otherworldly

And soulful tans. They had those bleached
Shag-cuts easy to make fun of, easy for me anyway.
Who knows what I said. But they took off,
And he got pissed. I don't care what he saw.

I down my cornflakes this morning, stare
At puffy red roses on the kitchen wallpaper.
Can't find my gloves, and meanwhile I'm late
For punch-in at the dye plant. So, outside,

I pretend at first I don't hear my father call
From his pickup. Road grit, bugs on the windshield.
On the dash, a crumpled race form: what's left
Of win-or-else shouts as three year olds hit

The wire at Suffolk Downs: a scream to be lifted clear,
Now. *Nothing,* I tell him, leaning on the truck door,
When he asks what I did last night. When what
He means is *what are you trying to prove, pal?*

And *smarten up.* This is how it will always seem to me.
As if a father always knows when his son lies,

And the son lies because he's sure of nothing
But the fact he's headed toward a factory,

Not even noticing why work is noisy and lonely
As the inside of a skull, or what drifts down
Into your blood from convoluted piping
Around fabric vats, or why that river flows

Past the plant, until, reaching sea twenty miles
Down, near a sandbar, it loses itself,
Now, while the beach haze starts to burn off.
While the day, swallow-delighting, already

Humid, shimmers like a smudged, heavy coin.

1966

Innocence? Soon as you try putting your finger on it
it zips off, a blur, like a slot car
plastered with oil and tire company decals,
like the low-slung Formula One winners that two boys,
thirteen, race over banked curves
and flats colored the tarmac gray of thunderclouds—
a track the olive-skinned boy built to mimic
the Daytona Grand Prix. Cool basement air,
ozone rasp of electric motors;
they hunch juicing the cars with black joysticks.

Across the room under old magazines is a book.
But the dark kid—he's pudgy, his mother says, "baby fat"—
well, he can't decide to tell his friend
about it. And beneath this debate with himself
swim images of sullen fashion models
from the book's trashy, soft-core, uptown romances.
Words, vaguely glamorous, like *valium,*
coitus interruptus, pouting girls, naked, half-naked,
all riding surging currents of possessiveness
or shame or ache until they fuse, inevitably,
into need. The need he feels, however

confusing, for secret. So that he bursts out, laughing,
punching, happily blaming the other boy
when, at a crisscross, their sleek racers smash up.

Later, his friend, a sandy-haired wiseass,
stands near the workbench littered by airplane kits,
plastic carcasses. He fiddles with a crimped tube of epoxy.
Hung on string, a camouflage-
coated B-52 banks above his head. Above a valley
and burning trucks and bodies, fires blending with sunlight
while the sun passes on to the next wilderness or pasture.

And, if only to buy that last line,
two boys smear the inside of a Stop & Shop bag with glue.
All right, says one, stick your head in.
Doesn't the darker boy tip his face to the sack?
Soon his chubby little heart seems to slam
not just in his chest but within the dim bag,
as, each long breath, the bag collapses and swells,
as if his heart pleads to punch out an opening, a hole.
Soon it does, soon
the fragrant and careless light streams in.

Fall River

When I wake now it's below ocherous, saw-ridged
pine beams. Haze streaks all three windows. I look up
at the dog-eared, glossy magazine photo
I've taken with me for years. It gets tacked
like a claim to some new wall in the next place—
Bill Russell & Wilt Chamberlain, one-on-one
the final game of the 1969 NBA championship,
two hard men snapped elbowing & snatching at a basketball
as if it were a moment one of them might stay inside
forever. I was with
my father the night that game played
on a fuzzy color television, in a jammed Fall River bar.
Seagram & beer chasers for hoarse ex-jocks,
smoke rifting the air. A drunk called him "Tiger"

and asked about the year he'd made all-state guard—
point man, ball-hawk, pacer. Something he rarely spoke
of, & almost always with a gruff mix of impatience
and shyness. Each year,
days painting suburban tract houses & fighting
with contractors followed by
night shifts at the fire station
followed by his kids swarming at breakfast
and my mother trying to stay out of his way,
each of the many stone-hard moments between 1941 & 1969—
they made up a city of granite mills
by a slate & blue river. That town was my father's
life, & still is. If he felt cheated by it,
by its fate for him,
to bear that disappointment, he kept it secret.
                                                    That
night, when he stared deep into a drunk's memory,
he frowned. He said nothing. He twisted on the stool,
and ordered this guy a beer.
Whatever my father & I have in common
is mostly silence. And anger that keeps twisting
back on itself, though not before it ruins,
often, even something simple
as a walk in the dunes at a warm beach.
But what we share too is a love so awkward
that it explains, with unreasoning perfection,
why we still can't speak
easily to each other, about the past or anything else,
and why I wake this far from the place where I grew up,
while the wall above me claims now
nothing has changed & all is different.

Torque

After his ham & cheese in the drape factory cafeteria,
having slipped by the bald shipping foreman
to ride a rattling elevator to the attic
where doves flicker into the massive eaves
and where piled boxes of out-of-style
cotton and lace won't ever be
decorating anyone's sun parlor windows.
Having dozed off in that hideout he fixed
between five four-by-six cardboard storage cartons
while the rest of us pack Mediterranean Dreams
and Colonial Ruffles and drapes colored like moons,
and he wakes lost—
shot through
into a world of unlocked unlocking light—
suddenly he knows where he is and feels half nuts
and feels like killing some pigeons with a slingshot.

That's all, and that's why he pokes
his calloused fingers into the broken machinery,
hunting for loose nuts a half inch wide—
five greasy cold ones that warm in his pocket—
and yanks back the snag-cut strip of inner tube
with a nut snug at the curve to snap it
at the soft chest of a dopey bird.
Then the noise of pigeons flopping down
to creosoted hardwood, and then a grin
the guy gives me & all his other pals later.
And afternoon tightens down on all
our shoulders, until the shift whistle
blasts, blowing through the plant like air
through lace. As it always has, as it does.
That bright. That stunned.

Firestone

Who would want to die defending Firestone Tire
and it's brick storage yards?
That night, at a plant torched by two laid-off steamfitters,
crawling the maze of a shipping dock, dazed, choking
on the floor with an empty oxygen tank,
my father would be discovered by another firefighter,
who would half-lead, half-drag him
by his collar to the outside.
No, my father didn't want to die there,
not even if every seed, each grain of sand, *is* numbered.
Just as ten years later nothing could explain it to him—
just why the man who'd saved him lay comatose
in a semi-private hospital room,
cancer resculpting every cell in his liver.
For weeks my father went around
wearing a miserable, distracted look,
as though carrying on constant arguments with fate,
as if it were some sentient lump or a postulating, querulous
wind loud as the Machine Age
furnace squatting at home in the basement corner.
At night, when its oil burners kicked on,
a glow filtered out the access hatch,
heavy glass the size of a dollar bill,
deep orange, flickering slightly, suffused.
Floorboards and air would hum. A base rumble that,
to my father, may have seemed filled with every loss
put in this world, to deny us, to crush.
The hell with that. He smashed a beer bottle
against the cellar wall. No cry for help.
The hell with that. Nine years old, the only thing I'd heard
when my father, back from Firestone, pushed into our house,
was the groan of the couch. Smoke and creosote,
stink of burning rubber. Soot
blackened his hair, soot eyebrows, soot forehead.
I'd stayed awake, listening as he nodded off and snored,
somehow imagining ash
got sucked into his lungs, or deeper.
How deep could it go?

One Too Many Mornings

—for Steve

After working the midtown ambulance night slot,
my brother drinks in a tavern, his back to thin bars
of lacquered sunlight, venetian blinds. In jeans
and a flannel cowboy shirt, & trying to down-shift
enough to head home. He sips a bourbon.
It carries him a little ways off,
not far enough. How can I get out, he thinks.
On the raised television, an ugly, yellow, manic cartoon bird
keeps escaping its cage,
only to be recaptured. No sound. But his partner, Franco,
jokes about this brunette emergency room nurse.
How she doesn't wear panties, how she asks
Does that mean you like me? when he stares too long.
My brother has heard it all before,
so the reply is an echo. One bad joke
then another. It's like asking *why*
when you know the one right answer is to repeat
the question. Why, last night, at the Hyatt

glitter palace, he had to pull a limp twelve year old
from the heated, chlorine-stinking swimming pool
He fingered the carotid for a pulse. It was there,
it wasn't. Some blood flecked an earlobe.
Kitchen noise, banged pots. Shouts from a distance.
Then a small crowd, uneasy murmurs.
When he locked fists & struck the boy's chest,
trying to make the heart flutter, switch on,
the rib cage cracked. A grunt came from the mouth,
a laugh, then silence. A laugh, he said. That's
what he remembers. Nobody
shut off the pool lights. The warm blue-green
planets under water became more
and more still, simplified & quiet.
Like a man in a bar who just doesn't want to talk,
because there are many wrong answers,
ways to soften failure. And no one wrong or close
enough, no one as far away as he is.

LIZ ROSENBERG

Photo by Eli Bosnick

A Suburban Childhood

Having a crush was how I existed—
how I spent recess; I wandered
dull fields gone brilliant
for one sullen boy who strolled scornfully by.
As if in a dream I boarded
strange buses, stepped down
and roamed through the flower-named
streets, past the one house lit up
from within; humming he loves me,
he loves me not yet . . .
past mounds of leaves burning
their acid of longing
till in the violet dusk headlights
would splash me; behind them my mother
propped up at the wheel—her mouth open,
the doors of the car flying out—
as she grabbed for me, already screaming.

The Story of My Life

It was my fate to help Billy Redanz learn how to read;
the bully king of second grade, left back three times,
head like a cinder block, with a dirty cowlick
and dirty nails he dug into the book
he pinned between us, torturing each word.

"So the Jews drink children's blood."
His eyes on mine were flat and bright. I drew back,
kicking a line of dirt across his shin,
and dragged him to the principal
who tightened her lipsticked mouth at me,
asked Billy to apologize. I saw in a flash how it was.

He showed up years later, holding a monkey wrench
—muscled, greasy, polite—to fix my father's car.
When I came to the door he grabbed me,
grinning, pressing his lips against my throat.

LIZ ROSENBERG / 243

"So you remember me?" he cried,
"You were so patient, so good, like a little nun."
He kissed my mouth, then off he went with his shining toolbox,
a last touch of his delicate broad fingers in my palm.
All day his cool, his birdlike whistle haunted the driveway,
that old conspiracy of kindness after me again,
another sweetness.

The Longing for Eternal Life

Tonight, after a rain
the insects' song comes washing clear
in air worn cool, so thin
I can hear the traffic
lights a block away clicking
and the faintest inclination of car wheels
bending right or left into dim streets.
My porch lamp beams on gourds
swelling by starlight,
groping slowly across the string.

Why is it hard to live like this,
simply to live?
Far off, on a highway dark as ocean water
woodchucks paddle across the road
to pass into eternal life.
I force myself to rest, unfold both fists,
and hear a weary tick-tick-tick—
the ambitious moth
testing her heart against the light.

Thanksgiving

The deer are just thankful it's over—
whole herds of them, grins sagging upside down,
stretched out on racks of wagons and trucks
huffing along Route 17 at dusk, in snow.
On vans, a few early Christmas trees strapped down.

Main Street at twilight is a skating rink
the adults maneuver down with dignity
clutching groceries, treading ice,
their arms filling with sleet.
But when the children are in bed,
uncles and aunts asleep
beside the fizzing TV set,
a drunk picks his slow way downtown.
He slides into the Donut Shoppe
and sips black coffee, his face an inch
above the cup. He eats
with two or three aproned bodies near.

And yes, beloved, you're right,
he's grateful
for the overhead pink
fluorescent lights, the sugary taste,
and all the gathered company.

The Accident

This is the young man, two cars ahead
who skidded across a double yellow line
and tumbled off his bike to lie with bent legs crossed
odd as a praying mantis or a fallen deer.

Young man, with your scruffy jeans, the sad dirt
brownish-gray and permanently poor, the black helmet
over your head, your gashed brow and the pool of crimson blood—
when they stripped away your shirt your chest had a thin
bone-china pallor, and when I walked close your fierce eyes
were rolled up like a dead gangster's or saint's, scorning the joke
till your pool of dark blood
ran toward my feet and chased me away.

Emmerich, rising toward heaven, Emmerich
already gone, hearing the scorched flare
struck and lit ten feet away,
feeling the blonde hysterical woman near,

the realtor who trembled violently but squatted
behind you gripping your helmet so your neck
could not roll back, her fingers splayed in terror,
red with blood she would not wipe off—
the drugged brown aura of hypnosis over it all.
Such chaos and collapsing of the earth's noises in you—
the dismal gathering and sirens collecting for the kill
one after another, blocked traffic, and you still
lying with your legs oddly crossed, your dirty boots,
the breath of life leaving through one crushed rib.

This is how you pushed
through your wife's smooth legs, your beer-breath fired
with sweetness and desire; your two jobs,
daylight time at E-Z Motors, and evenings, manager
at Bobby Dee's, that famous, noisy, hot, beer-brawling place.
Here lies your fine talent with machines,
the way your silky skin would soak up black oil,
and long days at the beach, the scratchy blanket,
the long smooth waves, your body hard
against a pillow age thirteen.
These are your bony knees, your broken tooth,
your straight brown hair
which the sunlight wore transfixed like a gold crown.

Emmerich Antoni, I prayed for you to rise
on your twisted feet, and hobble away like a bumped deer,
Emmerich Antoni, you lay there thinking nothing,
thinking black thoughts, thinking about your last meal,
about your first girl, your young wife,
thinking about your mother grieving—
Already with her as she studies the grass before your grave,
already reading the paper and the fine print,
sitting around the shaky kitchen table with your wife Regina
and all her brothers and sisters and the covered dishes they bring.
Say good-bye to your mother, who packed you off to school
with bent bologna sandwich, pickle and orange dew.
To your father, in another country now,
but who hears you call, and startled, looks up to see you pass.
Good-bye to your sisters, the lovely and the noisy one.
To your bosses, who will grimly hear the news.
Lean close to Regina's curving neck; farewell.

You are doing what you have to do; the earth's lamps
are turned down to twilight blue, you are sinking,
finding your way out and holding your breath, it's
easy, easy, the man in a blue shirt kneels in the road
and pumps your chest, the woman who held your head is gone.
Young man, with your neck so oddly thrown, and your broken leg
tossed over the other, with your long foot elegantly slanting down,
I was your guardian angel, I wasn't looking, I was busy praying,
and stepped back at the sight of your saintly dirty face,
your little collection of purplish blood, I was the one
moaning Breathe! Breathe! long after you'd come and gone
—and no one said, You are still you but changing fast.
We are taking you to the hospital, now we are lifting you,
It doesn't hurt, The traffic is stopped, It is September 30,
1983, In America which recedes beneath you Emmerich Antoni

sailing over the horizon of lost time.
Forgive my cowardice at the guardrail, and my self-pity.
You were on your way home; you slammed
into another car and flew; no one is hurt
but you. You sleep, but your spirit buzzes incandescently.
Something in you keeps flying, coming along
under the wing of the horse chestnut tree
at the corner of Conklin and the Exchange Street Bridge,
where the angel waits for you, gunning his engine—
under that fast blazing canopy
signal left in the green shade and go home.

MAXINE SCATES

Photo by Bill Cadbury

Angel's Flight

Memory is as narrow
as the porch where I sit next to my brother
over twenty years ago,
as the street my mother is crossing
with my grandmother to visit a neighbor,
as the track of the trolley
we rode that morning
in the city of angels.
My brother ten years older
and remembering it
when, on our way here,
to my grandparents' house,
my mother urged him to stop the car
so we could ride Angel's Flight
one last time. And so we rode
for a nickel, a rickety trolley
up a steep hillside no one lived on anymore.

And now we sit on the steps
watching my grandfather make his way
up Toluca Street,
the city below us layered in yellow haze.
Everything that is important to me is here,
everything I loved first:
the old man, my brother,
my mother leading her silent mother
across the street she will not cross alone,
and this dusty porch
and sagging house with all of its history,
the photographs on table and piano top
and the sunroom in front
piled with newspapers.
Because as a child, I loved
what had happened before me—
my father
rising through the unnatural light of the city
as he walked up this hill from the war,
my mother and small brother
waiting on this porch for him to return—

as a child loves looking back
because she cannot imagine the future.

I didn't know then
the history of my grandmother,
institutionalized at thirty-two
after giving birth to her seventh child
in fourteen years, of the years after that
when the old man
wouldn't let her come back to the house,
of the bigotry bred
so deeply into our family
that my grandmother,
the daughter of Lila Dolores Orozco,
was lost to us.

That old man,
the awful glow of the city,
and my father's awaited deliverance
on a bus from Long Beach
into a life that still wouldn't work,
were what I knew to love
because my mother had passed me
the best of her memories
letting me imagine this street,
deserted now too,
as a passage into another time
happier than the life we were living then,
and just as in her eyes
a rickety trolley became a dying angel
as it climbed a battered hillside
with no longer any place to go,
all of them seemed blessed for a moment
in some other light.

Working

All those women working,
laughing on their lunch break.
You found work the day after high school,
stopped for the first child
until war called you. Jarred
by a punch press, your own wounds were
bandaged hands resting on your knees.
Now there was something
just beyond your touch.

Standing in front of the police bulletin
pencil poised, pad in hand:
Back at work, I got pregnant with you.
The neighbors lean over chain link fences
where nothing's growing yet.
Wide open, at night the air smells
of ghost beanfields. The dairy calendar
reminds you of what mothers should know:
milk is important, recipes
for holding your man, notes to yourself
to call the dentist, record my first words,
feed the roses.

Thirty years later this gift,
a tablecloth that never touched your table:
you crocheted the same pattern
every night until I was old enough
for you to go back to work
and centerpieces for your mother,
sisters, every sister-in-law.
The stitches change from beginning to end.
It took so long and you were changing.

His dinner wasn't served,
notes for turning on the oven
and bringing in the clothes.
You had deserted.
I halfway believed him:
no milk and cookies, no aproned mother
bending over me. You paid for the only

vacation we ever had. You wore a bathing suit.
Intruders, my brother and I
found you sleeping in a clearing—
that blue dream of a lake.

Floor Plans

It was $8,000 with a GI loan
and thirty years to pay it off,
numbered streets to the south,
over to Hindry for catechism.

The house across the street
where the bachelor died, the same record
repeating for days like an echo
of his last cry, is Debbie Kimmel's
where a union picket, cornered
in an unfamiliar maze, was shot
beneath her bedroom window. And
Carol Jenson's past the front door
to her mother's bedclothes bunched
on the sofa.

North across Aviation to junior high,
Carol and Debbie wave or signal
something's wrong, that somnambulist
fumbling with his crotch walks
past me. Funny, until the afternoon
I'm alone. Then I run.

Two Kathys live in duplexes
at opposite ends of the tract.
One father riffling through train magazines;
the other a trail of grease on an armchair,
gone to the small hotels
where fathers stay downtown.
There, on a window of my grandparents' house
five stars for sons and sons-in-law
are still stuck to the pane.

Inside, a room smells of no one
having slept in it for years.
The bed pulls out from a bureau drawer,
like a relic bleeding on its saint's day,
it unwrinkles into place.

And beyond that house my cousins live:
four families, two in the same model,
Schwinns tangling in the driveway.
Their fathers, like mine,
march off to Water and Power every day.

Angel

This child is an angel . . .
The priest drank at her wake,
cassock swaying like big leaves falling in rain,
as he washed down
and was not meant for this world.

And what did she love but photos of the dead,
or the ebb of our grandfather's strength
as he grew close to a natural death?
Her parents could not bear this,
and she saw, as the adults gathered
on Sundays after church
that they did not want her,
that they all believed
she was the little offering,
the one in every generation who had seen
the other side.

Queen of Angels. Hospital
in a city ironic with names, nuns
still wearing habits then, trailing
the halls like her sisters' voices trail now
as they ask *What happened?*

What visible sign besides at seven
what she did to her body

that willed its release,
the call to dinner falling over our heads
in the corner of the yard,
one child saying to the other,
I don't eat.

Some make it through the little deaths,
but she had seen enough
and did not long for this world,
her bones sinking in that knowledge that knew,
that knew, and asked for nothing.

1956

In Nick Ray's "Bigger Than Life"
a poor schoolteacher's life is saved
by the miracle drug cortisone,
but still untested it gives him
delusions of grandeur: he buys
his wife expensive clothes
she won't ever wear in their
small house, hurls a football
at his chubby son for hours on end.
Finally he wants, like Abraham,
to sacrifice the boy for the sake
of discipline. He wakes
in a hospital bed. The diagnosis:
he took too much and wanted more.

A dose of too much hope, then
things got out of hand, or something
catches up with you. On weekends
father plants the perfect rose garden.
In a rainstorm he joins the neighbor men,
straining like the famous photograph
of raising the flag on Iwo Jima,
they push a Chinese elm
against the wind.

One afternoon he rescues
his old treasure, the Bataan knife,
and seeing no flag of surrender
tries to corner mother
between counter and sink.
The police leave him alone,
part of the conspiracy his family
can't understand. Now gifts:
the blue velvet rhinestone bathrobe,
the genuine hand-tooled leather purse.
But it's too late, nothing saves him.

As a child I stood next to my father
watching a lumberyard fire
and caught Eisenhower's eyes
on a campaign billboard hovering
above the flames. Nick Ray asks the question
of what it was—them, or something
in each of us waiting to go wild?
We were the little people,
those were our lives.

Going to Mass After Fifteen Years

Just off his motorbike
the boy rushed through his part
of the epistle.
His jeans and sweatshirt
already part of the life
in front of him,
the Latin he mumbled
like the language of childhood,
like the altar boys shifting
behind him on the steps of the altar,
like the months I've spent
away from home
where what had been present
and the past
all seem part of another life.

I knelt
I wanted to remember
that first litany,
Lamb of God,
to press my fist into my chest,
then make the casual sweeping sign
of the cross.
And the low sorrowing voice of the priest
did make me remember the death
that occurred every Sunday.

But kneeling alongside an elderly woman
I knew the best part of myself
wanted to be part of her,
part of the women
who lean together on street corners
and stand shading their eyes in doorways
and outlive their husbands.
And I remembered the last time
I'd been in a church
was the month my grandfather and a cousin
had died within weeks of each other.

I cried then
because no one had died before
or the words the priest said
weren't enough to make up for
a small child's life, even an old man's.
The only eloquence I remember
was my mother pressing a rose from his coffin
into my hand.

RICHARD SHELTON

Photo by David L. Hudnall

Job the Father

I have made my bed in darkness.
—Job 17:13

all his children in the same house
and a great wind comes
out of the wilderness

seven sons three daughters
all his eggs in one basket
and a great wind comes

reading the story I am paper
curling to avoid the flame

and no matter what I ask them
the stars say *yes yes yes*
all over the sky

I have but one son all my children
in one place always

and I am still here Lord
in the desert where even my fear
has grown a little courage of its own

saying *take me Lord*
take only me
and I will forgive you everything

Letter to a Dead Father

Five years since you died and I am
better than I was when you were living.
The years have not been wasted.
I have heard the harsh voices
of desert birds who cannot sing.
Sometimes I touched the membrane

---

between violence and desire
and watched it vibrate.
I learned that a man
who travels in circles
never arrives at exactly the same place.

If you could see me now
side-stepping triumph and disaster,
still waiting for you to say *my son*
my beloved son. If you could only see
me now, you would know I am stronger.

Death was the poorest subterfuge
you ever managed, but it was permanent.
Do you see now that fathers
who cannot love their sons
have sons who cannot love?
It was not your fault
and it was not mine. I needed
your love but I recovered without it.
Now I no longer need anything.

The Stones

I love to go out on summer nights and watch the stones grow.
I think they grow better here in the desert, where it is warm and
dry, than almost anywhere. Or perhaps it is only that the young
ones are more active here.

Young stones tend to move about more than their elders
consider good for them. Most young stones have a secret desire
which their parents had before them but have forgotten ages ago.
And because this desire involves water, it is never mentioned. The
older stones disapprove of water and say, "Water is a gadfly who
never stays in one place long enough to learn anything." But the
young stones try to work themselves into a position, slowly and
without their elders noticing it, in which a sizable stream of water
during a summer storm might catch them broadside and
unknowing, so to speak, and push them along over a slope or
down an arroyo. In spite of the danger this involves, they want

to travel and see something of the world and settle in a new place, far from home, where they can raise their own dynasties away from the domination of their parents.

And although family ties are very strong among stones, many have succeeded; and they carry scars to prove to their children that they once went on a journey, helter-skelter and high water, and traveled perhaps fifteen feet, an incredible distance. As they grow older, they cease to brag about such clandestine adventures.

It is true that old stones get to be very conservative. They consider all movement either dangerous or downright sinful. They remain comfortably where they are and often get fat. Fatness, as a matter of fact, is a mark of distinction.

And on summer nights, after the young stones are asleep, the elders turn to a serious and frightening subject—the moon, which is always spoken of in whispers. "See how it glows and whips across the sky, always changing its shape," one says. And another says, "Feel how it pulls at us, urging us to follow." And a third whispers, "It is a stone gone mad."

The Bus to Veracruz

The mail is slow here. If I died, I wouldn't find out about it for a long time. Perhaps I am dead already. At any rate, I am living in the wrong tense of a foreign language and have almost no verbs and only a few nouns to prove I exist. When I need a word, I fumble among the nouns and find one, but so many are similar in size and color. I am apt to come up with *caballo* instead of *caballero,* or *carne* instead of *casa.* When that happens, I become confused and drop the words. They roll across the tile floor in all directions. Then I get down on my hands and knees and crawl through a forest of legs, reaching under tables and chairs to retrieve them. But I am no longer embarrassed about crawling around on the floor in public places. I have come to realize that I am invisible most of the time and have been since I crossed the border.

All the floors are tile. All the tiles are mottled with the same disquieting pattern in one of three muddy colors—shades of yellow, purple, or green. They make me think of dried vomit, desiccated liver, and scum on a pond. The floor of my room is dried vomit with a border of scum on a pond, and like most of the floors it has several tiles missing, which is a great blessing to me. These lacunae are oases in the desert where I can rest my eyes. The nausea from which I suffer so much of the time is not caused by the food or water, but by the floors. I know this because when I sit in the town square, which is covered with concrete of no particular color, the nausea subsides.

The town is small, although larger than it would seem to a visitor—if there were any visitors—and remote. It has no landing field for even small planes, and the nearest railroad is almost one hundred kilometers to the east. The only bus goes to Veracruz. Often I stop at the bus terminal to ask about the bus to Veracruz. The floor of the bus terminal is scum on a pond with a border of desiccated liver, but there are many tiles missing. That terminal is always deserted except for Rafael and Esteban, sometimes sitting on the bench inside, sometimes lounging just outside the door. They are young, barefoot, and incredibly handsome. I buy them *Cocas* from the machine, and we have learned to communicate in our fashion. When I am with them, I am glad to be invisible, glad that they never look directly at me. I could not bear the soft velvet and vulnerability of those magnificent eyes.

"When does the bus leave for Veracruz?" I ask them. I have practiced this many times and am sure I have the right tense. But the words rise to the ceiling, burst, and fall as confetti around us. A few pieces catch in their dark hair and reflect the light like jewels. Rafael rubs his foot on the floor. Esteban stares out the filthy window. Are they sad, I wonder, because they believe there is no bus to Veracruz or because they don't know when it leaves?

"Is there a bus to Veracruz?" Suddenly they are happy again. Their hands fly like vivacious birds. *"¡Si, hay! ¡Por supuesto, Señor! ¡Es verdad!"* They believe, truly, in the bus to Veracruz. Again I ask them when it leaves. Silence and sadness. Rafael studies one of the tiles on the floor as if it contains the answer. Esteban turns back to the window. I buy them *Cocas* from the machine and go away.

Once a week I stop at the post office to get my mail from the ancient woman in the metal cage, and each week I receive one letter. Actually, the letters are not mine, and the ancient woman has probably known this for a long time, but we never speak of it and she continues to hand me the letters, smiling and nodding in her coquettish way, eager to please me. Her hair is braided with colored ribbons, and her large silver earrings jingle when she bobs her head, which she does with great enthusiasm when I appear. I could not estimate how old she is. Perhaps even she has forgotten. But she must have been a great beauty at one time. Now she sits all day in the metal cage in the post office, a friendly apparition whose bright red lipstick is all the more startling because she has no teeth.

The first time I entered the post office, it was merely on an impulse to please her. I was expecting no mail, since no one knew where I was. But each time I passed, I had seen her through the window, seated in her metal cage with no customers to break the monotony. She always smiled and nodded at me through the window, eager for any diversion. Finally one day I went in on the pretext of calling for my mail, although I knew there would be none. To avoid the confusion which my accent always causes, I wrote my name on a slip of paper and presented it to her. Her tiny hands darted among the pigeonholes, and to my astonishment she presented me with a letter which was addressed to me in care of general delivery. She was so delighted with her success that I simply took the letter and went away, unwilling to disillusion her.

As soon as I opened the letter, the mystery was solved. My name is fairly common. The letter was intended for someone else with the same name. It was written on blue paper, in flawless Palmer Method script, and signed by a woman. It was undated and there was no return address. But it was in English, and I read it shamelessly, savoring each phrase. I rationalized by convincing myself that the mail was so slow the man to whom the letter had been written was probably already dead and could not object to my reading his mail. But I knew before I finished the letter that I would return to the post office later on the chance there might be others. She loved him. She thought he was still alive.

Since then I have received one letter each week, to the enormous delight of my ancient friend in the post office. I take the letters home and steam them open, careful to leave no marks on the delicate paper. They are always from the same woman, and I feel by now that I know her. Sometimes I dream about her, as if she were someone I knew in the past. She is blond and slender, no longer young but far from old. I can see her long, graceful fingers holding the pen as she writes, and sometimes she reaches up to brush a strand of hair away from her face. Even that slight gesture has the eloquence of a blessing.

RICHARD SHELTON / 263

When I have read each letter until I can remember it word for word, I reseal it. Then, after dark, I take it back to the post office by a circuitous route, avoiding anyone who might be on the street at that hour. The post office is always open, but the metal cage is closed and the ancient one is gone for the night. I drop the letter into the dead letter box and hurry away.

At first I had no curiosity about what happened to the letters after they left my hands. Then I began to wonder if they were destroyed or sent to some central office where, in an attempt to locate the sender and return them, someone might discover that they had been opened. Still later, the idea that some nameless official in a distant city might be reading them became almost unbearable to me. It was more and more difficult to remember that they were not my letters. I could not bear to think of anyone else reading her words, sensing her hesitations and tenderness. At last I decided to find out.

It took months of work, but with practice I became clever at concealing myself in shadowy doorways and watching. I have learned that once each week a nondescript man carrying a canvas bag enters the post office through the back door, just as the ancient woman is closing her metal cage for the night. She empties the contents of the dead letter box into his canvas bag, and he leaves by the door he came in. The man then begins a devious journey which continues long into the night. Many nights I have lost him and have had to begin again the following week. He doubles back through alleys and down obscure streets. Several times he enters deserted buildings by one door and emerges from another. He crosses the cemetery and goes through the Cathedral.

But finally he arrives at his destination—the bus terminal. And there, concealed behind huge doors which can be raised to the ceiling, is the bus to Veracruz. The man places his canvas bag in the luggage compartment, slams the metal cover with a great echoing clang, and goes away.

And later, at some unspecified hour, the bus to Veracruz rolls silently out of the terminal, a luxury liner leaving port with all its windows blazing. It has three yellow lights above the windshield and three gold stars along each side. The seats are red velvet and there are gold tassels between the windows. The dashboard is draped with brocade of the richest shades of yellow, purple, and green; and on this altar is a statue of the Virgin, blond and shimmering. Her slender fingers are extended to bless all those who ride the bus to Veracruz, but the only passenger is an ancient woman with silver earrings who sits by the window, nodding and smiling to the empty seats around her. There are two drivers who take turns during the long journey. They are young and incredibly handsome, with eyes as soft as the wings of certain luminous brown moths.

The bus moves through sleeping streets without making a sound. When it gets to the highway, it turns toward Veracruz and gathers speed. Then nothing can stop it: not the rain, nor the washed-out bridges, nor the sharp mountain curves, nor the people who stand by the road to flag it down.

I believe in the bus to Veracruz. And someday, when I am too tired to struggle any longer with the verbs and nouns, when the ugliness and tedium of this place overcome me, I will be on it. I will board the bus with my ticket in my hand. The doors of the terminal will rise to the ceiling, and we will move out through the darkness, gathering speed, like a great island of light.

BETSY SHOLL

Photo by Ed Montalvo

Thinking of You, Hiroshima

Champagne goes straight to my head
so I hear beneath neat family hedges and lawns,
the dresses and ties we wear to dignify my 40th birthday,
how the trees with their long roots catch the city's throb
to release it above us in a dark sway. Jazzed up on the sky's
electric glare, I'm slow dancing with the whole night,
sweet gone music of willows. The patio

steadies my heels, but its cracks rise up and taunt
till I can't resist the shatter, a little break
in the perfect fit of things, a screech
to alleviate the silver strings emanating from the house.
No one follows me into the woods where I used to hide
as a kid, imagining a shadowy girl I never knew,
who knew shadowy things I couldn't imagine.

The party's relieved to glide around me, sisters
tracing each other's smiles, charming and calm,
brothers clustered, erupting in laughter. All these
beautiful people—no one wrings hands or glares wild eyed.
No one's grown fat. No one rubs my thigh, or crumbles
to blow like the bridges that summer I was born.
Sweet gone Hiroshima, I can't help thinking
each time I come home, something's got to give.
I can't get down to the music playing at my roots.

Which is not this muted rush of traffic's arteries
around the city, parts so barren I want to slam myself
into a tree. And not this little clink of ice in our glasses,
the murmur of voices that don't rise when they're angry
but fall, clenched and slow.

This can't be what they were saving the world for.
Something didn't grow as it should have, loose and generous,
like the tip ends of leaves barely distinguishing themselves
from air. There was a girl I didn't know, born the same day
as me, who was supposed to move as I move, root to my branches,
as mine would be root to her. I used to stand on the shore
singing to her on hers singing to me.

Something was stunted.
Lanterns clink on wires clenched to the trees.
One blink and her lids were fused to her eyes.
Sometimes I try to make myself see her
standing on a bridge whose far end is not visible
beyond the rise of its arc. When she turns to me
I try to say I am not alone with the darkness, lushed
and garrulous, listening to trees, trees leaning together
advanced, unbearably patient, like another race.

The Distinct Call of the Alligator

The first time I flew over Florida I was amazed
by all the green, and the blue crimp of waves
up and down the shore like a living relief map
only God could see wholly. Something about
the palm trees made me feel all I'd been taught
was true, it was possible to do something right.
Those elegant birds with long slender legs,
all those pelicans gliding smooth as TV ads,
made me want to reach into myself with both hands
and pull up my heart.

                But if I gave it to you,
you'd probably screw up your face as you always did
over turkey innards, and probably still do,
even in this strange Novemberless Florida,
this Florida where you no longer drive at night,
no longer see the stars, where you have more
doctors than days in the week, which is not
what they discovered it for.

                    This morning I set out
with a spiral notebook and blank tape to recover
my youth. I want my childhood, which you've saved
in a drawer under yellow linen monogrammed
with strange initials. I want something to prove
I wasn't adopted, am not a changeling whose thoughts

got crossed between a forgotten language
and the one you taught which is very stiff.

You claim you don't live in the past,
but it's written all over your face that the past
lives in you. And if you won't tell me
what you remember of your first lie, how can I ask
what entered your mind the moment I was conceived?
Or why, for so many years, you turned my name into
this persistent bird cry, which you repeated again
last night just because I let a map fly out the window
and slap against the windshield of another car.

Ah Florida, Florida. Not its beautiful name,
not its red birds singing all night in the gardenia,
not its oranges glowing in branches over smudge pots,
nor its white egrets perfectly balanced on one leg
can repair this visit. You want to be good,
I want to be honest. All we know to do is deny
each other, as if out of some deep terror
in the blood, some swampy place where creatures live
half in, half out of the water, creatures
with powerful jaws and very sly smiles
we had matching purses made out of once.

A Girl Named Spring

The only calm here is the trees, waiting
since childhood, where they never sighed
impatiently as I transposed the numbers
backward onto my work sheet, never snatched it
from my hands to do it right. Maple, mimosa,
razor-leafed Japanese elms, japonica—names
written in a tiny notebook hidden under the bed
along with dark angry words—

                        which must have
something to do with how I got from that childhood
to this girl, with a bunch of kids ditching school.

Hair dry from too much bleach and perm, thick
lipstick, black around her eyes, it's hard for her
to light a cigarette and walk at the same time
in high heels, a tight skirt, the wind.
The guys go loping off. Her girlfriend hesitates

then quick steps after them, leaving this one
alone with the match in rain. Fuck it, she mutters.
Then calls out, Wait, hobbling behind them.
And I remember something like that, hobbling
after my sister in wooden shoes on Halloween,
always having to be a Dutch girl or Bo-peep,
never a werewolf or witch. I was allowed out
one hour with my sister before dark.

                                        So maybe
inside this girl who was given more darkness
than she wanted, left alone in it, allowed to become
a little whore—maybe inside of her is a soft creature,
tender and skittish as her name, *Bambi*. And maybe
you could talk it out to the edge of a clearing,
if you were patient and calm, the way I imagine
they talked her sister off the bridge,

a jump-suited guy stretching his hand slowly,
no sudden moves, a flat voice telling her
what she didn't know, how to step back from the edge,
easy does it, one slick metal stair at a time. Nobody's
going to hurt you, it's OK—though her name is *Spring*
and she's got a long way to go starting from inside that van
with the word rescue written backward across its hood,
its windshield a crazed reflection of bare limbs.

The Hospital State

The smell of piss guides us down the halls,
strong aromatic to keep us scowling.
The doctor doesn't care how gracefully the blind boy
moves when allowed to walk in his preferred direction,

that is, backward to us: Just don't let him.
Make him go head-on, tripping over himself
because truth's not supposed to be pretty anymore.

Nevertheless, the hands of these spastic children
keep trying to effervesce, to lift off, chair and all—
grinning, nodding, drooling children who say *daaa daaa*,
meaning yes, in whatever language they speak
in this bald hospital where the gravity's all wrong.

Sometimes lining them up, tied to their green chairs,
my hands would laugh if I let them, just flap themselves
in huge guffaws, wanting to answer a question, any question,
like what drug would you have to take, what terrible
thoughts would you have to repeat for nine months
to produce a life so completely misconnected
it keeps jerking out of itself.

The doctor congratulates me after watching
an autistic girl yank out a patch of my hair.
From his office, over closed circuit TV
he seems to think we were trading pleasantries
in some dialect of Martian, her grabbing my hair,
my hand flying into her mouth.

In the worker's lounge, two orderlies
are out of their seats, fists jabbing the air
shouting yes YES
because—just seconds left—there's a steal,
a long pass, and a three point shot wins the game.
Bunched up in the doorway behind brooms
three smiling moon faces with almond eyes
try to understand this sudden burst of clarity.

No matter how far I drive from this place
I find I have left as collateral to a strange god
my right shoulder blade where the wing snapped off
at birth, and a certain piece of scalp that crawls
whenever I watch someone who perfectly fits,
as after a slam dunk, the guy comes back down
in slow-motion replay like a great heron folding
back exactly into himself, everything we wanted
to say. Take that.

A Small Patch of Ice

If I told you we could see nail polish stopping
a run in one skater's tights, a safety pin
in a zipper, that their patch of ice was the size
of my kitchen, no room to leap or spin—you might
agree with my daughter hissing fiercely, *Let's go*.
All they do is circle to tinny music, then stop
in a flourish of shaved ice. But the little mist
that makes reminds me of the gray flickering light
in those films where you come to care about
a balding aerialist, a clown weeping back stage,
the way they'll talk later in their van, in French
or Italian, with subtitles, about despair.

Maybe that's why I linger. Or is it the smell
of popcorn and cotton candy mixed with machine oil
from a hand-pushed Zamboni—the smell of boardwalks
from childhood, neck-jerk rides, tiered rows of teacups
you toss quarters into, those wiry barkers with burnt
cheekbones, voices snatching at your back—Hey, girl
in pink shorts. So we stay to the end.
Then while I scrape a thin crust of ice off
the windshield, my daughter says: *If you can't
do it right, you shouldn't do it at all.*
She's just seen the Olympics on TV and
doesn't like to think how far from grace things

can fall, or how most of us just circle and trudge,
like these skaters, in boots and jeans now, lugging
the heavy ice frame, the clunky machines out to
the U-Haul behind their van. Soon they'll doze,
or bitch, or razz each other about who gets the seat
by the wheel well. Someone will let out a long sigh
settling in by the window, longing for what
we call "the real thing"—the kind of ice you need
to work out fast and hard. In those movies, sometimes
the hard pressure of facing just how far we are
from our dreams, turns someone kinky and wise,
fills the screen with pungent images we remember

for years—the sweep of birds across a square,
clown suit hanging on a line. I'm telling you this
because my daughter doesn't want to hear it.
She doesn't want to know those boardwalks
were full of legless men, I guess from the war,
and one leaned toward me, an anchor tattooed
on his arm where his rolled up sleeve cradled
a pack of smokes. A stub of a man, with apish arms,
he jiggled a cigarette in my face, the way someone
does with a bone to make a dog come. *Girlie,*
he whispered, as I ran off, and what good would it do
to tell my daughter there's grace in falling too,

in that guy starting after me on his crutches
with huge strides like an ungainly bird that might
actually take off, or the way he threw back
his head and laughed—so loud I still see him
on those thin stilts in the middle of the boardwalk
flustering parents so they grab their kids
and step wide around him. I was twelve then,
the age my daughter is now, and maybe it isn't
cruel to believe you'll never get so wounded
or shoddy. Maybe to grow at all we have to
pretend they have nothing to do with us,
these dark pleasures, this dinky patch of ice.

Soup Kitchen

Ginny at a table of young men belly dancing
their tattoos: gray hair in braids circling her head,
and maybe it's the way they can't make her flinch
that finally soothes them. Maybe the way she
speaks with a *you* that is intimate, gets through
their skulls, and that's why they ask almost sweetly
for rags to clean the mess they've made,

which when I come back is a huge clump of wet napkins
resembling puke and a lot of talk about outer space
inside their heads, with Ginny saying *grow up,*

straight into their guffaws, not like my mother's
clenched teeth hissing that things are hard and it's
not fair, the way we spill our milk night after night.
Out of an old plastic bag she pulls a gull feather

and weaves it through a hole in her sweater.
Evolution, she muses, telling me that down under
the bridge by the ferry, on a hot day she went wading
and saw dragonflies more delicate than any lace
I'm likely to wear, bluer than that blouse over there
across the room. Something planned that, she says,
tapping the vein inside her wrist. She fingers

the embroidery on my blouse, which I got
down the block, used, three bucks, I say, and wonder
if the woman who owned it is here, if she sold it
the way heavier ones sell blood, to wire their veins
hot with liquor. One of the mouthier girls
from two tables away yells—Hey, gimme that shirt.
That's how it is these days, Ginny shakes her head—

as if a little gentleness would kill them. I wonder
through what kinds of gentle and killing she's passed,
under bridges, in train yards. Are there other time zones
where she's had children? But the rule is: don't ask,
don't make her look down and shred her napkin.
Just take what she's willing to give tonight,
which is how she discovered secrets once in a hidden file

her bosses warned her to overlook. They walked toward her.
She could smell the metal of the gun. And then—
she's looking away, fumbling in her purse
for a pair of multicolored mittens she knit by rote
in the darkness of boxcars. She holds them up to the light,
little x's on the thumbs so like my mother's, which she'd
pull out, start over, tightening her lips, while I sat

beside her asking why or what if, till she cried, Stop it,
and my face burned like this old guy Ginny nods to,
who looks plain drunk to me. That too, she says,
but he's got a terrible disease, and across the tables

---

she calls—God love you, to which he replies with a stiff
bow—Sweet lady, I cry out from my bed every night.
Yes you do, she tells him, and I believe her

since just then field lights come on in the next block
where school boys play soccer. That must be why,
returning her plate to the kitchen for seconds,
I forget I'm not her child. I pick up a piece
of crust pink with lipstick and put it into my mouth,
then stand there in that odd yellow light,
letting it soften.

PEGGY SHUMAKER

Photo by Kim Zumwalt

The Waitress's Kid

Before you left for the Lucky Strike
I ironed your outfit—straight black
indestructible skirt, low-cut ruffles
on the K-Mart blouse. I hated

the chore as you must have the job—
toting beer to the leagues, Al Ball's
Chevron, Addressograph-Multigraph.
Once, I made you late. You came

when I called, and held me,
fought for me against some pure
and adolescent pain. Most nights
we couldn't afford it.

You'd bring home the best
of a bad lot to dance till they fell,
the crashing bodies payment
against some larger debt.

I'd yell, then cry most school nights
till exhaustion tucked you in.
But one night my anger rose past
double-edged blades in the back bathroom,

and I uncapped the little white tube
free from the Avon Lady, Furious Passion,
my color, not yours, and wrote in virgin lipstick
three words on the mirror, then opened the window

and left. You held your lipstick smack
against your mouth, one wide pull
in each direction. You'd smear your lips
against each other, then kiss

a square of toilet paper, leaving always
surprised, a mouth. Under the oleanders
behind the public pool I waited
for you to miss me. I knew you would yell

I know you can hear me just like you used to
when I was little and you said stay
within hollering distance or else, and you did
yell *I know you can*

hear me, but I heard in your voice how much
you did not know. When you left, desperate,
to wake up my friends, I walked home up the arroyo,
sure the punishment would be swift.

The Circle of Totems

At Saxman, the totems slash down
through the mist, anchor themselves
deep in the Ketchikan muskeg
with one massive stomp
of each flat foot.
The ground, the people,
shiver, and look up.
                    The totems have chosen
this place, where alder and hemlock
crowd so thick a horse can't pass through
so tight the thick-skinned she-bear
swiping at salmonberries
must shove her cubs with the backside
of one blunt-clawed paw.
                    The totems have chosen
this rock, where chum and sockeye
whip upstream in a creek crammed full—
more fish than water—a creek where

eagles and ravens squawk, both clans
gorging themselves against the lean times
freshening mouths lately filled
by unread entrails
from the canneries' pilings.
                          The lowest mouth
on one tall pole clamps down on the wrist
of an anguished boy. He heads out on a morning
that's spitting at him, a fine drizzle
beading his eyelashes. Weaves down
at the lowest tide to hunt devilfish,
feeling already the slick circles against his tongue.
Chewy arms for seconds
coil in the cast iron stewpot.
He can tell from the sky
this will be a good day
for devilfish.

From the surface, bayside,
his eyes show him only himself,
wavering, squinting, hanging out
on a snag at the water's edge.
One branch cracks loose, so he
pokes around, jabbing into the mouths of stone
even this low tide covers. The branch
sings a thuck and scraping song,
hard bark against hard rock,
till the boy's arms grow heavy.
His stomach sings too now, an empty song,
and he sees in his mind the hand
of his mother, patting his shoulder,
loving him even when he brings her
nothing. He wades knee-high.

At first, it's the same story—
wood against stone under a loosening sky—
but on the third try, something
throws back his stick, a soft spitting out

of its splintering. Devilfish!
He reaches right down to grab its arm,
reaches back and down so he's bent
breathing hard, reaches far in,
fingers stretched and tickling—

    Then the whole world
                bites down!

For a moment he thinks this red-black cloud
is ink, squirted across his face
by the struggling one.
Only later does he claim it as pain,
his arm stuck in the frozen-hinged maw
of this stone-beast his fist and feet can't hurt.
He yanks and jimmies, tries relaxing
but feels only the distant spreading of his bones
traveling through his opening flesh.

    When he remembers to breathe,
he takes the deepest breath he can remember.
As soon as it's in, it wants out,
forces itself as a rippling long scream
up the hillside, through rocks and thickets,
past the work sheds where two Tlingit carpenters
are jacking up the roof of the carver's barn.
That scream clears the fog and brings the people,
his whole village, down.
                The strongest men
try with iron bars to break the face
of the great rock oyster.
But the water's coming home, as it does.
Up to his hips, his waist,
the boy knows this is his day,
straightens himself as much as he can.
He looks at his people,
at the eagle,

the raven,
the beaver-tail clan.
The water around his chest
lifts him a little, and he sings
his own song, a song of red and black,
of salmon shimmering in their buttons,
a song of fur buried under a stake
at the beach, so sand and water
can scrub it white, white fur
his mother will sew at the edges
of new moccasins,
the ones he will wear a long time
without any holes wearing through.

His people remember the song,
though it passed through the air
only once. They sing it
for the master carver who sharpens
his chisels and sets to work,
freeing the boy's spirit
from a five-ton trunk of cedar.
The carver's tools chant—

    Remember, remember, remember.
    Prepare. Prepare. Prepare.

First Winter: Joy

Yesterday at ten below
we tried to hang a bird feeder
to the lowest strong branch
of the birch outside the big window.

I held the little redwood
chalet by one eave.
He bent, and tucked his head
between my thighs, lifted me

laughing high enough to loop
blue filaments of fishing leader
into crooks in the bark.
Spilt seed nestled in his curls.

I tied one knot. By then,
my earlobes had stopped hurting.
The fingers in my gloves
weren't taking orders.

So I trussed it up
best I could, and we
ran, remembering why kids run
everywhere, back inside.

This morning, the seed
has all drained away,
a perfect heap in the snow,
the glass house
dangling by one corner.

Bush Navigator: The Last Morning of Hands

Dieter bit his sealskin mitts, and pulled.
Wind made ice in his knucklebones.

His maps spiraled out
into the copter's bubble—

he rolled them backwards
so they might lie flat.

Sheer as a salmon's eyelid
a windshear slashed
the jagged air,
whipped their bubble sideways
to the surface—
hacking blades stuttered
sparking against granite
three quarters up
a mountainside nobody owned.

The place had no name.
This offended him.

The last thing his hands felt
was the faint strum
of Leonid's pulse
quieting. One by one
he counted off his fingers
as the frost pointed out
uncharted boundaries, elevations, depths—
each graphic thing he would never touch.

The Inupiat Christmas Pageant

Under the red Korean banner
spanning the space above the altar
of the Episcopal Church
downtown in Fairbanks,
from way out in the bush
or just up from Two Street,
the faithful and the unfaithful gather.

The choir, like most choirs,
all women. Lining up to march in,
bright cotton calf-length

hooded dresses, silent
caribou foot coverings.

Flat drums, firm beat,
knee bends, grass fans.

Joseph's ermine
and squirrel tail coat,
ruff of hollow wolverine.

Hunters, not shepherds, searching
the night sky, tracing
string webs and stars
to mark a way
across sea ice.

Gifts of the whale captains:
a sealskin, mukluks,
tiny parka for the fur-swaddled child.

Glottal stopped, chopped
"Adeste Fidelis."

Kool-Aid, Oreos, and
bread born of lowbush cranberries.
Slices of raw turnip
dipped in seal oil.

Kiernan's jovial yank
breaks his mama's string
of blue beads—
we kneel to retrieve them—
shiny Siamese cats' eyes
skipping over dust
under straightbacked pews.

He laughs out loud,
this child conceived
when a sterile syringe let go
the milky rush and one
of millions whipped through

selfless whiteness to unite
with a small orb
traveling imperceptibly
through the lightless season.

JEFFREY SKINNER

Photo by Mario M. Muller

For Stuart Porter, Who Asked for a Poem That Would Not Depress Him Further

A joke the size of a small moon headed
for earth: it will decimate all talk of aging
schedules and quarterly projections. The dictators
will laugh themselves to death,
the crippled shall walk and the blind see.
Every heart shall open like rain
and the rivers flow
with gladness, oh my brother . . . I'm making
this up, of course, but you get the point—
imagination is a means of transport,
sometimes more real than any other, and I can see
you reading now, the smile beginning,
the corners of your lips raised,
slightly. And sometimes it's enough, a belly laugh's
redundant, the small
pleasure we can hold expands, takes up whole
moments of our lives. I think of your daughter
lying peaceful on the couch
in your lonely condo, her face like a perfected dream
of your own, translated into the feminine,
how your hands took on
a sudden grace I'd never seen
when you lifted her, turned her away
from the harsh light . . . It's coming! The astronomers
are already beginning to snicker! Close all doors
and windows, hustle to the cellar!
—How could we bear total joy when one small
speechless face transforms
our hearts, all our wounds forever-after bathed
in the light of that gaze so fresh from the other world. . . .

Earth Angel

Mica, if you peel carefully,
comes off in thin, clear panes,
lenses to see the angel. In my seventh year
I kept rocks in egg cartons, one

rock to replace each egg, and the angel
would sit at my elbow, still
as a diamond or the blue heart
of flame. He was a collector
too, and when I showed him my stamps,
the faces and flags embossed,
the tenderness of pastel greens,
reds and yellows, he danced
all whirl and elbows in the air
and a hay-scented breeze poured
from his sleeves. This was the year
satellites learned the word *orbit*
and the stars quivered in my telescope,
the angel impatient for his turn.
This was the year I showed
my father's gun to Ronnie (the angel,
not knowing what to feel, hovered
inside the willow); Ronnie
held the gun, his eyes fastened
to it, though the firing pin
had been removed, and was impressed,
was my friend. This was the
year Frankie Dunn blew off part
of his pinkie with a cherry bomb,
and the angel dragged me inside
where we watched the street
from the attic, the sparks flying
up from the dark as if the earth
were flint struck by invisible
steel. This was the year I remember
hiding in a circle of lilac
bushes, and the rain beginning
then, and the happiness of rain
in the smell of lilacs . . . This was
the year I woke up to the self
as history, and all the childish
forces took on names, and rocks
in the carton became quartz, schist,
pyrite, iron slag, limestone,

anthracite and mica. And the song,
Earth Angel, became a hit,
transistors bloomed on every pillow
and the angel went out into the world.

Late Afternoon, Late in the Twentieth Century

Dusk in Creason's Park comes on slow,
darkening the folds in the children's jackets,
the fall air beer-colored, thick
as remembrance, and the climbed trees shiver
down last leaves. I try to watch both kids
at once, though they tend to drift
from one steel-and-colored-plastic
jerryrig of slides, bridges and swings,
to another, independent, drawn to separate
peers, and I have to call them back
into one field of vision. There are other
parents here, sitting on the sawhorse
picnic benches, talking or smoking, their
arms spread the table's length, their legs
straight out. One man in his fifties
sits alone, an open briefcase before him,
making notes on a legal pad; office
alfresco . . . It is close to finished,
this century. Soon the 1 will change
to a simple 2, like a circuit changing
its mind from yes to no, like the short
step of a wounded soldier. We have filled
the universe with blood again, to no
one's surprise. And by the river's edge
we complained of thirst, we eyed
the forests and filled them with glare.
We said this edge will fit that space
and it did—the concrete oozed through
wooden forms, a thousand blank faces
rose above us, and we were happy
as a smooth surface, as a just-shot
arrow. We ridiculed the old questions,

stabbing our fingers in their leather chests
until they'd had enough, and headed back
to the salt caverns. We found love shivering
in a bus station and took her home,
tenderly sponging off the superficial
wounds. We gave her tea before the fire.
When she grew old we sold the company
and put her back on the bus. We died,
and the others were outraged, they pounded
fists, they petitioned, they did everything
but join us. Then they joined us. We
starved language, until the bones showed
through and the head dropped off
and rolled away, laughing like an idiot . . .
The dusk in Creason's Park comes on, slowly,
and the parents reel their children in
on the soft hook of their names, and they all
drift toward their cars and thoughts
of food and sleep. *Girls,* I yell, *let's
go!* and they come, breathless and glazed
from play. In them I am well pleased,
and would build a city for their future.
But I will not take credit for their failures.
Lord, they are close to me as my skin
and I snarl when the dress is torn, when
the milk spills. Hear me. I am still that lost.

Objects in Mirror are Closer Than They Appear

As thumb is genius of the hand,
able to touch each other with rapidity
and fly back home to his isolate bungalow

before you can say fly, say finger say Mozart,
so can I maneuver two thousand pounds
looking backward. Where is childhood? I'm not

asking for the hell of it, I really
have paid to know. Twilight was so long, ground
so far from father's eyes, difficult

to get where all that memory's kept,
to just say *now,* and *this* and *this* and *this* . . .
But I do it. Because how else. Because once

all that drift of shadows and grass in summer,
Ronnie practicing drums after dinner,
bike in street, bright slivers

of an airplane crashed before we moved
there, found and kept in the box guarded by ballerina,
tart cousin smell, her hair shiny and black

as a telephone, breasts we compared
and both found wanting, the boys' awkward,
electric leers . . . What you have to watch is

you don't trust what you see in that mirror
to be far as seems, that you don't cut in front
and pull the tonnage of what's passed right through you.

Silk Robe

Green as that summer fly,
the quick one who looks like a flying emerald,
that green. Embroidered flowers
on the back, wide sleeves and front
panels; must have taken forever.
Light, you said, trying it on,
like nothing. And though you never
wear it, I'm glad it hangs
in your closet, thin and dark as a leaf.
Because my gift
for the beginning of love, meant
to be worn alone, nothing
underneath, and only flesh
touching silk, silk
touching flesh—the way your name
still feels in my mouth—
remains.

Restoration

The childless couple
pour their hearts into the old house
and weekend by weekend,
as the contractors follow the wife's pointed
finger, the chipped and rotten falls
away, and the new—stone and plank
cut and placed to look old—
rises. She knows her mind,
and the door will be red with robin's-egg-blue
frame; the goldfish pond a rectangle
cut in the earth six feet from the flagstone
walk leading to dunes; a slat fence
dividing her land from
the Atlantic. How hard they work! In an emerald green
jumpsuit she moves like a hummingbird
through house and yard, hovering here, then
there, while her husband, cool-
skinned, sporting khaki shorts and a full
mustache, carts tiles from one room to another,
a slightly bewildered curl
to his lip. Finally, it's finished!
The house is on the town's historic tour,
the DAR nails a tin shield beside the robin's-egg-
blue doorframe. Now they can breathe salt
air every weekend, together, away from the well-paid
stress of international law, interior
design . . . In the upstairs
bedroom they draw lace curtains and switch
on a single yellow light. And make
love, thinking *Uhmmmmm, my house, just as*
it was two hundred years ago, but better,
our whole lives ahead of us!—as they move
upon each other, two creatures,
each half of one motion
older than the house, older than the town,
nearly as old as the moon and the sea,
that battered engine now boiling
and glistening in the freshly painted view
from their window.

The Starling Migration

Each morning they pass over
wiping their ragged scarf of cries
across the sky

and I am struck again by the miracle
of any voice,

even the blare of cat-fight
snarls in a drift of dead leaves,
even the crickets who sing the dry shadows.

         And the band marching
on distant fields, drums clumping
like some shaggy beast;

garbagemen who clatter their
        armor; squeal

of unseen tires; meaty bark
of a chained Lab, and the answer
from another yard—

all this should be worth praise
(he thought,
house quiet and the women asleep),

all this calling out
caught in the loop of time and sensation
(where
do they go, the starlings, do they know
a better here?),

each cry of travel and presence—

I give thanks, I lift up my eyes
to a sky
alive with fresh light and busy wings.

GARY SOTO

Photo by Scott Bartlett

Telephoning God

—for Jon Veinberg

Drunk in the kitchen, I ring God

And get Wichita,
Agatha drunk and on the bed's edge, undoing
Her bra.

Dial again, and Topeka comes through like snoring,
Though no one sleeps. Not little Jennifer
Yelling, "But Mommy,"
                              nor Ernie kissing
The inside of his wrist, whispering
"This is a Gorgeous Evening."

Dial again, and only the sound of spoons crashing
In a cafeteria in Idaho,

A little silence, then a gnat circling the ear
Of Angela beaten and naked in the vineyard,
Her white legs glowing.

The Morning They Shot Tony Lopez, Barber and Pusher Who Went Too Far, 1958

When they entered through the back door,
You were too slow in raising an arm
Or thinking of your eyes refusing the light,
Or your new boots moored under the bed,
Or your wallet on the bureau, open
And choking with bills,
Or your pockets turned inside out, hanging breathless as tongue
Or the vendor clearing his throat in the street,
Or your watch passed on to another's son,
Or the train to Los Banos,

The earth you would slip into like a shirt
And drift through forever.
When they entered, and shot once,
You twisted the face your mother gave
With the three, short grunts that let you slide
In the same blood you closed your eyes to.

The Elements of San Joaquin

Field

The wind sprays pale dirt into my mouth
The small, almost invisible scars
On my hands.

The pores in my throat and elbows
Have taken in a seed of dirt of their own.

After a day in the grapefields near Rolinda
A fine silt, washed by sweat,
Has settled into the lines
On my wrists and palms.

Already I am becoming the valley,
A soil that sprouts nothing
For any of us.

Wind

A dry wind over the valley
Peeled mountains, grain by grain,
To small slopes, loose dirt
Where red ants tunnel.

The wind strokes
The skulls and spines of cattle
To white dust, to nothing,

Covers the spiked tracks of beetles,
Of tumbleweed, of sparrows
That pecked the ground for insects.

Evenings, when I am in the yard weeding,
The wind picks up the breath of my armpits
Like dust, swirls it
Miles away

And drops it
On the ear of a rabid dog,
And I take on another life.

Wind

When you got up this morning the sun
Blazed an hour in the sky,

A lizard hid
Under the curled leaves of manzanita
And winked its dark lids.

Later, the sky grayed,
And the cold wind you breathed
Was moving under your skin and already far
From the small hives of your lungs.

Stars

At dusk the first stars appear.
Not one eager finger points toward them.
A little later the stars spread with the night
And an orange moon rises
To lead them, like a shepherd, toward dawn.

Sun

In June the sun is a bonnet of light
Coming up,
Little by little,
From behind a skyline of pine.

The pastures sway with fiddle-neck
Tassels of foxtail.

At Piedra
A couple fish on the river's edge,
Their shadows deep against the water.
Above, in the stubbled slopes,
Cows climb down
As the heat rises
In a mist of blond locusts,
Returning to the valley.

Rain

When autumn rains flatten sycamore leaves,
The tiny volcanos of dirt
Ants raised around their holes,
I should be out of work.

My silverware and stack of plates will go unused
Like the old, my two good slacks
Will smother under a growth of lint
And smell of the old dust
That rises
When the closet door opens or closes.

The skin of my belly will tighten like a belt
And there will be no reason for pockets.

Fog

If you go to your window
You will notice a fog drifting in.

The sun is no stronger than a flashlight.
Not all the sweaters
Hung in closets all summer

Could soak up this mist. The fog:
A mouth nibbling everything to its origin,
Pomegranate trees, stolen bicycles,

The string of lights at a used-car lot,
A Pontiac with scorched valves.

In Fresno the fog is passing
The young thief prying a window screen,
Graying my hair that falls
And goes unfound, my fingerprints
Slowly growing a fur of dust—

One hundred years from now
There should be no reason to believe
I lived.

Daybreak

In this moment when the light starts up
In the east and rubs
The horizon until it catches fire,

We enter the fields to hoe,
Row after row, among the small flags of onion,
Waving off the dragonflies
That ladder the air.

And tears the onions raise
Do not begin in your eyes but in ours,
In the salt blown
From one blister into another;

They begin in knowing
You will never waken to bear
The hour timed to a heart beat,
The wind pressing us closer to the ground.

When the season ends,
And the onions are unplugged from their sleep,
We won't forget what you failed to see,
And nothing will heal
Under the rain's broken fingers.

Field Poem

When the foreman whistled
My brother and I
Shouldered our hoes,
Leaving the field.
We returned to the bus
Speaking
In broken English, in broken Spanish
The restaurant food,
The tickets to a dance
We wouldn't buy with our pay.

From the smashed bus window,
I saw the leaves of cotton plants
Like small hands
Waving good-bye.

Hoeing

During March while hoeing long rows
Of cotton
Dirt lifted in the air
Entering my nostrils
And eyes
The yellow under my fingernails

The hoe swung
Across my shadow   chopping weeds
And thick caterpillars
That shriveled
Into rings
And went where the wind went

When the sun was on the left
And against my face
Sweat   the sea

That is still within me
Rose and fell from my chin
Touching land
For the first time

Harvest

East of the sun's slant, in the vineyard that never failed,
A wind crossed my face, moving the dust
And a portion of my voice a step closer to a new year.

The sky went black in the 9th hour of rolling trays,
And in the distance ropes of rain dropped to pull me
From the thick harvest that was not mine.

Summer

Once again, tell me, what was it like?
There was a windowsill of flies.
It meant the moon pulled its own weight
And the black sky cleared itself
Like a sneeze.

What about the farm worker?
He had no bedroom. He had a warehouse
Of heat, a swamp cooler
That turned no faster than a raffle cage.

And the farms?
There were groves
Of fig trees that went unpicked.
The fruit wrinkled and flattened
Like the elbows
Of an old woman.

What about the Projects in the Eastside?
I can't really say. Maybe a child

Burned his first book of matches.
Maybe the burn is disappearing
Under the first layer
Of skin

And next summer?
It will be the same. Boredom,
In early June, will settle
On the eyelash shading your pupil from dust,
On the shoulder you look over
To find the sun rising
From the Sierras.

History

Grandma lit the stove.
Morning sunlight
Lengthened in spears
Across the linoleum floor.
Wrapped in a shawl,
Her eyes small
With sleep,
She sliced papas,
Pounded chiles
With a stone
Brought from Guadalajara.

                              After
Grandpa left for work,
She hosed down
The walk her sons paved
And in the shade
Of a chinaberry,
Unearthed her
Secret cigar box
Of bright coins
And bills, counted them
In English,
Then in Spanish,

And buried them elsewhere.
Later, back
From the market,
Where no one saw her,
She pulled out
Pepper and beet, spines
Of asparagus
From her blouse,
Tiny chocolates
From under a paisley bandana,
And smiled.

That was the '50s,
And Grandma in her '50s,
A face streaked
From cutting grapes
And boxing plums.
I remember her insides
Were washed of tapeworm,
Her arms swelled into knobs
Of small growths—
Her second son
Dropped from a ladder
And was dust.
And yet I do not know
The sorrows
That sent her praying
In the dark of a closet,
The tear that fell
At night
When she touched
Loose skin
Of belly and breasts.
I do not know why
Her face shines
Or what goes beyond this shine,
Only the stories
That pulled her
From Taxco to San Joaquin,
Delano to Westside,
The places
In which we all begin.

LESLIE ULLMAN

Running

1

Lately my neighbor wheezes
pounding dough, her forearms
glazed with sweat and flour.
"At your age," my mother
writes, "I wanted babies
and got pregnant
each time one of you
learned to walk."
I circle the block again
and again, until I run
outside my body.
This time last year
my husband stopped
speaking of the other woman
who slept poorly inside him.

She promised in another town
to give him up. All night she
tossed and tried to speak
until he spoke of his
father, who drank himself
into the cracked
well of his voice
and never touched bottom.
She made him wake sweating
and brooding in the closed
room of his departure
while I ran myself past
my neighbor's lawn and plump
loaves settling in their heat
to an early shape of myself.

2

I'd forgotten the apartment
that stretched like a tunnel,
shapeless and dark

the way my good dress hung
too large, a formal
body outside my body.
The other men drifted
alike behind their drinks
while he stood in one place
and spoke to me of *The Moviegoer*
which spoke, he said, to his very soul.

Sometimes I run in Louisiana
where I've never been,
where the hero saw an egret gather
itself over swamp mist
and settle in a single oak
that rose to meet it.
Later he married his cousin
whose agile mind wandered,
glittering at the family table.
The dense mahogany.
The black butler
wheezed as he passed the beans.
She couldn't sleep, she
said, without pills.
Sometimes she slept for two days.
She promised she could
be like anyone, if he
would tell her each morning
how to pass that day.

That night, my skin
held me like liquid glass.
I wanted to slip
my hand beneath his elbow,
to dance, to see the other women
naked inside their clothes.

3

Every morning I run
through pollen, late summer
haze, and rain. My husband

is an illness I had
in another country.

The day he left
again and again he said
it wasn't your fault.
I circle the block, pump
and sweat until I run
outside my body.
My ribs ache.
He brushed his hands
gently over them.

Inside my running
I write to him, breaking
the silence we keep
for his new wife:
I saw the sun disappear
into mist as it reached
the horizon. And an egret
airborne, circling all
this time.

The morning bus gathers
husbands and children
and leaves for a moment
a soft rope of exhaust.
I draw breath over breath
as the children

must breathe in their sleep.
My neighbor waves
from her doorway, follows my
easy stride: "Your waist,"
she says wistfully,
"fits the dress I wore as a bride."

Dreams by No One's Daughter

1

Daylight. For everyone but me. *Nap*
is a night word, a shade they pull
every afternoon against sunlight and speckled leaves
which come to my room anyway
with the telephone ringing downstairs, the boy
across the street, in a tree, shouting
to his friends, and cars' tires
heavy on gravel. *I'm not tired.*

My hand suddenly is a friend
opening and closing like a secret plan
on its silent hinges. It is not
fat anymore like my brother's,
this hand growing up by itself,
this hand hugged in skin the color of sand,
this hand that blooms from my wrist
in a world of chance. *Hand.* Mine.

Something fills me now, like water
but not water—a feeling
in my head. *Idea* of hand.
I float over the bed while everyone
thinks I'm asleep
and my hand begins to remember growing
in the dark, finger by finger,
then the dream, the swim, parting
the dark to touch skin, face, cup, flame,
my mother's sharp red nails,
my grandmother's creased map of veins
and her mother's ring
so green it turns my eyes into stones.

2

Emerald. It anchored my grandmother's hand
at the head of the table. At her touch
the brass bell sang, the consommé arrived
and disappeared in its scalloped tureen, and glass plates
floated on the maid's hands like mirrors.
It leaked sea light through the fingers
of her other hand, clasped over it in dimmed Carnegie Hall
while music swelled toward the busy ceiling.
It flashed under chandeliers at receptions and
foreign hotels, splitting the air into rainbow
and ice like the stars, the bubbles in
crystal, laughter in the night.
Now it smolders over my mother's thickening knuckle
in the house where I grew up, all those long afternoons
of trump cards and tea. Someone's gardener
burning the last of the leaves. It slips in and out
of its velvet box. It slips in and out of Sundays.
It waits under her black gloves at funerals.

3

That was another life, when it found its way
to my third finger, right hand.
I wore black silk
and painted my nails coral.
I took my coffee
without honey, sherry at five,
and brandy from a slender glass before bed.
I did not live between
two fields, one cotton and one alfalfa.
The sky did not fill the days with
silence and depths of blue
while the skin loosened slowly about my knuckles.
I moved among symphonies, dinners
served by strangers, and buildings
that pressed like thieves against each other's windows.
I did not measure oats every morning
for two chestnut geldings.
I did not watch the sun vanish
every night in its nest of coals.

I locked my doors. I left on all the lamps
against the soft, mysterious night.
I did not tell story after story to
myself, like a child believed to be asleep.

Living Near the Plaza of Thieves

Three floors up, I fall
asleep to footsteps rising.
Somebody's door lets out
syllables whose music thickens the air.
All night traffic breathes
water, sound through a shell, and I
follow the Sexta, the Quinta,
the Avenida del Rio, where language
flows past me in the careless
currency of speech.

The words, the whole country
I'm chipped from, dissolve.
I leave nothing behind as I follow
the dusty child who sometimes
follows me—maybe he sleeps
under a bridge, maybe the smell
of cooking draws him
closer to guarded doors.

The man who watches this building
blows his whistle, barely
nudging the air. He reminds me
to look for myself where
I am—next door to a woman
whose husband I've never seen
and a plump bachelor who keeps
rattling his keys. A radio
fills suddenly with tambourines
and I am wrapped around my purse,
staring into the dark
that is not a window. The real

window takes shape against a streak
of dawn as the watchman mutters sharp
words, pebbles flung into the street.
All night I try to finish
a sentence in another language,
the silence I break in letters home.

CONSTANCE URDANG

Old Wives' Tales

1. The Well

It was a real well, real
As any in a fairy tale
Where a frog might sit
On its mossy lip, dreaming of princesses;
Far below the stone rim
Mantled in velvet verdigris
A single watery eye stares up,
Unwinking, hypnotic, blinkered
By a wooden lid. At its side
A mundane bucket remembers the kitchen
And the stout farmwife, hoarse as a frog,
Warning of depths unplumbed, scraping crusted pots.

2. The Hedge

Higher than my head
Thicker than my outstretched arm
—Uncle had to stand on a chair
To clip it with giant shears—
How could a prince
Ever wrench his way through it?
Ah, but close to the ground
Leafy passageways and tunnels
Have been opened by the small animals of darkness.
I myself have crept out that way, unseen
By those who don't lower their eyes
Or glance sideways
But stand at attention, looking straight ahead.

3. The Slipper

Twenty years later
How could it fit a foot
Broad, calloused, no longer accustomed
To dancing? On the dusty shelf
Rackety girls, heartless and innocent,
Find mysterious souvenirs.
A wedding dress

Evokes incredulous laughter,
And as for the dancing shoes,
Surely Mother could never
Have worn something so dainty, so fragile,
So fine.

The Muse Is Always the Other Woman

He courts her up there on the roof.
Among the chimneys and flowering vines,
In the pale, lucid air
Crowded with invisible presences
He is looking for something;
He believes that, womanlike,
She will help him find it.
He is a rational man
In search of his madness,
Although all art is an illusion
And music and dance
Do not, in fact, make the corn grow
Or assist the crops to ripen.

He cries, without her the world is meaningless
As music to the tone deaf
Or the rainbow to the color blind!
He thinks today he will build
Such a curious cage
She will creep inside of her own accord;
But she has escaped him before,
Many times, on the border
Between two lives, or in the caesura
Between reason and unreason,
And makes her way alone
Through his long dream.

Back Far Enough, Down Deep Enough

Who she was:
  the old woman rocking, impatient for her kingdom
Whence she sprang:
  from soiled loins
How she looked:
  like a maiden in May
What she wore:
  a crown of cress and gown of gossamer
Where she lived:
  in stony streets
Did she, nevertheless, laugh and sing?
  yes
The gift she coveted:
  flowers that would not fade
Where she hunted for it:
  in the mirror's blonde reflection
What she feared to find:
  the room without echoes
Why she cried:
  so someone would hear her
Who comforted her:
  no one

All Around Us

How many pallid Christs, with painted blood
And real hair, does it take to explain
A single boy spread-eagled on the floor
Of the police station, blind, baffled eyes
Still not believing what has happened to him?
There are a thousand tragedies all around us.
There is the tragedy of the dog with three legs
And the tragedy of the old uncle lying, or dying, in bed
Who turns his head away on the comfortless pillow;
The tragedy of the young girl afraid of the life within her.
I think of the tragedy of barren women,
Of the poor, who never starve, but are always hungry;
I think of the tragedy of having visions,

And that of never having visions,
And what a miracle it is that the dog still hops to his dinner
On his three legs, and the rain comes in its season
All around us, and waters weeds and garden alike.

My Father's Death

He knew it was waiting for him   somewhere
His own death   that he had sailed to meet
Years ago in Flanders   he never spoke
Of that broken appointment
But throughout the years that followed
He looked for it   among the frail shells
On the beaches of Maine and Connecticut
Or in the pages he loved   of books heady with mildew
Sometimes he forgot it
Till it nipped at his leg   almost playfully
Where the shrapnel still festered
When he was a boy, weak-eyed   in long black stockings
He heard its voice in the sound of milk carts
Grumbling over the cobbles   in his mother's breathy sighs
In the clatter of the el trundling over the points   later
He thought he had outfaced it at the Polyclinic
But he still had a thousand miles to go
To find it   reaching out to take my hand
His own grew cold   and stiffened in the clasp
Of the inevitable last embrace

This Poem

If you are cold, this poem will not warm you.
If you are hungry, you will not be fed
By this poem; if you are sick
It will not cure you. If you are alone
The poem won't take your hand.

This poem lives in warm houses.
It has never known hunger. All it can do
Is, from a pocket of loose change
Select a coin to drop into your palm,
The cold coin of compassion in this poem.

At Frank 'n' Helen's

It's Nostalgia Week at Frank 'n' Helen's:
The two cops at the table near the door
Ordering pepperoni pizza have hung up
Their two blue coats, and on their brawny thighs
Their blunt black holsters dream. Under tinsel stars
Left over from Christmas, a party of seven,
Every one a senior citizen,
Is making itself at home. Over baskets
Of steaming fried chicken or shrimp
Carried by waitresses gently perspiring,
Sweethearts and strangers catch one another's eye.

Here, in the odor of down-home hospitality
Dispensed for a price (but reasonable),
America rediscovers itself, all the homely virtues
Displayed in the mirrors behind the booths
Where time has been arrested, and everything
Remains what we recall, as Frank—or Helen—
Dreamed it. Here we are all fed, we can all
Love one another. Let the scarlet hearts
Festoon the ceiling, let the walls leaf out
With mammoth cardboard shamrocks, greener far
Than anything in nature, under the dreaming stars.

Returning to the Port of Authority: A Picaresque

Some New Yorkers refer to the Port Authority Building, where all buses enter and leave New York, as the "Port of Authority."

1

Where are they going, the crowds that pass in the street?
I had not thought life had undone so many,
So many men and women, seeking the Port of Authority,
Safe anchorage, harbor, asylum.
                          Late at night

Theirs are the voices on the radio, asking the hard questions;
Or they don't ask. The homeless, the hunted,
The haunted, the night-watchers
Who can't wait any longer for morning, where are they going?

2

Returning, revenant, I see Eighth Avenue is a poem,
Seventh and Broadway are epics, Fifth an extravaganza
From the winos and freaks at its feet in Washington Square
(Past once-white buildings, long-ago sidewalk cafés
Behind grimy privet, Fourteenth Street's brash interruption)
To the crossover at Twenty-third.
                                        At Thirty-fourth
The mammoth parade of department stores begins,
And, on the pavement, a cacophony of hawkers
That stretches beyond the stone lions, the bravura
Of Forty-second, to a kind of apotheosis
At Fifty-ninth.
                        O prevalence of pinnacles!
O persistence of uniformed doormen sounding, in the rain,
Your lordly whistles! On Madison and Third
I am assaulted by florists' windows
Bursting with tropical blooms, I'm magnetized
By the windows of jewelry shops, by vegetables
Displayed like jewels, I'm buffeted
By the turbulence of this stream
Of life, this lyric, this mystery,
This daily miracle-play.

3

What impossible collaborations
Are being consummated in cloud-high offices!
How many sweaty love-acrobatics are being performed
Behind a thousand windows
In the tall imperturbable hotels!
                                        And all day long
The restless crowds continue in the street,
Ebbing and flowing like the tidal rivers,
And I am carried, flotsam like the rest,
Riding the crest of the flood down to the sea.

4

Certain images I take with me,
Rescuing them from the flood;
Cast ashore, like so many others,
In a landscape I never imagined
But have come to recognize
I need something to define my life.

Coming back to the narrow island
Between the two rivers, on my right
The sweet river of memory,
And on my left the sweet river
Of forgetfulness, I see what I have become,
A woman in a blue dress,
Carried along on my own tides.

5

Wherever I go, the river accompanies me;
It flows through my earliest dreams, its satiny surface
Fretted with lyrical little waves, or garnished
In winter, with baroque islands of ice.
Alongside, on the windswept upper deck
Of a bus, I rode to womanhood.
Now, around countless corners, in drafty offices,
Gleaming lobbies, or decorous apartments
Suspended in midair like the fabulous hanging
Gardens, I breathe its breath, and feel
Its salty undertow, tugging me home.

RONALD WALLACE

Photo by Emily Wallace

The Facts of Life

She wonders how people get babies.
Suddenly vague and distracted,
we talk about "making love."
She's six and unsatisfied, finds
our limp answers unpersuasive.
Embarrassed, we stiffen, and try again,
this time exposing the stark naked words:
penis, vagina, sperm, womb, and egg.
She thinks we're pulling her leg.
We decide that it's time
to get passionate and insist.
But she's angry, disgusted.
Why do we always make fun of her?
Why do we lie?
We sigh, try cabbages, storks.
She smiles. That's more like it,
We talk on into the night, trying
magic seeds, good fairies, god. . . .

Sestina for the House

October. They decide it is time to move.
The family has grown too large, the house
too small. The father smokes his pipe.
He says, I know that you all love
this house. He turns to his child
who is crying. She doesn't want to leave.

Outside in the large bight yard the leaves
are turning. They know it is time to move
down onto the ground where the child
will rake them together and make a house
for her dolls to play in. They love
the child. A small bird starts to pipe

his song to the leaves while the pipe
in the father's hand sputters. The father leaves
no doubt that he's made up his mind. He loves
his family; that's why they must move.
The child says, this is a wonderful house.
But nobody listens. She's only a child.

The father continues to talk. The child
cries, staring out at the Indian pipes
in her backyard, wondering if the birds of this house
will pack up their children, their nests, and leave
the old yard. Do birds ever move?
Do they know her sadness, her love?

Her father is smoking and talking of love.
Does he know what it's like being a child?
He knows she doesn't want to move.
She hates him sitting there smoking his pipe.
When has he ever been forced to leave
something he loved? He can't love this house.

The father sits by himself in the house
thinking how painful it is to love
a daughter, a house. He's watched her leave
saying she hates him. She's just a child
but it hurts nonetheless. Smoking his pipe
he wonders if he is wrong about the move.

Outside the bird pipes: Don't move. Don't move.
The bright leaves fall on the wonderful house.
And the child sits crying, learning about love.

Thirteen

Gent, Nugget, Swank, and *Dude:*
the names themselves were lusty, crude,
as I took my small detour from school,
my breath erect, my manner cool.

In Kranson's Drugstore, furtive, alert,
stiff in my khakis I'd sneak to the back,
unzip the new issue from its thick stack,
and stick it in my quick shirt.

Oh, I was a thief for love,
accompliced by guilt and thrill,
mystery and wonder my only motive.

Oh, that old Kranson could be there still!
I'd slip in and out, liquid, unseen,
out of my mind again, thirteen.

State Poetry Day

The mayor couldn't be here, but he sends his grand whereases,
and his best regards take their places in the rear.
Another year closes with a villanelle's razzmatazzes.

Outside, in sunlight, with their stunted squash and radishes,
farmers wonder what the going rate is for crop failure and despair.
The mayor couldn't be here but he sends his grand whereases.

In the legislative chambers with their dactyls and caesuras
the local poet laureates sing in praise of cheese and beer.
Another year closes with a villanelle's razzmatazzes.

On the South Side, poverty makes another of its passes.
A bag lady lifts her breakfast from a trash can on the square.
The mayor couldn't be here but he sends his grand whereases.

RONALD WALLACE / 323

Now the poetry club presidents show their poems off like badges
to the hard-of-hearing, blue-haired citizens gathered here.
Another year closes with a villanelle's razzmatazzes.

No one mentions Nicaragua, acid rain, cocaine, or Star Wars,
as the couplets and quatrains maintain a pleasant atmosphere.
The mayor couldn't be here, but he sends his grand whereases.
Another year closes with a villanelle's razzmatazzes.

Building an Outhouse

Is not unlike building a poem: the pure
mathematics of shape; the music of hammer
and tenpenny nail, of floor joist, stud wall,
and sill; the cut wood's sweet smell.

If the Skil saw rear up in your unpracticed hand,
cussing, hawking its chaw of dust,
and you're lost in the pounding particulars
of fly rafters, siding, hypotenuse, and load,
until nothing seems level or true
but the scorn of the tape's clucked tongue,

let the nub of your plainspoken pencil prevail
and it's up! Functional. Tight as a sonnet.
It will last forever (or at least for awhile)
though the critics come sit on it, and sit on it.

Basketball

The ball, almost
as big as she is,
hefted above her head,
she looks up into
the bright orange rim
of the sun. She's six

and the backboard sky
might just as well be
93 million miles away.
Stubs of burdock erupt
all around us
on our court of dirt and hay.
Hurry up, I shout.
We don't have all day.
And we don't.
The next time I look
she's sixteen, the years
arcing up and falling
with a curt swish,
her laughter spinning off
her fingertips, as
the future, all elbows and hips,
sets its practiced pick.

The Makings of Happiness

> *If a man can't be happy on a little farm in*
> *Wisconsin, he hasn't the makings of happiness*
> *in his soul.*

Until you have looked at something so long
it grows so familiar you can't see it—
the alp that all but disappears in dailiness;
the sea that common routine conceals;
the little farm in Wisconsin that seems
painted in oil on your long picture window,
its thick cow turned toward you, wryly
rolling its eyes, stymied by all this hoopla,
its stiff farmer, pinned to his blue ribbon,
pressed in his Sunday best, levitating,
its grinning photographer, tipping
what could be a black beret,
as if this were Marseilles or Paris
and not Hollandale, Wisconsin, 1922,
the war to end all wars now over,

the barn more like a hearth than a barn,
a mother, who could be your mother,
in the doorframe across the way,
bread in the oven and time on her hands,
the little girl, who could be a boy,
roped to her calf, which could be a dog,
waving to her cat, which could be a stoat,
apples in her cheeks and honey in her hair,
the church in the permanent center,
the townspeople happy as larks,
the scene flat and perspectiveless,
a child's colorful cutout—
you'll not know the soul's work:
to keep the man floating, the girl
smiling, the calf changing, the cow rolling
its eyes, the blue Frenchman tipping
his hat at you who live so far off
in the vanishing point of the future.

Nightline: An Interview with the General

The retired general is talking about restraint,
how he could have blown them all to kingdom come.
Read between the lines: this man's a saint.

War is, after all, not for the faint-
hearted. It's more than glory, fife, and drum,
and tired generals talking of restraint.

Make no mistake. He's never been one to paint
a rosy picture, mince words, or play dumb.
Caught behind the lines no man's a saint.

But why should strong offensives ever taint
a country pressed by Leftist, Red, and Hun?
He's generally tired of talking about restraint,

tired of being muzzled by every constraint
put on him. He thinks the time has come
to draw the line between the devil and the saint,

RONALD WALLACE / 326

to silence protest, demonstration, and complaint,
beneath a smooth, efficient, military hum.
The general's retired all talk of restraint.
He aligns himself with God. And God's no saint.

BELLE WARING

Photo by Richard Hurst

Reprieve on the Stoop

If your first memory was the arms of your father
about to chuck you out the window of that catpiss
apartment in Downingtown, you couldn't dream.
You don't remember dreams, like when I got
robbed, the scumface
broke in my room while I was alone
asleep and naked and when he left
I woke up
untouched. Now if the sun

abides in these brassy leaves
quivering over my ankles which talk
to you and you ask me to sit
so I do—you and I
were both alive and how bad is that—on the stoop
like a girl with her front door key on two feet of green
string around her neck, watching the boys shoot
hoops, how they crouch and leap extending to the rim
and sweat on the sweet lunette of neck over their T-shirts

only now we're not slinking
home for supper in time to boil a pork dog
and watch dad throw his liquid obituary in mom's
face. We sit down on the stoop and watch the earth
swing her hips to the next dance hit and the dark
slide his arms around her waist. Listen
—I'm not romantic, baby, but I do
know grace when I see it.

Baby Random

tries a nosedive, kamikaze,
when the intern flings open the isolette.

The kid almost hits the floor. I can see the headline:
DOC DUMPS AIDS TOT. Nice save, nurse,

Why thanks. Young physician: "We have to change
his tube." His voice trembles, six weeks

out of school. I tell him: "Keep it to a handshake,
you'll be OK." Our team resuscitated

this Baby Random, birth weight
one pound, eyelids still fused. Mother's

a junkie with HIV. Never named him.
Where I work we bring back terminal preemies,

No Fetus Can Beat Us. That's our motto. I have
a friend who was thrown into prison. Where do birds

go when they die? Neruda wanted to know. Crows
eat them. Bird heaven? Imagine the racket.

When Random cries, petit fish on shore, nothing
squeaks past the tube down his pipe. His ventilator's

a high-tech bellows that kicks in & out. Not
up to the nurses. Quiet: a pigeon's outside,

color of graham crackers, throat oil on a wet street,
wings spattered white, perched out of the rain.

I have friends who were thrown in prison, Latin
American. Tortured. Exiled. Some people have

courage. Some people have heart. *Corazon.*
After a shift like tonight, I have the usual

bad dreams. Some days I avoid my reflection in store
windows. I just don't want anyone to look at me.

Breeze in Translation

Me, I like to putz in the kitchen and regard
fat garlic and hum about nothing. Make it up. Word
for *blues*. Like dragging down the street
in a hundred-and-four heat—you know
when air temp tops body temp, how buzzed and weird

you get? Word for *trance*. So this character
taps me: remember me, *mon amie?* Name's
Breeze. Then she dictates most fabulous. I'm
blessed. She's benign. Word for *pixilated*.

She's a scholarship girl at the School of Fine Arts
so she drags me down the line to an out-of-town
show. Rattle express. Word for

kismet. This lady with the face of an old walnut
sits by us making lace with an eye-fine
hook and when the train dives into the tunnels
she keeps on working in the dark. Word's

exquisite. Breeze sings
scat all the way to the opening:
sculpture of heating ducts, stovepipes and stones.
Breeze is prole to the bone. The tablecloth's

spattered with blood of the lamb,
wine on the lace. The critic pronounces optimism
vulgar, and asks: Why have there been so few
great women artists?
                    We ask ourselves. The word is
jerkoff. Breeze, who is terrifyingly fluent,

challenges him to sew a bride's dress. From
scratch. *Femmes aux barricades!* The critic can't weave
a cat's cradle. Breeze spits: By hand. French lace.

When a Beautiful Woman Gets on the Jutiapa Bus

babies twist in their mothers' arms. The men
yearn so the breath snags, Ai! in their chests.
The women flick their eyes over her,
discreet, and turn back to each other.
                                       When
a beautiful woman steps on the bus, she scowls
with the arrogance of the gorgeous. That face,
engrave it on commemorative stamps. A philatelist's
dream. That profile should be stamped on centennial
coins. Somebody, quick, take a picture of her,
la señorita in the azure frock. Sculpt her image
to honor Our Lady.
                      Just how did she land here,
Miss Fine Mix? As a matter of course, her forefather,
El Conquistador, raped a Mayan priestess,
Anno Domini 1510. At the moment of her own conception,
her parents met each other's eyes. Don't stare.

What's she doing squeezed in here with campesinos
carrying chickens? Squawk. Save that face.

When a beautiful woman gets off the bus, everyone
sighs, Ai! and imagines her fate: she's off
to Sunday dinner with mama who's groomed her
to marry an honest farmer happy to knock her up
every spring. Her looks (no doubt) will leach out,
washing the dead, schlepping headloads of scavenged
firewood, grinding, grinding, grinding corn,
hanging the wash in the sun and wind, all
by hand, all by her graceful brown hand.

The Tip

It was boss cook's fault. He left
the window wide open and now
the stockroom was crawling with cicadas.
He yelled and stomped them with his big
boot feet. "Stop!" I said, and ran for the broom.

Out front the regulars hollered for coffee.
One cicada escaped and made an emergency
landing on the counter. Pernell, who worked
graveyard shift at the power plant,
coaxed the thing onto his hand.

The trustful creature
didn't dart like a roach. It perched
right on Pernell's knuckles
calm as a man who's worked a tough shift
with a clear conscience.
                            "He don't eat
much," said Pernell.
                            The cicada had a body like a dog poop,
crystal wings and orange eyes that broke the light
weird, like a 3-D postcard of Jesus. Miz Boulden
cringed. Her lipstick was on crooked
again. The cicada rubbed its hindparts
on its wings and chirred. Outside,
its tribe revved up the heat, like a UFO.

I said, "How do they know when to
come back?"

            "God tells them," said Pernell.

"God nothing," Miz Boulden said. "Last time they came
my son was still living. That was when?"

" '53," Pernell said. Boss cook hollered at me
to get sweeping. Pernell clucked: "Why
you work for that stringy-hair sucker?
You too sweet."

           I swept and swept.
The cicadas backflipped and scratched
the air. I threw them all
—living and dead—out
the back door, and let it
slam.
       The sun cut through the pines.
I wished I was back in the woods with the bugs,
listening.

When I got back to the counter, Pernell had left.
"He took his pet with him," Miz Boulden said.
"That boy's not right. Now, where's my eggs,
missy?"
       Up the hen's butt, I thought.
I bit my tongue and cleared Pernell's
cup. Underneath, crisp as an insect's
wing, I found the new five.

Nothing Happened

Tyler scuffs oak leaves to frisk
the scent walking through Malcolm X Park.
First date. The arms of our jackets
graze, sweet puff of romance. Then boom
I step on a syringe, the needle
quick as a pit viper hits my boot.

If this were a movie, I'd laugh, but I've got
works stuck into my tread. "Jesus,
don't touch it," says Tyler, and whips out
his hankie to yank it.

          "Please,
I'm fine," but he started to fuss,
hailed a cab, told the hack to drive fast,
got me home, sat me down to examine
The Foot; a scrap of red toe polish
left over from August, skin intact. Then
he held my foot in both hands.

                 People say
Nothing Happened when they mean No Sex,
when the fact is every look counts. The sun
quivered in the wind outside whaling
the trees, and shimmered over the wall. When I met
Tyler's eyes in that witchy light, I breathed
off the beat and choked, like I was fourteen.

I used to be depressed all the time,
and romance, by the way was not the cure.
I don't mind winter because I know
what follows. There are laws.

Refuge at the One Step Down

Shrapnel lives in Morton's neck, so his head stays
cocked to the left. We've changed generations,
man. Our waitress, sporting seven different
earrings, was born the year Morton pitched
his Purple Heart over the White House fence & then
split for Cuba & then came home to report: Nixon's
an asshole, Fidel's an asshole. It does
further one to have somewhere to go.

               When Morton
OD'd and got the tubes slapped down him without
one single splendid vision of his own white light,
sure, I went to see him. We used to sneak into
the One Step Down, underage, where Monk's still on
the jukebox. Then I busted out on a scholarship.
Morton went to Nam.

Right now Monk's playing "Misterioso"
and Morton's feeding me coffee and his arms
smooth and clean as a puppy's underbelly
making me laugh. Wide awake for swing
shift at the halfway house, he leans across the table
and says real soft, "I could teach you to meditate." Me
I want to be unconscious. Morton says, "That ain't
quite right."

The fog is rolled up into my head. Sunday
night always gets me depressed—dragging down Columbia Road
the winos holler Lady! Talk, Lady! in Spanish & English
the pigeons hover in the torched-out windows and then

I hear my name and HEY GIRL—big hug. Let's say
you give up and ride the bus eighteen hours sore and sad.
This time nobody's talking. Morton is the moment
you open the door after a long ride home in the dark.

Our Lady of the Laundromat

Me and Marlene sit tight in her truck
parked right outside the Laund-o-rama.
Marlene's just quit her Persian lover
who kisses like a barnful of electric
swallows. She says her wedded husband doesn't
kiss.
    So LEAVE.
Can't.
      Why NOT?
He'd get the kids.

She sure needs a Kleenex but all I have is a mini pad
wrapped in pink plastic. Inside, the Laund-o-rama

steams like a Carolina swamp. As kids
we built tree forts, safe from our parents' godlike
opinions. We thought we would prevail, garrisoned.
We would never be as sad as our parents.

If we moved to Vancouver with the kids, the men could visit
if they behaved. How practical is that? Marlene sobs
into the mini pad. See that girl at the bus stop,
hugging her viola tight? Maybe
Back on the brain. Maybe not.

MICHAEL S. WEAVER

Photo by Michael Bergman

The Missing Patriarch

She peeked out from under
the old foot-powered sewing machine
a frightened cat, her eyes
still and aflame, her hair
darting about the iron curls
of the frame, her buttocks
filling the wide pedal, her daughters
twirling their fingers in their hair.
He pushed her there
when she accused him of loving
a schoolteacher, a light woman
of grace and power the men
eyed with scratching hands
from the wooden handles
of their ploughs. He slammed
her down until the wood
of the house set her marrow
to dancing and the waters
swallowed the shores that were her eyes.
He slammed her down
and strode out into the yard,
unmindful of the crisp fingers
of the sun poking his cheeks,
or the slow rustle of white sand
around his black shoes, deaf
to the dominant wail
of my grandmother behind him
or the screeching of my aunts and mother
like frenzied chicks beside her.

Beginnings

The house on Bentalou Street
had a cemetery behind it,
where the white hands of ghosts
rose like mist when God
tapped it with his silver cane.

There were giant pine trees
out front that snapped when
we hit them from the porch,
jumping like big squirrels
from the stone ledge.

Inside it had no end;
the stairs led to God's tongue;
the basement was the warm door
to the labyrinth of the Earth.
We lived on the rising chest of a star.

And on one still day,
I hammered a boy until
he bled and ran, the blood
like red licorice on my small hand.
The world became many houses,

all of them under siege.

The Dogs

You killed the Dalmatian puppy
with the wheel of your truck,
driving backwards over it until
the white with black spots popped
in the soft ooze of baby dog.
It was a simple and unexpected
flop of the wheel, and the children
cried, the children of the man
who owned the dog, the laziest farmer
in Woodstock, the man who let
pig shit collect until it was
three-feet thick and looked like
bad deviled eggs. The children
carried the dead puppy to ground
hallowed enough to wait for those spirits
who attend to the soulless, and
the truck spattered exhaust and oil

on the place where he left this earth,
as we drove off. In another year,
you killed another dog, this time
with the shotgun you ordered me
to bring to you, and I took his body
to the burn pile in a wheelbarrow,
watching how the flesh quivered
like the soft arm of your wife sleeping
in the yellow pickup, riding out
to where time is pregnant with surprise.

My Father's First Baseball Game

You lumbered along the stadium
like a sinner being marshaled to baptism,
your head high and certain of convictions,
the busy chatter of the crowd beside you.

The radio is better, you declared,
and baseball is baseball regardless.
The wooden seat held you erect and mute,
glancing at the tiny figures in the field.

The open wealth of your first live game
came at you singly as the Negro Leagues
came up as you spoke of Satchel Paige,
Jackie Robinson and your ancient radio.

After the 9th, you fought the crowd,
fingering the ticket stubs in your shirt,
as we floated out into the night
with the deep river of white faces.

The Message on Cape Cod

We have slept in
the wide electric arms
of love. At noon we pass
a wedding of celebrities,
count the limousines
as we stalk the souvenir shops.
An invisible and peculiar wire
holds this life together,
and we cling to a molecule
proudly. In the restaurant
we chant a child's lullaby
over the clam chowder,
and you remember another
tune and still another
until the light dims
in the eye of the baked fish,
and the waitress retires
to her stool, wrapped in smiles.
We move down the beach
in the evening, always
one failing step ahead
of the March wind, looking
out on the vast tongue
of the ocean to where
whales passed. A sweep
of the fog light circles around;
the smug authority of the water
allows us a sudden privacy,
and we make love behind
a giant log washed to softness.
A boat eases past, investigating,
and, dressing, we ease back
to the wooden stairs of the cliff,
counting the eyes that see.

My Father's Geography

I was parading the côte d'Azur,
hopping the short trains from Nice to Cannes,
following the maze of streets in Monte Carlo
to the hill that overlooks the ville.
A woman fed me pâté in the afternoon,
calling from her stall to offer me more.
At breakfast I talked in French with an old man
about what he loved about America—the Kennedys.

On the beaches I walked and watched
topless women sunbathe and swim,
loving both home and being so far from it.

At a phone looking to Africa over the Mediterranean,
I called my father, and, missing me, he said,
"You almost home boy. Go on cross that sea!"

ROBLEY WILSON

The Mechanical Cow

Marvelous four-cylindered beast:
switch on her tail and she muses
butterfat, clanking a brass bell,
between her armored quarters oil
gathers and runs to the shed floor—
watch your step. Every spring and fall
the co-op man dismantles her,
checks points and brushes, changes plugs
and sets her timing; once a month
the man from the commission stops
to analyze her milk—as if
anything could go wrong with *that*.
She ruminates on low-test gas,
combustion chambers so designed
as to be practically silent
in operation; she will run
night after night flat out, and is
(if there are children) tamper-proof.
Early mornings the farmer comes
into her stall, sets down his pails,
and strikes white sparks from her dugs.

Say Girls in Shoe Ads:
"I go for a man who's tall!"

Me, for example,
a skinny kid
skyrocketed to skinny manhood—
my mother as a girl nicknamed
"Spindleshanks,"
my father off at Exeter
called "Master Bones"—

Me, the shy get of their clacking
sharp-hipped love,
who scowled school corridors

in trousers cuffless
and too tight at the crotch,
who ducked for awnings,
cracked his skull through exits,
stuck like two warped planks
out of bunk beds and camp cots—

Me, wickedly inside my slats,
taught in the nick of time
this lanky aphrodisia of height,
this lusty vertigo—
crying to the runt world:
Jump! ladies soft and small.
Shinny up for kisses.
Hang on for love.

Envoi

Sun in the mouth of the day,
Moon in the teeth of night—
Taste everything, they say;
Swallow nothing but light.

The Rejoicing That Attends the Murder of Famous Men

The anonymous handsome
woman in the evening newsfilm
neither weeps nor bows.
Amid a general grief
she is some unbeliever
who looks out at us
past the shoulders of the stricken
and with tight lips and clear eyes
overbears us. She is ageless.
She has come among the first
to stand witness to tragedy,
the first whose mission it is
to teach us the rejoicing.

We find her offensive.
In the rainbows of our own
restricted visions, we curse
her detachment. If
we could put out our hands
and bridge the distance
between our chaos and her repose,
we would throttle her
and make her eyes bulge tears
like our own. If no one
stopped us, we would learn
the power sorrow confers
into the empty hands
we presently clench in our laps.

We see in this woman
the perverseness of history
and the unshatterable, solemn
dispassion of time—as if
indifference to evil were
the secret of immortality. She
is an insult to the mind,
cannot be got back at,
will not even tell her name.

If only she would go home
and in the privacy of her rooms
break down utterly!
But what we expect of history
we expect of her.

She is truly unshakeable;
in her heart's arrogance
she is glad for portentous death.
The anonymous handsome woman
in the newsfilms
is one of God's various faces,
so we do not know her
though we have seen her
everywhere—letting murder
happen, letting the cameras grind—
the one of us always
untouched, rejoicing, claiming
it is for the sake of love.

Sparrow Hills

(After Boris Pasternak)

God, how my mouth swam
your nipples—Can't it be
like this forever? Endless
muggy summer, and night
after night the schmaltz
of that same accordion
we heard when we stood up
out of breath, slapping
the dust off our clothes?

People go queasy over time,
they make age scary as hell,
they talk all holy—you
don't fall for that drivel,
do you? You don't catch
nature on its knees praying;
the fields don't simper,
the ponds don't turn salty.
God doesn't care. Instead

let's crack our souls
wide open; today is all
time—the world's high noon;
use your eyes, look hard.
Whatever the two of us
touch turns to a muddle:
wood-birds, balsam, sky—
is it passion that colors
the pine spills like blood?

Forget the city; streetcars
stop miles from here, the woods
are trackless—anyway
nothing runs on Sundays.
We'll break down boughs
to rest on, play kid games
on the squirrel paths;

you slip on the needles,
I'll fall on top of you. . . .

God, the blindness of noon
this Sunday, being alone—
The woods say: this world
will never be civilized.
The pines believe in that,
and the wild fields—and so
should you. Here: hug me
under this crazy quilt
the clouds unfold for us.

The Military-Industrial Complex

On his free weekends he took
from its patent holster
the black sidearm, clicked
the safety off halfway
across the back lot, and sat
—we could see him, his legs
dangling over the edge of
the roof—sat on the hencoop.

After the first round or two
the chickens stayed inside
and gossiped the thunder
above their witless heads;
he would shoot, and the hens
echo, and another shell case
shine in the hot sun—the yard
a litter of brass and dung.

Flies. Green flies were what
he murdered from his perch,
brushing them from his face,
scowling them down to earth,
taking aim. He hammered them
into the dirt, into the wood

frame the wire was nailed to.
Hours this lasted—weekends.

At the start we had thought
it was the rats that raided
the coop from time to time—
and it all made sense: noise
and the panic of the fowl,
the killer in his khaki shirt
sitting at ease on the roof,
waving the sun from his eyes.

When it was not rats, we saw
this was none of our affair
and got used to it—weekdays
called him *Sir* and envied him
ribbons and rank. So what if
the chickens choked to death
on the spent casings, and men
working nights got no sleep?

DAVID WOJAHN

Photo by David B. Sutton

"Satin Doll"

It's probably the year her marriage
fails, though the photo, blackened now
on the edges of its sepia, doesn't say:
my aunt on the hood of the blue Chevy coupe,

straw hat and summer dress. It's the year
she carries the novels and notebooks
into the backyard to burn them, and when she finishes
her dress and apron are covered with ashes, rising

in what she wants to call a pillar of fire
but it is only smoke on a damp day.
She walks back to the house and her first
sickly daughter, feeling the one

inside her kick. She thinks of going
back to her maiden name, and the daughter
cries in her crib like the passionless
wind up the St. Croix River bluffs.

And when she was a child there, the day
of the grade school picnic, they found
a woman drowned on the banks. Everyone stared
and no one closed the eyes staring back.

But now it's raining on the first spring night
of 1947, six years to my birth,
and I don't want to leave her here. I want
the kitchen radio to murmur

some slithering big band and "Satin Doll"
from the Casablanca ballroom, high in Chicago's clouds.
I want her to see the women floating
in their taffeta, chilly red corsages from

their pencil-mustached men, ivory tuxedos, lotion,
and bay rum. She can almost touch them now. Duke Ellington
rises from the sprawling Steinway as the four
trombones begin their solo, horns glittering

under the spinning globe of mirrors. And now
she's dancing, isn't she? Until the cupboards shake,
until the window, already trembling with rain,
hums its vibrato, and she's holding herself in her arms

so tightly she can feel the veins
in her shoulders throb to their separate music,
until this is a song she can dance with too,
and I can let her go.

EXCERPTS FROM "Mystery Train: A Sequence"

Homage: Light from the Hall

It is Soul Brother Number One, James Brown,
Chanting, "It wouldn't be nothing, noth-iiiiinnnnnggg. . . . "
Dismembering the notes until everything hangs
On his mystical half-screech, notes skidding 'round
Your brain as you listen, rapt, thirteen,
Transistor and its single earphone tucked
With you beneath the midnight covers, station WKED,
Big Daddy Armand, The Ragin' Cajun,
"Spinning out the *bossest* platters for you all,"
Golden Age trance, when New Orleans stations
Traveling two thousand miles shaped distance
Into alchemy. Beneath the door, a light from the hall
Bathing the bedroom in its stammering glow:
Cooke and Redding risen, James Brown quaking the Apollo.

Buddy Holly Watching *Rebel Without a Cause,*
Lubbock, Texas, 1956

He's played hookey to see the flick again,
Though it's only showing at The Alhambra,

The run-down joint in the barrio. Spanish version,
Tawdry trashed marquee: *Rebelde Sin Causa.*

Dean staggers into Juvey, playing a credible drunk,
Though his dubbed voice squeaks like Mickey Mouse.

Me llamo Jaime Stark. But Dean's trademark smirk
Obliterates the dialogue. Buddy studies every gesture,

Hornrims sliding the bridge of his nose,
Though the smirk doesn't save that punk in the car,

Crashing to some stock-footage ocean, doesn't save Sal Mineo's
Benighted life. But Buddy, walking home, wants a *trademark.*

In shop window reflections, he practices the Jim Dean strut.
Some of us, he thinks, will never get it right.

Matins: James Brown and His Famous Flames
Tour the South, 1958

"Please, Please, Please" on the charts permits
Four canary yellow sequined suits
And a hulking Coupe de Ville—bought on credit—
For the Alabama-Georgia roadhouse circuit.
Half last night they drove from Athens, taking turns
At the wheel. The radio hissed National Guards
In Little Rock, static filling Jackie Wilson's
"Lonely Teardrops." Parked near Macon in a soybean field,

They sleep with heads in towels to protect
Their kingly pompadours, and as the predawn
Mist burns off, they wake to knocks against
The windshield. A cruiser with its siren on
Dyes the fog bright red. *Don't you niggers know your place?*
A billy club, a face, the windshield breaks.

Custom Job: Hank Williams, Jr., and the Death Car, 1958

We know this story: how his daddy died of drink
On New Year's Eve, comatose in his Cadillac,
Black fins and boots splayed out the window in a grim quartet.
And in his will the car is all that's left

His son, who makes the best of it. Custom
Paint job with orange flames, chopped and channeled,
Bedazzling chrome valves and fuel injection.
Seventeen, he's cruising downtown Nashville,

Midnight, sipping sour mash from a silver flask.
He's been to see *Attack of the Teenage Werewolves*.
But there's no one out to race. He pounds time on the dash
To Carl Perkins from the radio. Neon unravels

Its Little White Way before him. Beyond it, the dark
He will cruise into, singing with it all night.

Tattoo, Corazon: Ritchie Valens, 1959

He has three singles on the charts and in
Six weeks will be dead,
     the Piper Cub that also kills

Big Bopper, Buddy Holly, and almost Dion,
Skidding to pieces in an Iowa field.

Easy to imagine premonitions—
That he wakes in night-sweats from dreams of falling—
But no.
   Harder to say he's seventeen
And buys, with cash, a house in West L.A.,

Where he's sprawled tonight, sculpting in his bedroom
A gift for his new wife. His left hand turns

The knife in circles on his right. Where thumb
And index finger meet, he cuts and squirms,

Replacing blood with ink. Cotton stops the flow.
She'll wake to heart shape,
     circling TE AMO.

Fab Four Tour Deutschland: Hamburg, 1961

"Und now Ladies und Gentlemun, *Der Peedles!*"
The emcee oozes pomade, affecting the hip American,

But the accent twists the name to sound like *needles.*
Or some Teutonic baby's body function.

The bassist begins, nodding to the drummer,
Who flaunts his movie-star good looks: Pete Best,

Grinning as the drums count four. "Roll Over
Beethoven" 's the opener. McCartney's Elvis

Posturing's too shrill, the playing sloppy,
But Lennon, stoned on Romilar, doesn't care.

Mild applause, segue into "Long Tall Sally. . . . "
One will become a baby-faced billionaire,

One a film producer, one a skewed sort of martyr,
And this one, the drummer, a Liverpool butcher.

Woody Guthrie Visited by Bob Dylan: Brooklyn State Hospital, New York, 1961

He has lain here for a terrible, motionless
Decade, and talks through a system of winks
And facial twitches. The nurse props a cigarette
Between his lips, wipes his forehead. She thinks
He wants to send the kid away, but decides
To let him in—he's waited hours.
Guitar case, jean jacket. A corduroy cap slides
Down his forehead. Doesn't talk. He can't be more
Than twenty. He straps on the harmonica holder,
Tunes up, and begins his "Song to Woody,"
Trying to sound three times his age, sandpaper
Dustbowl growl, the song interminable, inept. Should he
Sing another? The eyes roll their half-hearted yes.
The nurse grits her teeth, stubs out the cigarette.

The Trashmen Shaking Hands with Hubert Humphrey at the Opening of Apache Plaza Shopping Center, Suburban Minneapolis, August 1963

Well-uh Bird, Bird, Bird, Bird is the Word:
The opening of their current—and what will be

Their only—hit, a ditty called "Surfin' Bird,"
Though the band was formed in Shakopee,

Minnesota, and the drummer confesses, sheepishly,
He has never seen the ocean, or even

The Great Salt Lake. Senator Humphrey
Does his balding unctuous best with them,

Stumping for next year's presidential bid.
Should Kennedy choose not to run again,

He'll be ready. And the cancer that will kill,
Slowly, and in public, this smiling public man,

Must already cruise his cells.
                    They exchange signed photographs.

"What's a Surfin' Bird?" he asks.

"Mystery Train": Janis Joplin Leaves
Port Arthur for Points West, 1964

Train she rides is sixteen coaches long,
   The long dark train that takes the girl away.
The silver wheels
                    click and sing along

   The panhandle, the half-assed cattle towns,
All night until the misty break of day.
   Dark train,
                    dark train, sixteen coaches long.

Girl's looked out her window all night long,
   Bad dreams:
                    couldn't sleep her thoughts away.
The wheels click, mournful, dream along.

   Amarillo, Paradise,
                    Albuquerque still a long
Night's ride. Scrub pine, cactus, fog all gray
   Around the dark train
                    sixteen coaches long.

A cardboard suitcase and she's dressed all wrong.
   Got some cousin's address,
                    no skills, no smarts, no money.
The wheels mock her as they click along.

A half-pint of Four Roses,
                    then she hums a Woody song,

"I Ain't Got No Home,"
                              The whistle brays.
The Mystery Train is sixteen coaches long.

    The whistle howls, the wheels click along.

At Graceland with a Six Year Old, 1985

It's any kid's most exquisite fantasy,
To have his name
                    emblazoned on a private jet.

So Josh stares through the cockpit of
                              The Lisa Marie,

Its wings cemented to the Graceland parking lot.

The kitsch?
                All lost on him, the gold records and cars,
Dazzling as the grave's eternal flame.

And I read him the epitaph's Gothic characters.
"A gift from God . . . " etc. Daddy Presley's wretched poem.

Colonel Parker was asked, after Elvis's death,
What he'd do now to occupy his time:
                              "Ah guess

Ah'll jus' keep awn managin' him." He's really *Dutch.*
The accent, like the colonel tag, is a ruse,

Like the living room's wall of mirrors—rigged immensity,
Pipsqueak Versailles,
                where Josh makes faces, grinning at me.

Colorizing: Turner Broadcasting Enterprises, Computer Graphics Division, Burbank, California, 1987

The process calls for twenty heads to stare
All winter at *Hard Day's Night,*
                    to transfer

Color to *Can't Buy Me Love,* to Ringo
Bobbing at his BEATLES kit. And so,

With MFA in studio art (watercolor),
Lani's now employed, nonunion, by Ted Turner,

Applying "color sense" on a computer screen.
Today,
        it's John's face in the train coach scene:

She wants the flesh lifelike, a British pale,
While he croons "I Should Have Known Better," wails

Through his harmonica,
                     alive almost. Next cubicle,
Lani's friend fills in another scene, beaming Paul

Chased through alleys by his pimply fans.
She's shading his peach-fuzz,
                  the lips that form "Where's John."

The Assassination of John Lennon as Depicted by the Madame Tussaud Wax Museum, Niagara Falls, Ontario, 1987

Smuggled human hair from Mexico
Falls radiant around the waxy O

Of her scream. Shades on, leather coat and pants, Yoko
On her knees—like the famous Kent State photo

Where the girl can't shriek her boyfriend alive, her arms
Windmilling Ohio sky.
                     A pump in John's chest heaves

To mimic death throes. The blood is made of latex.
His glasses: broken on the plastic sidewalk.

A scowling David Chapman, his arms outstretched,
His pistol barrel spiraling fake smoke

In a siren's red wash, completes the composition,
And somewhere background music plays "Imagine"

Before the tableau darkens. We push a button
To renew the scream.
                     The chest starts up again.

PAUL ZIMMER

Photo by Michael Pettit

Zimmer in Grade School

In grade school I wondered
Why I had been born
To wrestle in the ashy puddles,
With my square nose
Streaming mucus and blood,
My knuckles puffed from combat
And the old nun's ruler.
I feared everything: God,
Learning and my schoolmates.
I could not count, spell or read.
My report card proclaimed
These scarlet failures.
My parents wrung their loving hands.
My guardian angel wept constantly.

But I could never hide anything.
If I peed my pants in class
The puddle was always quickly evident,
My worst mistakes were at
The blackboard for Jesus and all
The saints to see.
                    Even now
When I hide behind elaborate masks
It is always known that I am Zimmer,
The one who does the messy papers
And fractures all his crayons,
Who spits upon the radiators
And sits all day in shame
Outside the office of the principal.

Zimmer's Head Thudding Against the Blackboard

At the blackboard I had missed
Five number problems in a row,
And was about to foul a sixth,
When the old, exasperated nun
Began to pound my head against
My six mistakes. When I cried,
She threw me back into my seat,
Where I hid my head and swore
That very day I'd be a poet,
And curse her yellow teeth with this.

The Day Zimmer Lost Religion

The first Sunday I missed Mass on purpose
I waited all day for Christ to climb down
Like a wiry flyweight from the cross and
Club me on my irreverent teeth, to wade into
My blasphemous gut and drop me like a
Red hot thurible, the devil roaring in
Reserved seats until he got the hiccups.

It was a long cold way from the old days
When cassocked and surpliced I mumbled Latin
At the old priest and rang his obscure bell.
A long way from the dirty wind that blew
The soot like venial sins across the schoolyard
Where God reigned as a threatening,
One-eyed triangle high in the fleecy sky.

The first Sunday I missed Mass on purpose
I waited all day for Christ to climb down
Like the playground bully, the cuts and mice
Upon his face agleam, and pound me
Till my irreligious tongue hung out.
But of course He never came, knowing that
I was grown up and ready for Him now.

The Eisenhower Years

for my father

Flunked out and laid-off,
Zimmer works for his father
At Zimmer's Shoes for Women.
The feet of old women awaken
From dreams, they groan and rub
Their hacked-up corns together.
At last they stand and walk in agony
Downtown to Zimmer's fitting stool
where he talks to the feet,
Reassures and fits them with
Blissful ties in medium heels.

Home from work he checks the mail
For greetings from his draft board.
After supper he listens to Brubeck,
Lays out with a tumbler of Thunderbird,
Cigarettes and *From Here to Eternity*.

That evening he goes out to the bars,
Drinks three pitchers of Stroh's,
Ends up in the wee hours leaning
On a lamppost, his tie loosened,
Fedora pushed back on his head,
A Chesterfield stuck to his lips.

All of complacent America
Spreads around him in the night.
Nothing is moving in this void,
Only the feet of old women,
Twitching and shuffling in pain.
Zimmer sighs and takes a drag,
Exhales through his nostrils.
He knows nothing and feels little.
He has never been anywhere
And fears where he is going.

Zimmer Drunk and Alone, Dreaming of Old Football Games

I threw the inside of my gizzard out, splashing
Down the steps of that dark football stadium
Where I had gone to celebrate the ancient games.
But I had been gut-blocked and cut down by
A two-ton guard in one quarter of my fifth.
Fireflies broke and smeared before my eyes,
And the half-moon spiraled on my corneas.
Between spasms the crickets beat halftime to
My tympanum, and stars twirled like fire batons
Inside the darkness. The small roll at my gut's end,
Rising like a cheer, curled up intestine to the stomach,
Quaking to my gullet, and out my tongue again.
Out came old victories, defeats and scoreless ties,
Out came all the quarters of my fifth,
Until exhausted, my wind gone and my teeth sour,
I climbed the high fence out of that dark stadium,
Still smarting from the booing and hard scrimmage.
I zigzagged down the street, stiff-arming buildings,
And giving flashy hip fakes to the lampposts.
I cut for home, a veteran broken field drunkard,
With my bottle tucked up high away from fumbles.

The Duke Ellington Dream

Of course Zimmer was late for the gig.
Duke was pissed and growling at the piano,
But Jeep, Brute, Rex, Cat and Cootie
All moved down on the chairs
As Zimmer walked in with his tenor.
Everyone knew that the boss had arrived.

Duke slammed out the downbeat for "Caravan"
And Zimmer stood up to take his solo.
The whole joint suddenly started jiving,
Chicks came up to the bandstand

To hang their lovelies over the rail.
Duke was sweating but wouldn't smile
Through chorus after chorus after chorus.

It was the same with "Satin Doll,"
"Do Nothing Till You Hear from Me,"
"Warm Valley," "In a Sentimental Mood";
Zimmer blew them so they would stay played.

After the final set he packed
His horn and was heading out
When Duke came up and collared him.
"Zimmer," he said, "You most astonishing ofay!
You have shat upon my charts,
But I love you madly."

Zimmer Imagines Heaven

for Merrill Leffler

I sit with Joseph Conrad in Monet's garden.
We are listening to Yeats chant his poems,
A breeze stirs through Thomas Hardy's moustache,
John Skelton has gone to the house for beer,
Wanda Landowska lightly fingers a clavichord,
Along the spruce tree walk Roberto Clemente and
Thurman Munson whistle a baseball back and forth.
Mozart chats with Ellington in the roses.

Monet smokes and dabs his canvas in the sun,
Brueghel and Turner set easels behind the wisteria.
The band is warming up in the Big Studio:
Bean, Brute, Bird and Serge on saxes,
Kai, Bill Harris, Lawrence Brown, trombones,
Little Jazz, Clifford, Fats on trumpets,
Klook plays drums, Mingus bass, Bud the piano.
Later Madam Schumann-Heink will sing Schubert,
The monks of Benedictine Abbey will chant.
There will be more poems from Emily Dickinson,

James Wright, John Clare, Walt Whitman.
Shakespeare rehearses players for *King Lear*.

At dusk Alice Toklas brings out platters
Of Sweetbreads à la Napolitaine, Salad Livonière,
And a tureen of Gaspacho of Malaga.
After the meal Brahms passes fine cigars.
God comes then, radiant with a bottle of cognac,
She pours generously into the snifters,
I tell Her I have begun to learn what
Heaven is about. She wants to hear.
It is, I say, being thankful for eternity.
Her smile is the best part of the day.

Notes on the Poets

CLARIBEL ALEGRÍA was born in Estelí, Nicaragua, in 1924, and grew up in Santa Ana, El Salvador. In 1948 she received her B.A. in philosophy and letters at George Washington University. She has published twelve volumes of poetry, five novels, and a book of children's stories. In collaboration with her husband, the American writer Darwin J. Flakoll, she has published another novel, several books of testimony and contemporary Latin American history, as well as several anthologies. In 1978 her book of poems *Sobrevivo* won the Casa de las Americas Prize of Cuba. During the past forty years she has lived in various Latin American and European countries. In recent years, she and her husband have divided their time between Majorca, Spain, and Managua, Nicaragua.

DEBRA ALLBERY was born in Lancaster, Ohio, in 1957. She studied at Denison University and the College of Wooster, where she earned a B.A. in English, at the University of Iowa, where she received her M.F.A. in creative writing, and in the graduate English program at the University of Virginia. She has been writer-in-residence at Interlochen Arts Academy and Phillips Exeter Academy. *Walking Distance,* her first book, won the 1990 Agnes Lynch Starrett Poetry Prize. She lives in Charlottesville, Virginia.

MAGGIE ANDERSON was born in New York City in 1948 and moved to West Virginia when she was thirteen years old. She has taught in the creative writing programs at the University of Pittsburgh, the Pennsylvania State University, the University of Oregon, and Hamilton College. She was coeditor of the poetry magazine *Trellis* from 1971 to 1981, and in 1991 she edited *Hill Daughter,* a collection of new and selected poems by West Virginia poet laureate Louise McNeill. Currently she teaches creative writing at Kent State University.

ROBIN BECKER was born in Philadelphia in 1951. She attended a Quaker day school there and received her B.A. and M.A. from Boston University. Her poems have appeared in many journals, including *AGNI, American Poetry Review, The Kenyon Review,* and *Ploughshares.* She lives in Cambridge, Massachusetts, where she teaches poetry and fiction writing courses in The Program in Writing and Humanistic Studies at the Massachusetts Institute of Technology and serves as poetry editor for *The Women's Review of Books.*

SIV CEDERING was born in 1939 near the Arctic Circle in Sweden and as a teenager moved to the United States. She has worked as a nursemaid, a pilot, a balloonist, a professor, a housewife, and a writer. Her writing has appeared in *Harper's Magazine, Ms., The New Republic, The New York Times, Paris Review, Partisan Review,* and *Science.* She is the author of ten collections of poetry, two novels, six books for children, four books of translations, and several screenplays. A Swedish film based upon her second novel, *The Ox,* was nominated for a 1992 Academy Award for Best Foreign Language Film. Cedering is also a visual artist who has illustrated five books and has participated in several art exhibitions, including three recent one-woman shows. She lives in Amagansett, New York.

LORNA DEE CERVANTES was born in 1954 in San Francisco and grew up in San Jose, where she studied at San Jose City College and San Jose State University. *Emplumada,* her first book, was winner of the 1982 American Book Award of the Before Columbus Foundation. Active in Chicano community affairs, she has been a member of the Chicana Theatre Group and organizer for the Centro Cultural de la Gente. She teaches at the University of Colorado, Boulder.

NANCY VIEIRA COUTO was born in 1942 in New Bedford, Massachusetts, and grew up in that city and the nearby town of Dartmouth. She studied at Bridgewater State College and later worked as a fifth grade teacher, an insurance claims investigator, and a secretary at a TV station. At Cornell University she received her M.F.A. in 1980. Her poems have appeared in *American Poetry Review, The Iowa Review, Poetry Northwest, Prairie Schooner,* and other literary magazines. Her book *The Face in the Water* was selected by Maxine Kumin as the winner of the 1989 Agnes Lynch Starrett Poetry Prize. She lives in Ithaca, New York.

KATE DANIELS was born in Richmond, Virginia, in 1953. She studied English literature at the University of Virginia, where she received her B.A. and M.A., and writing at Columbia University, where she received her M.F.A. in 1980. Her first book, *The White Wave,* won the 1983 Agnes Lynch Starrett Poetry Prize. She lives in Durham, North Carolina, and teaches at Wake Forest University.

TOI DERRICOTTE was born in Detroit in 1941. Educated at Wayne State University, where she received her B.A. in special education, for several years she taught mentally retarded and disturbed children in the Detroit public schools. She also received a masters degree in literature and creative writing from New York University. For nearly twenty years she worked as a master teacher in the New Jersey Poets-in-the-Schools Program. Her poems have been published widely, including poems in *American Poetry Review, Callaloo, The Iowa Review, Paris Review,* and *Ploughshares.* She is associate professor of English at the University of Pittsburgh.

SHARON LURA EDENS DOUBIAGO was born in Long Beach, California. She holds a M.A. degree in English from California State University, Los Angeles, and for many years has traveled the American West as an itinerant writer and artist-in-residence at numerous schools and colleges. She received the 1991 Hazel Hall Oregon Book Award for Poetry for *Psyche Drives the Coast, Poems 1974–1987.* She considers the West Coast of the United States—San Diego to Seattle, Ramona to Port Townsend—her home.

STUART DYBEK was born in Chicago in 1942 and grew up there. Later he worked as a caseworker on Chicago's South Side. He has a M.F.A. from the University of Iowa where he studied in both the poetry and fiction workshops. His poems have been widely published in magazines such as *Paris Review, Poetry,* and *TriQuarterly.* Besides *Brass Knuckles,* his collection of poems, he is also the author of two prize-winning collections of fiction, *Childhood and Other Neighborhoods* and *The Coast of Chicago.* He teaches in the creative writing program at Western Michigan University.

JANE FLANDERS was born in Waynesboro, Pennsylvania, in 1940. She was educated at Bryn Mawr College, where she studied musicology, and at Columbia University, where she studied English literature. Her poems have appeared in *The New Republic, The New Yorker, Poetry, Prairie Schooner,* and other magazines. She has taught at a variety of institutions, including Clark University and the University of Cincinnati, where she was Elliston Poet-in-Residence. Currently she teaches poetry workshops in the Writing Institute at Sarah Lawrence College. She lives in Pelham, New York.

GARY GILDNER was born in West Branch, Michigan, in 1938. He has contributed a number of poems and stories to *Antaeus, The Nation, The North American Review, Paris Review, Poetry,* and other magazines. He is the author of five volumes in the Pitt Poetry Series, two collections of short stories, a novel, and a nonfiction book about his year coaching a Polish baseball team—The Warsaw Sparks. He teaches at Drake University in Des Moines, Iowa.

ELTON GLASER was born in New Orleans in 1945 and grew up in nearby Slidell, Louisiana. He holds degrees from the University of New Orleans (B.A., M.A., English) and the University of California,

Irvine (M.F.A., creative writing). More than 400 of his poems and translations have appeared in such magazines as *The Georgia Review, Parnassus: Poetry in Review,* and *Poetry.* Professor of English at the University of Akron, he lives in Akron, Ohio, with his wife and two children.

DAVID HUDDLE was born in 1942 in Ivanhoe, Virginia. He was educated at the University of Virginia, Hollins College, and Columbia University. He served in Vietnam as an enlisted man in the U.S. Army. His poetry, fiction, and essays have appeared in *Esquire, Harper's Magazine, Los Angeles Times Book Review, The New York Times Book Review, The New York Times Magazine,* and other magazines. He teaches at the University of Vermont and at the Bread Loaf School of English, where in 1991 he was Robert Frost Professor of American Literature.

LAWRENCE JOSEPH was born in Detroit in 1948. His grandparents were Lebanese and Syrian Catholic immigrants. He was educated at the University of Michigan, where he received the Hopwood Award for Poetry; Cambridge University, where he read English literature; and the University of Michigan Law School. His first book, *Shouting at No One,* won the 1982 Agnes Lynch Starrett Poetry Prize. His poems, reviews, and essays have appeared in *The Kenyon Review, The Nation, Paris Review, Partisan Review, Poetry, The Village Voice,* among other magazines. He presently is professor of law at St. John's University School of Law. Married to the painter Nancy Van Goethem, he lives in New York City.

JULIA KASDORF was born in Lewistown, Pennsylvania, in 1962. Both of her parents were from nearby Mifflin County, one of the oldest Amish/Mennonite settlements in the country. Her family later moved to western Pennsylvania, where she grew up, and she studied at Goshen College in Indiana and New York University, where she received the Thomas Wolfe Memorial Prize for Poetry. Her first book, *Sleeping Preacher,* won the 1991 Agnes Lynch Starrett Poetry Prize. She currently works in the Development Office at New York University and lives in Brooklyn.

ETHERIDGE KNIGHT was born in rural Mississippi in 1931 and received little formal education. He served as an army-trained medical technician during the Korean War and was badly wounded. Later convicted of armed robbery, he spent six years in prison. "I died in Korea from a shrapnel wound," he wrote, "and narcotics resurrected me. I died in 1960 from a prison sentence and poetry brought me back to life." He was awarded fellowships by the Guggenheim Foundation and the National Endowment for the Arts, and in 1985 received the Shelley Memorial Award by the Poetry Society of America in recognition of distinguished achievement in poetry. *The Essential Etheridge Knight* was published in the Pitt Poetry Series in 1986 and it won a 1987 American Book Award of the Before Columbus Foundation. Knight died in 1991 at his home in Indianapolis.

BILL KNOTT was born in Michigan in 1940 and grew up there and in Illinois. He teaches in the M.F.A. program at Emerson College in Boston, but he considers himself "essentially a Midwestern poet."

TED KOOSER was born in Ames, Iowa, in 1939. He was educated in the Ames public schools, at Iowa State University, and the University of Nebraska. His awards include two National Endowment for the Arts Fellowships, the Stanley Kunitz Prize from *Columbia* magazine, and the 1981 Society of Midland Authors Award for Poetry for *Sure Signs*. His poems have appeared in many magazines including, most recently, *The Antioch Review, The Hudson Review,* and *The Kenyon Review*. He lives on an acreage near Garland, Nebraska, and makes his living as a life insurance executive. He is also adjunct professor at the University of Nebraska where he teaches occasional courses in poetry writing.

LARRY LEVIS was born in Fresno, California, in 1946. He received his B.A. in English at California State University, Fresno, his M.A. in creative writing at Syracuse University, and in 1974 a Ph.D. in modern letters at the University of Iowa. His first book of poems, *Wrecking Crew,* was selected by Philip Booth and Robert Mezey as the winner of the 1971 United States Award of the International Poetry Forum. His second book, *The Afterlife,* won the Lamont Award of the American Academy of Poets in 1976. In 1981 *The Dollmaker's Ghost* was the winner of the Open Competition of the National Poetry Series. Levis teaches at Virginia Commonwealth University in Richmond, Virginia.

IRENE MCKINNEY was born in Belington, West Virginia, in 1939. She received her B.A. from West Virginia Wesleyan College, her M.A. from West Virginia University, and her Ph.D. from the University of Utah. She has taught poetry and literature at the University of California, Santa Cruz, the University of Utah, and Hamilton College. She is currently a visiting scholar at the University of Virginia.

PETER MEINKE was born in Brooklyn in 1932 and educated at Hamilton College (A.B.), the University of Michigan (M.A.), and the University of Minnesota (Ph.D.). His poems and stories have appeared in *The Atlantic, The New Republic, The New Yorker, Poetry,* and other magazines. He is married to artist Jeanne Clark and they have four children. After directing the Writing Workshop at Eckerd College in St. Petersburg, Florida, for twenty-seven years, he retired this year to devote more time to his writing.

CAROL MUSKE was born in St. Paul, Minnesota, in 1945 and attended Creighton University and San Francisco State, where she received her M.A. in Creative Writing in 1970. She lived in Manhattan for twelve years, teaching in the graduate writing program at Columbia University, working as assistant editor of *Antaeus* magazine, and teaching creative writing in New York prisons in a program she founded called Art Without Walls. In 1983 she married actor David Dukes and moved to Los Angeles. Currently she teaches writing and literature at the University of Southern California.

LEONARD NATHAN was born in Los Angeles in 1924. He served in the U.S. Army during World War II and earned his Ph.D. in English at the University of California, Berkeley. His poems have appeared in many magazines including *The Kenyon Review, The New Yorker,* and *Prairie Schooner.* He has received a National Institute of Arts and Letters award in poetry and a Guggenheim Fellowship. He retired in 1991 from the Department of Rhetoric of the University of California, Berkeley, where he taught for thirty years.

SHARON OLDS was born in 1942 in San Francisco and educated at Stanford University and Columbia University. Her poems have appeared in *The Nation, The New Yorker, Paris Review, Poetry,* and other magazines. Her first book of poems, *Satan Says,* was selected by Ed Ochester and published in 1980 in the Pitt Poetry Series. Subsequently it won the inaugural San Francisco Poetry Center Award in 1981. Her second book, *The Dead and the Living,* was both the 1983 Lamont Poetry Selection and winner of the National Book Critics Circle Award. She teaches poetry workshops at New York University and Goldwater Hospital on Roosevelt Island in New York.

ALICIA SUSKIN OSTRIKER was born in New York City in 1937, and studied at Brandeis University and the University of Wisconsin. She has published seven volumes of poetry, most recently *The Imaginary Lover,* which won the 1986 William Carlos Williams Award of the Poetry Society of America, and *Green Age,* both in the Pitt Poetry Series. Her poetry appears in *American Poetry Review, The Atlantic, The Nation, The New Yorker,* and other magazines. As a critic she is the author of *Vision and Verse in William Blake* and editor of Blake's *Complete Poems,* and has written two books on American women's poetry, *Writing Like a Woman* and *Stealing the Language: The Emergence of Women's Poetry in America.* She lives in Princeton, New Jersey, and is a professor of English at Rutgers University.

GREG PAPE was born in Eureka, California, in 1947. He received his B.A. from Fresno State College, his M.A. from California State University, Fresno, and his M.F.A. from the University of Arizona. His poems have appeared in *Antaeus, Field, The Nation, The New Yorker, Poetry,* and many other publications. Associate professor of English and creative writing at the University of Montana, he lives in Stevensville, Montana.

KATHLEEN PEIRCE was born in Moline, Illinois, in 1956 and grew up in Rock Island. She worked the late shift in a Catholic hospital for eight years before attending the University of Iowa, where she earned her B.A. and M.F.A. Her first book, *Mercy,* was selected by Ellen Bryant Voigt as the winner of the 1990 Associated Writing Programs' Award Series in Poetry. Peirce lives in Iowa City, Iowa, with her husband and son.

DAVID RIVARD was born in Fall River, Massachusetts, in 1953. He was educated at Southeastern Massachusetts University and Princeton University, where he studied anthropology, and at the University of Arizona, where he received an M.F.A. in creative writing. His poems have appeared in *The North American Review, Ploughshares, Poetry,* and other magazines. *Torque,* his first book of poems, won the 1987 Agnes Lynch Starrett Poetry Prize. He teaches at Tufts University and in the M.F.A. in writing program at Vermont College.

LIZ ROSENBERG was born in Glen Cove, New York, in 1955. She was educated at Bennington College and Johns Hopkins University. Her poems have been published in *The Nation, The New Republic, The New Yorker, Paris Review,* and elsewhere. Her first book, *The Fire Music,* won the 1985 Agnes Lynch Starrett Poetry Prize. She teaches creative writing and English at the State University of New York, Binghamton, where she lives with her husband and son.

MAXINE SCATES was born in Los Angeles, California, in 1949. She studied English literature at California State University, Northridge, where she earned a B.A., and writing at the University of Oregon, where she received her M.F.A. In 1988 she received an Ed.M. in adult education (literacy, development writing, English as a second language) from Oregon State University. From 1981 to 1985 she was poetry editor of *Northwest Review.* Her first book of poems, *Toluca Street,* won the 1988 Agnes Lynch Starrett Poetry Prize, and subsequently the 1990 Oregon Book Award for Poetry. She has taught poetry throughout the state of Oregon in the Artists-in-the-Schools Program, as poet-in-residence at Lewis and Clark College, and currently at Lane Community College. She lives in Eugene, Oregon.

RICHARD SHELTON was born in Boise, Idaho, in 1933. He received his B.A. from Abilene Christian University in 1958 and his M.A. from the University of Arizona in 1961. His first book, *The Tattooed Desert*, was chosen by Mark Strand, May Swenson, and Richard Wilbur as the winner of the 1970 United States Award of the International Poetry Forum. His most recent prose book, *Going Back to Bisbee*, won the Western States Award for Creative Nonfiction. He is a Regent's Professor in the English department of the University of Arizona. Since 1972 he has worked in the Arizona state prison system directing creative writing workshops. He lives in Tucson.

BETSY SHOLL was born in Lakewood, Ohio, in 1945 and grew up in Brick Town, New Jersey. She was educated at Bucknell University, the University of Rochester, where she was a Woodrow Wilson Fellow, and Vermont College. Her poems have appeared in *The Beloit Poetry Journal, Field, The Massachusetts Review, Ploughshares, West Branch*, and other magazines. Her book *The Red Line* won the 1991 Associated Writing Programs' Award Series in Poetry. She lives with her family in Portland, Maine, and teaches at the University of Southern Maine.

PEGGY SHUMAKER was born in La Mesa, California, in 1952. She grew up in Tucson, Arizona, and received her B.A. and M.F.A. from the University of Arizona. In 1989 she was awarded a National Endowment for the Arts Poetry Fellowship. For 1992–93 she is president of the Associated Writing Programs Board of Directors. She teaches in the M.F.A. program at the University of Alaska, Fairbanks, where she is head of the Department of English. She lives in a log house near Ester, Alaska.

JEFFREY SKINNER was born in Buffalo, New York, in 1949. He was educated at Rollins College and Columbia University. His poems have appeared in *The Atlantic, The Nation, The New Yorker, Paris Review*, and other magazines. His book *A Guide to Forgetting* was chosen by Tess Gallagher for the 1987 National Poetry Series. He is associate professor of English at the University of Louisville.

GARY SOTO was born in 1952 in Fresno, California. He received his B.A. at California State University, Fresno, and his M.F.A. in creative writing at the University of California, Irvine. *The Elements of San Joaquin,* his first book of poems, won the 1976 United States Award of the International Poetry Forum. He teaches at the University of California, Berkeley.

LESLIE ULLMAN was born in Chicago, Illinois, in 1947. She received her B.A. from Skidmore College and her M.F.A. in 1974 from the University of Iowa Writers' Workshop. *Natural Histories,* her first book, won the Yale Series of Younger Poets Award in 1978. She lives in southern New Mexico and directs the creative writing program at the University of Texas, El Paso, and is also on the faculty of the Vermont College nonresident M.F.A. program.

CONSTANCE URDANG was born in New York City in 1922. She received her B.A. from Smith College and her M.F.A. from the University of Iowa. She is the author of ten volumes of poetry and fiction, including *The Lone Women and Others* and *Only the World,* both published in the Pitt Poetry Series. Among her awards are a National Endowment for the Arts Poetry Fellowship and the Delmore Schwartz Memorial Poetry Award. She divides her year between St. Louis, Missouri, and San Miguel de Allende, Mexico.

RONALD WALLACE was born in Cedar Rapids, Iowa, in 1945, and grew up in St. Louis, Missouri. He was educated at the College of Wooster and the University of Michigan, where he won a Hopwood Award for Poetry and received his Ph.D. His poems have appeared widely in such magazines as *The Atlantic, The Nation, The New Yorker, Poetry,* and *Poetry Northwest.* He directs the creative writing program at the University of Wisconsin, Madison, and serves as series editor of the Brittingham Prize in Poetry of the University of Wisconsin Press. He divides his time between Madison and a forty-acre farm in Bear Valley, Wisconsin.

BELLE WARING was born in Warrenton, Virginia, in 1951. She holds degrees in nursing and English, and in 1988 she received her M.F.A. in creative writing at Vermont College. She is now on the field faculty of the Vermont College M.F.A. program, but for many years worked as a registered nurse. Her first book, *Refuge,* was selected by Alice Fulton as the winner of the 1989 Associated Writing Programs' Award in Poetry. Subsequently it was cited by *Publishers Weekly* as one of the best books of 1990 and it also won the 1991 Award of the Poetry Committee of Washington, D.C., selected by Mark Strand. She lives in Washington, D.C.

MICHAEL S. WEAVER was born in 1951 in Baltimore, Maryland, where his parents, themselves the children of Virginia farmers, had moved during World War II. He received his B.A. from the University of the State of New York and his M.A. from Brown University. His poems have appeared in *African-American Review, Callaloo, Indiana Review, The Kenyon Review, Pequod,* and other magazines. An assistant professor of English at Rutgers University, Camden, he lives in Philadelphia, where he is active in theatre as a playwright.

ROBLEY WILSON was born in Brunswick, Maine, in 1930. He received his B.A. degree from Bowdoin College in 1957, after service in the U.S. Air Force, and earned his M.F.A. from the University of Iowa in 1968. His first book of poems, *Kingdoms of the Ordinary,* won the 1986 Agnes Lynch Starrett Poetry Prize; his second, *A Pleasure Tree,* won the 1990 Society of Midland Authors Award for Poetry. He is also the author of a novel and four collections of short stories. Since 1969 he has edited *The North American Review,* and he is professor of English at the University of Northern Iowa.

DAVID WOJAHN was born in St. Paul, Minnesota, in 1953, and educated at the University of Minnesota and the University of Arizona. His first poetry collection, *Icehouse Lights,* was selected by Richard Hugo as the 1981 winner of the Yale Series of Younger Poets Award, and it subsequently won the Poetry Society of America's William Carlos Williams Book Award. He has taught at the University of New Orleans, the University of Arkansas, and the University of Houston. He presently teaches at Indiana University, where he is Lilly Associate Professor of Poetry, and in the M.F.A. writing program of Vermont College. Married to poet Lynda Hull, he lives in Chicago.

PAUL ZIMMER was born in Canton, Ohio, in 1934. For twenty-five years he has worked in scholarly publishing, and he has been founding editor of poetry series at three university presses (Pittsburgh, Georgia, and Iowa). Seven full-length books of his poetry and five chapbooks have been published. *Family Reunion: Selected and New Poems* (Pitt Poetry Series, 1983) won an Award for Literature from the American Academy and Institute of Arts and Letters. *The Great Bird of Love* was selected by William Stafford for the National Poetry Series. He has received three Pushcart Prizes and two National Endowment for the Arts Poetry Fellowships. Director of the University of Iowa Press, he lives in Iowa City.

About the Editors

ED OCHESTER was born in Brooklyn, New York, in 1939 and was educated at Cornell University, Harvard University, and the University of Wisconsin. His nine books of poetry include *Changing the Name to Ochester, Miracle Mile,* and *Dancing on the Edges of Knives,* which won the Devins Award for Poetry. His poems have appeared in *American Poetry Review, The North American Review, Ploughshares, Poetry, Virginia Quarterly Review,* and many other magazines. He has received fellowships in poetry from the National Endowment for the Arts and the Pennsylvania Council on the Arts, and won a Pushcart Prize in 1992. Since 1978 he has served as general editor of the Pitt Poetry Series, and he is also general editor of the Drue Heinz Literature Prize for short fiction. For most of the past fifteen years he has been director of the writing program at the University of Pittsburgh, and he has twice been elected president of the Associated Writing Programs. He is a founding editor of the poetry magazine *5 AM.*

PETER ORESICK was born in 1955 in Ford City, Pennsylvania. He earned both a B.A. in education and a M.F.A. in writing from the University of Pittsburgh. While a student he worked on the line in a glass factory, followed by stints as a high school teacher in the Pittsburgh Public Schools and as a writer-in-residence for the Pennsylvania Council on the Arts. In 1985 he joined the staff of the University of Pittsburgh Press, where he is assistant director and promotion and marketing manager. His books of poetry are *Definitions, An American Peace, Other Lives,* and *The Story of Glass.* He is coeditor, with Nicholas Coles, of the anthology *Working Classics: Poems on Industrial Life* and a forthcoming companion volume focusing on jobs in the service economy. He lives in Pittsburgh with his wife, Stephanie Flom, and three sons.

Pitt Poetry Series
Chronological Series List 1968–1992

The Pitt Poetry Series was established in 1968, receiving initial funding through the generosity of the A. W. Mellon Educational and Charitable Trust and its president, Theodore L. Hazlett, via the agency of the International Poetry Forum and its director, Samuel Hazo. Dr. Hazo also secured additional funding for books in translation published during the first ten years of the Series.

From the mid-1970s to the present, volumes by individual authors published in the Series have been supported by juried grants from the National Endowment for the Arts and the Pennsylvania Council on the Arts. These have been essential to underwriting the cost of book manufacturing and in helping the Series maintain its consistent growth in distribution and sales. During the past ten years nearly every year has seen a new record set in sales of Series books.

During its twenty-five year history the Series has had two general editors. Paul Zimmer, now director of the University of Iowa Press, was editor from 1968 to 1978. Samuel Hazo was instrumental during these years with the selection of translated volumes and the winners of the United States Award of the International Poetry Forum. Ed Ochester was appointed editor in 1978 and continues in that position.

1968
Looking for Jonathan, Jon Anderson
Learning the Way, James Den Boer
The Homer Mitchell Place, John Engels
Blood Rights, Samuel Hazo

1969
The Invention of New Jersey, Jack Anderson
Fazil Hüsnü Dağlarca: Selected Poems, Fazil Hüsnü Dağlarca, translated by Talât Halman
First Practice, Gary Gildner
Body Compass, David Steingass
Sweating Out the Winter, David Young

1970
Death & Friends, Jon Anderson
Another Kind of Rain, Gerald W. Barrax
Collected Poems, Abbie Huston Evans
Dear John, Dear Coltrane, Michael S. Harper
The Floor Keeps Turning, Shirley Kaufman
When Thy King Is a Boy, Ed Roberson

1971

The Blood of Adonis: Selected Poems of Adonis (Ali Ahmed Said), Adonis, translated by Samuel Hazo
Trying to Come Apart, James Den Boer
Alehouse Sonnets, Norman Dubie
Digging for Indians, Gary Gildner
The Tattooed Desert, Richard Shelton

1972

Song: I Want a Witness, Michael S. Harper
Once for the Last Bandit: New and Previous Poems, Samuel Hazo
Wrecking Crew, Larry Levis
Of All the Dirty Words, Richard Shelton
Windows and Stones: Selected Poems, Tomas Tranströmer, translated by May Swenson

1973

Gold Country, Shirley Kaufman
A Canopy in the Desert: Selected Poems, Abba Kovner, translated by Shirley Kaufman
101 Different Ways of Playing Solitaire and Other Poems, Belle Randall
Uncle Time, Dennis Scott
American Handbook, David Steingass
48 Small Poems, Marc Weber

1974

In Sepia, Jon Anderson
After Our War, John Balaban
The Lost Heroes, Michael Culross
The Axion Esti, Odysseus Elytis, translated by Edmund Keeley and George Savidis
No Time for Good Reasons, Brendan Galvin
Quartered, Samuel Hazo
Eskimo Poems from Canada and Greenland, Tom Lowenstein, translator
Lake Songs and Other Fears, Judith Minty
Disguises, Herbert Scott
Learning to Count, Alberta T. Turner

1975

In the Dead of the Night, Norman Dubie
Signals from the Safety Coffin, John Engels
Nails, Gary Gildner
Special Effects, Gwen Head
The Great American Fourth of July Parade, Archibald MacLeish
The New Body, James Moore
Camouflage, Carol Muske
Exile, Thomas Rabbit
Etai-Eken, Ed Roberson
You Can't Have Everything, Richard Shelton

1976

First Selected Poems, Leo Connellan
Backroads, Mark Halperin

The Terror of the Snows: Selected Poems, Paul-Marie Lapointe, translated by
   D. G. Jones
In Lieu of Mecca, Jim Lindsey
Groceries, Herbert Scott

1977

Collected Poems, Dannie Abse
Toward the Liberation of the Left Hand, Jack Anderson
Blood Mountain, John Engels
The Minutes No One Owns, Brendan Galvin
Reading the Ashes: An Anthology of the Poetry of Modern Macedonia, Milne Holton
   and Graham W. Reid, editors
The Night Train and the Golden Bird, Peter Meinke
The Lifeguard in the Snow, Eugene Ruggles
The Elements of San Joaquin, Gary Soto
Lid and Spoon, Alberta T. Turner

1978

A Festering Sweetness: Poems of American People, Robert Coles
The Runner, Gary Gildner
The New Polish Poetry: A Bilingual Collection, Milne Holton and Paul Van-
   gelisti, editors
Woman Before an Aquarium, Patricia Hampl
The Climbers, John Hart
Border Crossings, Greg Pape
The Bus to Veracruz, Richard Shelton
The Tale of Sunlight, Gary Soto

1979

Brass Knuckles, Stuart Dybek
The Ten Thousandth Night, Gwen Head
Paper Boy, David Huddle
From One Life to Another, Shirley Kaufman
A Romance, Bruce Weigl
The Names of a Hare in English, David Young

1980

*The Badminton at Great Barrington; or, Gustave Mahler & the Chattanooga Choo-
   Choo,* Michael Benedikt
Sure Signs: New and Selected Poems, Ted Kooser
Dear Blood, Leonard Nathan
Satan Says, Sharon Olds
The Lone Woman and Others, Constance Urdang
The Salamander Migration and Other Poems, Cary Waterman

1981

Ruby for Grief, Michael Burkard
Emplumada, Lorna Dee Cervantes
Trying to Surprise God, Peter Meinke
In the Presence of Mothers, Judith Minty
The Middle of the World, Kathleen Norris
Where Sparrows Work Hard, Gary Soto
Northern Spy, Chase Twichell

1982

Flowers from the Volcano, Claribel Alegría, translated by Carolyn Forché
Heart of the Garfish, Kathy Callaway
January Thaw, Bruce Guernsey
Holding Patterns, Leonard Nathan
Selected Poems, 1969–1981, Richard Shelton

1983

Shouting at No One, Lawrence Joseph
Living in Code, Robert Louthan
Express, James Reiss
Only the World, Constance Urdang
Tunes for Bears to Dance To, Ronald Wallace
Family Reunion: Selected and New Poems, Paul Zimmer

1984

Letters from the Floating World: Selected and New Poems, Siv Cedering
The White Wave, Kate Daniels
Blue Like the Heavens: New & Selected Poems, Gary Gildner
Black Branches, Greg Pape
Black Hair, Gary Soto

1985

One World at a Time, Ted Kooser
Winter Stars, Larry Levis
Wyndmere, Carol Muske
Carrying On: New & Selected Poems, Leonard Nathan
Elegy on Independence Day, Arthur Smith

1986

Cold Comfort, Maggie Anderson
The Essential Etheridge Knight, Etheridge Knight
The Imaginary Lover, Alicia Suskin Ostriker
Faultdancing, William Pitt Root
The Fire Music, Liz Rosenberg
The Odds, Chase Twichell

1987

Night Watch on the Chesapeake, Peter Meinke
Temporary Dwellings, Phyllis Janowitz
Dreams by No One's Daughter, Leslie Ullman
People and Dog in the Sun, Ronald Wallace
Kingdoms of the Ordinary, Robley Wilson
Glassworks, David Wojahn

1988

Woman of the River, Claribel Alegría, translated by Darwin Flakoll
The Niobe Poems, Kate Daniels
Timepiece, Jane Flanders
Curriculum Vitae, Lawrence Joseph
Torque, David Rivard
The Circle of Totems, Peggy Shumaker

1989

Captivity, Toi Derricotte
Poems: 1963–1988, Bill Knott
Six O'Clock Mine Report, Irene McKinney
Applause, Carol Muske
Green Age, Alicia Suskin Ostriker
Toluca Street, Maxine Scates

1990

Giacometti's Dog, Robin Becker
The Face in the Water, Nancy Vieira Couto
Alternative Lives, Constance Urdang
Refuge, Belle Waring
Pleasure Tree, Robley Wilson
Mystery Train, David Wojahn

1991

Walking Distance, Debra Allbery
The Widening Spell of the Leaves, Larry Levis
Liquid Paper: New and Selected Poems, Peter Meinke
Mercy, Kathleen Peirce
The Makings of Happiness, Ronald Wallace

1992

A Space Filled with Moving, Maggie Anderson
South America Mi Hija, Sharon Doubiago
Color Photographs of the Ruins, Elton Glaser
Sleeping Preacher, Julia Kasdorf
Storm Pattern, Greg Pape
The Red Line, Betsy Sholl
The Company of Heaven, Jeffrey Skinner
My Father's Geography, Michael S. Weaver

Forthcoming in 1993–1994

M-80, Jim Daniels
Lynchburg, Forrest Gander
The Flying Garcias, Richard Garcia
The New World, Suzanne Gardinier
The Domestic Life, Hunt Hawkins
The Pittsburgh Book of Contemporary American Poetry, Ed Ochester and Peter
    Oresick, editors
Children of Paradise, Liz Rosenberg
Short History of One Hour's Desire, Peggy Shumaker
School Figures, Cathy Song
Tall Birds Stalking, Michael Van Walleghen

Pitt Poetry Series
Complete Series List 1968–1992

Dannie Abse, *Collected Poems*
Adonis, *The Blood of Adonis: Selected Poems of Adonis (Ali Ahmed Said),* translated by Samuel Hazo
Claribel Alegría, *Flowers from the Volcano,* translated by Carolyn Forché
Claribel Alegría, *Woman of the River,* translated by Darwin Flakoll
Debra Allbery, *Walking Distance*
Jack Anderson, *The Invention of New Jersey*
Jack Anderson, *Toward the Liberation of the Left Hand*
Jon Anderson, *Looking for Jonathan*
Jon Anderson, *Death and Friends*
Jon Anderson, *In Sepia*
Maggie Anderson, *Cold Comfort*
Maggie Anderson, *A Space Filled with Moving*
John Balaban, *After Our War*
Gerald W. Barrax, *Another Kind of Rain*
Robin Becker, *Giacometti's Dog*
Michael Benedikt, *The Badminton at Great Barrington; Or, Gustave Mahler & the Chattanooga Choo-Choo*
Michael Burkard, *Ruby for Grief*
Kathy Callaway, *Heart of the Garfish*
Siv Cedering, *Letters from the Floating World: Selected and New Poems*
Lorna Dee Cervantes, *Emplumada*
Robert Coles, *A Festering Sweetness: Poems of American People*
Leo Connellan, *First Selected Poems*
Nancy Vieira Couto, *The Face in the Water*
Michael Culross, *The Lost Heroes*
Fazil Hüsnü Dağlarca, *Fazil Hüsnü Dağlarca: Selected Poems,* translated by Talât Sait Halman
Kate Daniels, *The White Wave*
Kate Daniels, *The Niobe Poems*
James Den Boer, *Learning the Way*
James Den Boer, *Trying to Come Apart*
Toi Derricotte, *Captivity*
Sharon Doubiago, *South America Mi Hija*
Norman Dubie, *Alehouse Sonnets*
Norman Dubie, *In the Dead of the Night*
Stuart Dybek, *Brass Knuckles*
Odysseus Elytis, *The Axion Esti,* translated by Edmund Keeley and George Savidis
John Engels, *The Homer Mitchell Place*
John Engels, *Signals from the Safety Coffin*
John Engels, *Blood Mountain*
Abbie Huston Evans, *Collected Poems*
Jane Flanders, *Timepiece*
Brendan Galvin, *No Time for Good Reasons*

Brendan Galvin, *The Minutes No One Owns*
Gary Gildner, *First Practice*
Gary Gildner, *Digging for Indians*
Gary Gildner, *Nails*
Gary Gildner, *The Runner*
Gary Gildner, *Blue Like the Heavens: New & Selected Poems*
Elton Glaser, *Color Photographs of the Ruins*
Bruce Guernsey, *January Thaw*
Mark Halperin, *Backroads*
Patricia Hampl, *Woman Before an Aquarium*
Michael S. Harper, *Dear John, Dear Coltrane*
Michael S. Harper, *Song: I Want a Witness*
John Hart, *The Climbers*
Samuel Hazo, *Blood Rights*
Samuel Hazo, *Once for the Last Bandit: New and Previous Poems*
Samuel Hazo, *Quartered*
Gwen Head, *Special Effects*
Gwen Head, *The Ten Thousandth Night*
Milton Holton and Graham W. Reid, editors, *Reading the Ashes: An
     Anthology of the Poetry of Modern Macedonia*
Milton Holton and Paul Vangelisti, editors, *The New Polish Poetry: A
     Bilingual Collection*
David Huddle, *Paper Boy*
Phyllis Janowitz, *Temporary Dwellings*
Lawrence Joseph, *Shouting at No One*
Lawrence Joseph, *Curriculum Vitae*
Julia Kasdorf, *Sleeping Preacher*
Shirley Kaufman, *The Floor Keeps Turning*
Shirley Kaufman, *Gold Country*
Shirley Kaufman, *From One Life to Another*
Etheridge Knight, *The Essential Etheridge Knight*
Bill Knott, *Poems: 1963–1988*
Ted Kooser, *One World at a Time*
Ted Kooser, *Sure Signs: New and Selected Poems*
Abba Kovner, *A Canopy in the Desert: Selected Poems,* translated by Shirley
     Kaufman
Paul-Marie Lapointe, *The Terror of the Snows: Selected Poems,* translated by
     D. G. Jones
Larry Levis, *Wrecking Crew*
Larry Levis, *Winter Stars*
Larry Levis, *The Widening Spell of the Leaves*
Jim Lindsey, *In Lieu of Mecca*
Robert Louthan, *Living in Code*
Tom Lowenstein, translator, *Eskimo Poems from Canada and Greenland*
Archibald MacLeish, *The Great American Fourth of July Parade*
Irene McKinney, *Six O'Clock Mine Report*
Peter Meinke, *The Night Train and the Golden Bird*
Peter Meinke, *Trying to Surprise God*
Peter Meinke, *Night Watch on the Chesapeake*
Peter Meinke, *Liquid Paper: New and Selected Poems*
Judith Minty, *Lake Songs and Other Fears*
Judith Minty, *In the Presence of Mothers*
James Moore, *The New Body*
Carol Muske, *Camouflage*

Carol Muske, *Wyndmere*
Carol Muske, *Applause*
Leonard Nathan, *Dear Blood*
Leonard Nathan, *Holding Patterns*
Leonard Nathan, *Carrying On: New & Selected Poems*
Kathleen Norris, *The Middle of the World*
Sharon Olds, *Satan Says*
Alicia Suskin Ostriker, *The Imaginary Lover*
Alicia Suskin Ostriker, *Green Age*
Greg Pape, *Border Crossings*
Greg Pape, *Black Branches*
Greg Pape, *Storm Pattern*
Kathleen Peirce, *Mercy*
Thomas Rabbit, *Exile*
Belle Randall, *101 Different Ways of Playing Solitaire and Other Poems*
James Reiss, *Express*
David Rivard, *Torque*
Ed Roberson, *When Thy King Is a Boy*
Ed Roberson, *Etai-Eken*
William Pitt Root, *Faultdancing*
Liz Rosenberg, *The Fire Music*
Eugene Ruggles, *The Lifeguard in the Snow*
Maxine Scates, *Toluca Street*
Dennis Scott, *Uncle Time*
Herbert Scott, *Disguises*
Herbert Scott, *Groceries*
Richard Shelton, *The Tattooed Desert*
Richard Shelton, *Of All the Dirty Words*
Richard Shelton, *You Can't Have Everything*
Richard Shelton, *The Bus to Veracruz*
Richard Shelton, *Selected Poems, 1969–1981*
Betsy Sholl, *The Red Line*
Peggy Shumaker, *The Circle of Totems*
Jeffrey Skinner, *The Company of Heaven*
Arthur Smith, *Elegy on Independence Day*
Gary Soto, *The Elements of San Joaquin*
Gary Soto, *The Tale of Sunlight*
Gary Soto, *Where Sparrows Work Hard*
Gary Soto, *Black Hair*
David Steingass, *Body Compass*
David Steingass, *American Handbook*
Tomas Tranströmer, *Windows and Stones: Selected Poems,* translated by May
    Swenson
Alberta T. Turner, *Learning to Count*
Alberta T. Turner, *Lid and Spoon*
Chase Twichell, *Northern Spy*
Chase Twichell, *The Odds*
Leslie Ullman, *Dreams by No One's Daughter*
Constance Urdang, *The Lone Woman and Others*
Constance Urdang, *Only the World*
Constance Urdang, *Alternative Lives*
Ronald Wallace, *Tunes for Bears to Dance To*
Ronald Wallace, *People and Dog in the Sun*
Ronald Wallace, *The Makings of Happiness*

Belle Waring, *Refuge*
Cary Waterman, *The Salamander Migration and Other Poems*
Michael S. Weaver, *My Father's Geography*
Marc Weber, *48 Small Poems*
Bruce Weigl, *A Romance*
Robley Wilson, *Kingdoms of the Ordinary*
Robley Wilson, *A Pleasure Tree*
David Wojahn, *Glassworks*
David Wojahn, *Mystery Train*
David Young, *Sweating Out the Winter*
David Young, *The Names of a Hare in English*
Paul Zimmer, *Family Reunion: Selected and New Poems*

Pitt Poetry Series
Sponsored Awards and Prizes

The United States Award of the International Poetry Forum

1967	*Learning the Way*	James Den Boer
1968	*Sweating Out the Winter*	David Young
1969	*The Floor Keeps Turning*	Shirley Kaufman
1970	*The Tattooed Desert*	Richard Shelton
1971	*Wrecking Crew*	Larry Levis
1972	*48 Small Poems*	Marc Weber
1973	*Lake Songs and Other Fears*	Judith Minty
1974	*Exile*	Thomas Rabbit
1975	*Backroads*	Mark Halperin
1976	*The Elements of San Joaquin*	Gary Soto

Agnes Lynch Starrett Poetry Prize

1981	*Heart of the Garfish*	Kathy Callaway
1982	*Shouting at No One*	Lawrence Joseph
1983	*The White Wave*	Kate Daniels
1984	*Elegy on Independence Day*	Arthur Smith
1985	*The Fire Music*	Liz Rosenberg
1986	*Kingdoms of the Ordinary*	Robley Wilson
1987	*Torque*	David Rivard
1988	*Toluca Street*	Maxine Scates
1989	*The Face in the Water*	Nancy Vieira Couto
1990	*Walking Distance*	Debra Allbery
1991	*Sleeping Preacher*	Julia Kasdorf
1992	*The Domestic Life*	Hunt Hawkins

Acknowledgments

The idea for this anthology originated with Catherine Marshall, assistant director and editor-in-chief of the University of Pittsburgh Press. Thanks is due to her and also to Frederick A. Hetzel, director, who has steadfastly supported and advanced the Pitt Poetry Series during its entire twenty-five years.

Thanks to Sara Games, advertising and publicity coordinator, who helped to compile the biographical notes on the poets, the series lists, and who prepared the manuscript for editing and production. Luisa Bonavita, promotion and marketing assistant, assembled the many author photographs, and Stephanie Flom assisted the editors with the tedious proofreading. Frank Lehner, assistant promotion and marketing manager, and Jennifer Matesa, direct mail and exhibits coordinator, worked to plan and implement the promotion and marketing campaign for the book.

Special thanks to Elizabeth Detwiler, editorial assistant, who copyedited the manuscript with great care and who made many valuable suggestions throughout this process.

Thanks to Jerry Minnich, who served as production coordinator, to Jane Tenenbaum, the book's designer, and to Marcy Weiland for her typesetting skill.

Other unsung heroes on this project include our University of Pittsburgh Press sales representatives, who offered sound advice on the formatting and pricing of this book. Day in and day out they sell Pitt Poetry Series titles to booksellers throughout the world. Thanks to George Dawson (New England); Fran Lee Frank, Bill Jordan, Mark Gates, and Dan Fallon (Middle Atlantic States); Roger Sauls and Corey Mesler (the South); Theron Palmer, Jr. (Texas); Bruce Miller and Eric Miller (the Midwest); Duke Hill, Nancy Bye, and Pat Malango (the West); Michael Romano (Canada); Royden Muranaka and the group at East-West Export Books (Hawaii, Asia, and Oceania); and Danny Maher, Michael Geelan, Kate Symonds, and the crew at Eurospan University Press Group, Ltd. (United Kingdom, Europe, and Israel).

Finally, thanks to the forty-five poets of this collection for their help, patience, and enthusiasm.

All poems in this anthology are reprinted from books published by the University of Pittsburgh Press in its Pitt Poetry Series and that are in print as of December 1992, when this volume is going to press.

We hope that readers will seek out individual collections of poetry by these poets at bookstores and libraries. To order any Pitt Poetry Series title directly from the University of Pittsburgh Press, call toll free 800–666–2211 or write to the Marketing Department, University of Pittsburgh Press, 127 North Bellefield Avenue, Pittsburgh, Pa. 15260.

Specific book titles and copyright information follow.

CLARIBEL ALEGRÍA. Both poems reprinted from *Woman of the River*. © 1988 by Claribel Alegría.

DEBRA ALLBERY. All poems reprinted from *Walking Distance*. © 1991 by Debra Allbery.

MAGGIE ANDERSON. "The Invention of Pittsburgh" and "Closed Mill" reprinted from *A Space Filled with Moving*. © 1992 by Maggie Anderson. "Country Wisdom" and "Spitting in the Leaves" reprinted from *Cold Comfort*. © 1986 by Maggie Anderson.

ROBIN BECKER. All poems reprinted from *Giacometti's Dog*. © 1990 by Robin Becker.

SIV CEDERING. All poems reprinted from *Letters from the Floating World: New and Selected Poems*. © 1984 by Siv Cedering.

LORNA DEE CERVANTES. All poems reprinted from *Emplumada*. © 1981 by Lorna Dee Cervantes.

NANCY VIEIRA COUTO. All poems reprinted from *The Face in the Water*. © 1990 by Nancy Vieira Couto.

KATE DANIELS. "Ethiopia" and "Bus Ride" reprinted from *The Niobe Poems*. © 1988 by Kate Daniels. "Not Singing" reprinted from *The White Wave*. © 1984 by Kate Daniels.

TOI DERRICOTTE. All poems reprinted from *Captivity*. © 1989 by Toi Derricotte.

SHARON DOUBIAGO. Excerpt reprinted from *South America Mi Hija*. © 1992 by Sharon Doubiago.

STUART DYBEK. All poems reprinted from *Brass Knuckles*. © 1979 by Stuart Dybek.

JANE FLANDERS. All poems reprinted from *Timepiece*. © 1988 by Jane Flanders.

GARY GILDNER. All poems reprinted from *Blue Like the Heavens: New and Selected Poems*. © 1984 by Gary Gildner.

ELTON GLASER. All poems reprinted from *Color Photographs of the Ruins*. © 1992 by Elton Glaser.

DAVID HUDDLE. All poems reprinted from *Paper Boy*. © 1979 by David Huddle.

LAWRENCE JOSEPH. "Curriculum Vitae," "In the Age of Postcapitalism," and "That's All" reprinted from *Curriculum Vitae*. © 1988 by Lawrence Joseph. "Then" and "Do What You Can" reprinted from *Shouting at No One*. © 1983 by Lawrence Joseph.

JULIA KASDORF. All poems reprinted from *Sleeping Preacher*. © 1992 by Julia Kasdorf.

ETHERIDGE KNIGHT. All poems reprinted from *The Essential Etheridge Knight*. © 1986 by Etheridge Knight.

BILL KNOTT. All poems reprinted from *Poems: 1963–1988*. © 1989 by Bill Knott.

TED KOOSER. "Flying at Night" and "At the Office Early" reprinted from *One World at a Time*. © 1985 by Ted Kooser. All other poems reprinted from *Sure Signs: New and Selected Poems*. © 1980 by Ted Kooser.

LARRY LEVIS. "The Widening Spell of the Leaves" reprinted from *The Widening Spell of the Leaves*. © 1991 by Larry Levis. "The Poem You Asked For" reprinted from *Wrecking Crew*. © 1972 by Larry Levis.

IRENE McKINNEY. All poems reprinted from *Six O'Clock Mine Report*. © 1989 by Irene McKinney.

PETER MEINKE. All poems reprinted from *Liquid Paper: New and Selected Poems*. © 1991 by Peter Meinke.

CAROL MUSKE. "The Wish Foundation," "The Eulogy," "Intensive Care," and "Pediatrics" reprinted from *Applause*. © 1989 by Carol Muske. "Wyndmere, Windemere" and "August, Los Angeles, Lullaby" reprinted from *Wyndmere*. © 1985 by Carol Muske.

LEONARD NATHAN. All poems reprinted from *Carrying On: New and Selected Poems*. © 1985 by Leonard Nathan.

SHARON OLDS. All poems reprinted from *Satan Says*. © 1980 by Sharon Olds.

ALICIA SUSKIN OSTRIKER. "A Meditation in Seven Days" reprinted from *Green Age*. © 1989 by Alicia Suskin Ostriker. "In the Twenty-fifth Year of Marriage, It Goes On" and "I Brood about Some Concepts, for Example" reprinted from *The Imaginary Lover*. © 1986 by Alicia Suskin Ostriker.